Roots & Wings

Roots & Wings

Affirming Culture in Early Childhood Programs

STACEY YORK

Redleaf Press
St. Paul, Minnesota
www.redleafpress.org

© 2003 Stacey York
Cover and interior design by Kristina Kachele
Typesetting by Dorie McClelland, Spring Book Design

Photo credits:
Cover and page 34 © Ariel Skelley/CORBIS
Frontispiece © Paul Barton/CORBIS
page viii © Digital Vision/Getty Images
page xvi © Annie Griffiths Belt/CORBIS
page 10 © ThinkStock/Getty Images
page 58 © ThinkStock/Getty Images
page 82 © Kevin Fleming/CORBIS
page 104 © John Feingersh/CORBIS
page 122 © Getty Images
page 146 © Digital Vision/Getty Images
page 178 © CORBIS

Redleaf Press books are available at a special discount when purchased in bulk (1,000 or more copies) for special premiums and sales promotions. For details, contact the sales manager at 800-423-8309.

Published by Redleaf Press
      a division of Resources for Child Caring
      450 N. Syndicate, Suite 5
      St. Paul, MN 55104
Visit us online at www.redleafpress.org.

Library of Congress Cataloging-in-Publication Data
  York, Stacey, 1957–
   Roots and wings : affirming culture in early childhood programs / by
Stacey York.— Rev. ed.
     p. cm.
  Includes bibliographical references.
  ISBN 1-929610-32-7 (pbk.)
  1. Early childhood education—Activity programs—United States. 2.
Multicultural education—Activity programs—United States. 3.
Curriculum planning—United States. I. Title.
   LB1140.35.A37Y675 2003
   372.21—dc21
               2003006731

This book is dedicated to my family of origin:

Cornelia Marilee Bijland
William Edwin York
Maria Strooker Bijland
Martinus Bijland
Essie Octavia Tillery York
Marion Nicholas York

Acknowledgments

Many thanks to all of the people who have supported me and contributed to *Roots & Wings,* especially the following:

All of the people who responded to the first edition of *Roots & Wings.* Your comments, questions, and disagreements affirmed and challenged me. It has been an amazing eleven years.

The Culturally Relevant and Anti-Bias Education Leadership Project—Louise Derman-Sparks, Sharon Cronin, Sharon Henry, and Cirecie Olatunji, and all of the Minneapolis participants. The project was a wonderful experience resulting in great personal and professional growth. It was clearly a privilege to work with you all.

Folks I've had the pleasure of training with—Julie Bisson, Claire Chang, Linda Coleman, Becky Goze, Linda Jimenez, Mary Loven, Nedra Robinson, Meg Thomas, Kathy Watanabe, Katie Williams, and Marcia Ziemes. I've learned so much from you.

My students at Minneapolis Community and Technical College, who create the most incredibly diverse and accepting learning community. It is such an honor to be in your presence and watch you grow into skillful teachers.

Beth Wallace, an awesome editor who knows early childhood folks and understands culturally relevant and anti-bias issues. Thanks for bringing greater clarity to my work while respecting my voice.

My family, who hates it when I'm always working on "books"—but eagerly and lovingly embraces our cultures and human diversity.

Contents

We become not a melting pot but a beautiful mosaic. Different people, different beliefs, different yearnings, different hopes, different dreams.

Jimmy Carter

Introduction

Welcome! This is a book about implementing culturally relevant and anti-bias education with young children. It provides a practical introduction to working with diverse children and families in early childhood settings. But first, let's clarify the basics: What does "culturally relevant" mean? What does "anti-bias" mean?

The phrase **culturally relevant** means the caregiving routines, teaching strategies, and curriculum match the child's home culture. The term "culturally relevant" is placed first in the title of this book because providing culturally relevant care and education is the foundation of high-quality child care and early education. **Anti-bias** refers to teaching children to respect, appreciate, and positively interact with people who are different from them. This also includes teaching children to avoid teasing and name-calling, and to stand up for themselves and others who are experiencing bias. Children learn to reject bias through our modeling, classroom materials, and classroom activities.

See glossary.

The best way to think about culturally relevant and anti-bias teaching is to understand the topics presented in this book: *culture, prejudice, racism, culturally responsive care, bilingual education, and multicultural education.* Whole books have been written about each of these complex topics. *Roots & Wings* attempts to present the prevailing theories and best practices in a clear and simple manner, without losing the true meaning. We all need a place to enter the dialogue and rethink our understanding of diversity and early childhood education. Before we begin, let's explore common misconceptions, my working assumptions, and the benefits of affirming culture in early childhood programs.

Misconceptions

Many misconceptions exist about culturally relevant and anti-bias education. You may find yourself doubting the importance of multicultural education for young children. Perhaps you aren't sure if exploring such issues with your children is developmentally appropriate. Maybe you are afraid that you'll make matters worse. Here are some of the most common misconceptions teachers have about culturally relevant and anti-bias education:

Misconception: Children are too young to notice differences among people.

Fact: Children notice differences and form attitudes about human diversity in the early years.

Misconception: Pointing out or talking about human differences with children will only make cross-cultural relations worse.

Fact: Including human diversity in the curriculum and giving children simple, accurate information helps them see differences as normal. It prevents them from developing negative or fearful attitudes toward diversity.

Misconception: Multicultural education is only necessary if there are different cultures in the school.

Fact: Culturally relevant and anti-bias education is relevant for all children, in all grades. Children in all-white (racially segregated) classrooms are at risk for growing up without the social skills and knowledge base needed to live in a diverse country and work in a global marketplace.

Misconception: Multicultural education will create separatism and weaken national unity.

Fact: Culturally relevant and anti-bias curriculum reinforces patriotism, democracy skills, and citizenship skills—all of which promote a sense of national unity.

Misconception: Multicultural education is an attack on white people.

Fact: Culturally relevant and anti-bias education seeks to recognize and honor the ethnic identities and cultural traditions of all people. It does challenge the exclusive European American orientation of child development theories, caregiving and teaching practices, and curriculum, but it doesn't attack anyone.

Goals

This book was written for early childhood teachers, program directors, teacher trainers, and parents. The goals of this book are the following:

1. To introduce culturally relevant and anti-bias curriculum in a simple and organized way

2. To challenge prevailing misconceptions, stereotypes, and "isms" that affect child care and early childhood curriculum

3. To invite you to reflect on and clarify your own cultural identity and attitudes toward other races, cultures, and language groups

4. To empower you to develop cross-cultural competence, culturally responsive caregiving and teaching, and anti-bias curriculum

5. To present many practical ideas for implementing culturally relevant and anti-bias education in early childhood settings

Assumptions

This book does not include everything there is to know about culturally relevant and anti-bias education for young children. The information and topics covered in *Roots & Wings* reflect child development theory, established early childhood education practices, and current accreditation standards. The decisions to emphasize some information about culturally relevant and anti-bias education and to leave out other information is a product of my values and thinking, and the limitations of space and time.

This book deals with such controversial issues as racism, prejudice, and oppression. The content is emotionally charged, and it is likely that you will have moments of discomfort as you read through this book. There is mass confusion when it comes to multicultural education. Be prepared to rethink your own beliefs and assumptions. It is an incredibly complex issue. I have attempted to present a clear, simple approach that remains true to complexity without getting lost or immobilized by it.

Although the following assumptions are not discussed in this book, I want you to know that I believe in them and that they are important to me. These assumptions greatly influence my perspective on culturally relevant and anti-bias education.

1. In its fullest expression, culturally relevant and anti-bias education includes addressing the issues of discrimination against individuals in all areas, including religion, gender, economic class, age, ability, and sexual orientation. I have chosen to focus on culture and race because so few early childhood programs successfully deal with this issue. I believe that if a program can successfully incorporate multicultural values, it can incorporate the other equally important components of diversity and equity.

2. Life in the United States is not fair for everyone. All kinds of discrimination keep individuals from having equal access to society's services and opportunities. Education is not neutral. Schools and child care centers are institutions, and as such, they are part of the social structure that discriminates against individuals. As part of the social structure, early childhood programs inadvertently teach white supremacy and perpetuate European American, middle-class values. In the classroom, teachers pass on their values to children through their choice of bulletin board displays, toys, activities, celebrations, unit themes or projects, and through their interactions with the children and with other adults.

3. Everyone needs training in this area and one-time workshops aren't enough. We are all on a lifetime journey of learning about ourselves and others. There are no simple solutions or easy answers to these difficult issues. No quick fixes or "recipe book" solutions exist for designing and implementing culturally relevant and anti-bias education. Everyone means well. But many people are ignorant or misinformed. Don't get stuck in self-judgment. Let go of the past and embrace the present and the future.

4. The process is the product. If you come to this book focused solely on the outcome of having a culturally relevant and anti-bias curriculum, you won't be open to the possibility of discovery and personal growth. Put aside your preconceived notions of what culturally relevant and anti-bias education should be. Let go of your worries about implementing it in

your program. As you read this book, focus on the here and now. Open yourself up to your feelings. Take in the information bit by bit. Ask questions, stop for reflection, watch others around you, gather some materials and create some activities, and talk with children and parents. As you do these things, you will create a greater understanding of yourself, your culture, prejudice, and racism. And you will have begun the steps of implementing culturally relevant and anti-bias education in your classroom.

How This Book Is Organized

This book is divided into two main parts, one aimed at helping you understand the issues and the other designed to help you put these concepts into practice in your classroom or child care setting. Part one, "Understanding Multicultural and Anti-Bias Issues in the Classroom," will give you information and insight that will help you understand the many issues involved. You will explore how multicultural and anti-bias issues affect today's classrooms, what multicultural education is, and what culturally responsive care and education looks like on a day-to-day basis in the classroom. You will also have a chance to think through the ways that prejudice, racism, and bilingualism affect children. And finally, you will learn more about the interactions of community, culture, and family in relation to multicultural and anti-bias issues that affect the children you deal with every day.

Part two, "Implementing Multicultural and Anti-Bias Issues in the Classroom," provides concrete ideas and activities you can use to start implementing culturally relevant and anti-bias education in your classroom. These activities will be of value for teachers who are relatively new to these ideas as well as for those of you who have already implemented them, but need new and fresh ways to provide culturally relevant and anti-bias care and education.

Each chapter is a building block that creates a solid foundation of understanding. Chapter 1, "The Changing Face of Our Classrooms," provides an overview of issues in classrooms right now. What has changed in early childhood education that warrants a good, hard look at multicultural and anti-bias issues? Immigration, integration, and ethnic and racial diversity are just a few of the topics that contribute to new challenges and opportunities in today's classrooms.

Chapter 2, "Children and Prejudice," challenges the widely held belief that children are too young to understand bias. It's easier to believe they don't notice differences than to consider that young children are aware of differences and form strong attitudes toward themselves and others. This chapter challenges you to look at your assumptions about children's awareness of and attitudes toward human differences, and to think about prejudice in new ways.

Chapter 3, "Racism," poses some key questions about racism: Are we as early childhood professionals able to recognize and understand how the environment shapes children's development? How do external environmental factors such as racism affect children's development? The fields of early education and child development have long ignored the issues of race in the development of children. There are few resources to help teachers minimize the impact racism has on their classrooms. This chapter examines race, racism, children's racial identity development, and how to create a nonracist classroom.

Differences between children and teachers or parents and teachers often cause problems. Chapter 4, "Culturally Responsive Care and Education," helps teachers realize that differences may be a result of culture. Culture influences how families raise children and how a child behaves, communicates, and learns. These behavior patterns and child-rearing practices reflect a specific culture's history, values, beliefs, and current situation. This chapter will help you work successfully with children from diverse cultures by identifying ways in which culture and family patterns mold the children you serve.

Chapter 5, "Bilingual Education," explores how children acquire a second language and provides classroom strategies you can use to support second language learners. Second language learners are one of the fastest-growing populations in early childhood classrooms. Today, a classroom will very likely have at least one child who does not speak English and a few children whose parents speak more than one language. Often, second language learners may attend early childhood programs in which no adults speak their home language. Moreover, the staff have little knowledge of how children learn a second language and no idea how to foster the development of a second language. The result is that most children who speak a language other than English do not receive developmentally appropriate language instruction and, as a result, are less likely to succeed in school.

Chapter 6, "Family, Culture, and Community," explores the idea that culturally relevant and anti-bias education requires us to understand the families, neighborhoods, and communities in which we work. This chapter provides an understanding of the context including the social, political, and historical environment. The community context is viewed in terms of geographic region, type of community, and the community economy, diversity, history, events, and issues. The family context includes a look at the diversity of the families served. And the program context includes the program mission, particularly in relation to race, culture, home language, economic class, religion, and sexual orientation.

The remaining three chapters of the book form a guide to implementing multicultural and anti-bias care and education in the classroom or child care setting. Chapter 7, "Multicultural Education," defines such important words as "multicultural" and "anti-bias." These words mean many different things to people, including varying approaches and descriptive terms. This chapter sorts things out by examining the nature of multicultural education, listing its goals, and explaining the basic approaches. Chapter 8, "A Culturally Relevant, Anti-Bias Classroom," explains that the quickest and easiest way to add or improve culturally relevant and anti-bias education is to improve the classroom by changing its environment as well as the people who teach in it. Chapter 9, "Culturally Relevant and Anti-Bias Activities," provides over eighty culturally relevant and anti-bias activities for use in your classroom.

These are exciting times, full of new challenges and opportunities. Culturally relevant and anti-bias education can renew and rejuvenate your teaching and caregiving. I hope *Roots & Wings* introduces you to new ideas, and challenges and empowers you to put this new knowledge to work today in your classroom or in your work with children.

E pluribus unum—
out of many, one.
(United States motto)

The Changing Face of Our Classrooms

Today, teaching is more complex and more challenging than it was a few decades ago. When I reflect back on the classrooms of children I taught over twenty years ago, I smile as I think about the things that seemed so difficult. A child going through a divorce, a child with ADHD, or a child whose family had just arrived from Iran seemed like major disruptions in my quiet, settled classroom. Today, we expect to have children who experience crisis in their lives, children with special needs, and children from many different cultures and language groups.

As I grow older, it seems there are two things I can always count on in life: change and diversity. Change and diversity are the essence of life—be it plant life, animal life, or humanity. Living in the upper Midwest, I am so aware of changing seasons. In my garden and the woods beyond there is a rich diversity of plant and animal life in my little half acre. I have been teaching at the same school for seven years now and I am truly amazed at how our student population has changed. We were always one of the more diverse campuses in the state, but now there is a much wider range of cultural diversity among our students. Every school year brings students from new countries and new language groups. Just as I would miss the changing seasons or diversity of plants in my garden, I can't imagine teaching in a setting where everything stays the same or is expected to stay the same. To deny change or to reject diversity is to deny life. If anything, we need classrooms, schools, and child care centers that are full of life.

Three points are critical to understanding the impact of diversity on early childhood classrooms: (1) the United States is a racially, ethnically, and linguistically diverse country, and that diversity is increasing, not diminishing; (2) most education in the United States does not take this diversity into account, and as a result it is ineffective for students of color; and (3) professional standards in the early childhood field increasingly require that early childhood teachers view diversity as a strength and provide culturally relevant programs.

Racial Diversity in the United States

Census 2000 data confirmed what demographers have been telling us: America is racially diverse. European Americans make up 77 percent of the total population. The South and Midwest have the highest population of white people. The Midwest also has the highest proportion of white people to other racial groups.

African Americans number 36.4 million people in this country and make up 12.9 percent of the total population. Almost 55 percent of all African Americans live in the South. States with the largest African American populations include New York, California, Florida, Georgia, Illinois, North Carolina, Maryland, Michigan, and Louisiana.

Latinos make up 13 percent of the total U.S. population, numbering 35.3 million. The largest number of Latinos are Mexican followed by Puerto Rican, Cuban, Central American, and South American. Three-fourths of Latino people in the United States live in the West or the southern regions of the United States, and one-half live in California or Texas.

Asian Americans number 11.9 million, representing 4.2 percent of the total population. Chinese is the largest ethnic group followed by people from India, Korea, the Philippines, and Vietnam. Cities with the largest Asian American populations include Los Angeles, New York, San Francisco, San Jose (California), and Honolulu.

American Indians and Alaskan natives make up 1.5 percent of the total population. There are 4.1 million people who identified themselves as American Indian or Alaskan Native, or American Indian in combination with another race. The state of California has the highest American Indian population followed by Oklahoma, Alaska, New Mexico, and South Dakota.

Census 2000 offered the first chance for people to report biracial identity, and 6.8 million people took advantage of that opportunity. Ninety-three percent of them identified themselves as coming from two racial or ethnic groups. The most common combinations were white and American Indian or Alaska Native, white and Asian, and white and African American.

There are 28.4 million people living in the United States who were born in a foreign country. One-fifth of the total population are foreign-born or have a parent who was foreign-born. Children under the age of eighteen who live in a household with a foreign-born parent number 72.1 million. Of that 72.1 million, 35 percent are under the age of six.

Many of our classrooms reflect both the cultural and linguistic diversity present in the United States today. In 1993, California Tomorrow, a California organization that does research and policy advocacy on the topic of diversity, randomly surveyed 435 child care centers in five California counties. They found that 96 percent of the centers cared for children from more than one racial group, and 80 percent cared for children from more than one language group.

Minorities Are Becoming the Majority

Look at what's happening in California, Florida, New York, and Texas. Among California's population, there is no clear racial majority. Today the majority of school children in California are members of a minority group. In 1980, 70 percent of America's school-age children were European American—today that number is 64 percent. In the next eighteen years, European American children will make up 56 percent of the school-age population. And thirty years from now, children of color will make up the majority of school-age children in the United States. The number of Latino children is increasing the most rapidly of any racial group. By 2025, nearly one in four schoolagers will be Latino. America's children are more diverse than the general U.S. population By 2050, half of all Americans will be people of color, which means that, according to the National Association for the Education of Young Children (2001), "U.S. babies born today will reach adulthood in a country in which no one ethnic group predominates."

Immigration

Immigration has always been a major force shaping America's history, economy, and social life. Currently, we are experiencing one of the largest waves of immigration. About one million people immigrate to the United States each year. In the past, immigrants came from Europe. Today they come mostly from Asia, and Central and South America. Today's immigrants are younger: about 22 percent of all immigrants are under twenty-five. One in five immigrants come from Mexico.

Do immigrants have distinct educational needs? Many of them do. Less than one-third of Mexican immigrants have a high school diploma. Children of refugee families may have missed out on schooling due to political turmoil and war in their home country. They may be coming to school without knowing English and without being literate in their home language. One of the challenges facing teachers today is how to improve the educational outcomes for children of immigrants and refugees.

Diversity Is Spreading beyond the Inner City

While much of the diversity is concentrated in a few states, the search for jobs and quality of life results in diversity throughout our country. Many small and rural communities as well as Midwestern and southern communities are experiencing an increase in diversity like never before. Historically, inner-city neighborhoods were often home to immigrant communities. Today's immigrants are settling in suburban and rural areas. Food processing plants and manufacturing plants located in small towns and rural areas provide a source of employment to recent immigrants. As a result, rural school districts in Alabama, Kansas, Nebraska, North Carolina, and Minnesota reported a 400 percent or greater increase in the number of English as a Second Language (ESL) students. In many cases, change in the ethnic makeup of these communities occurred rapidly and was not predicted. It caught community leaders, administrators, and teachers by surprise. They must now rethink their practices and change the way they provide services.

Teacher-Student Mismatch

While researchers foresee a slight demand for elementary school teachers in the next ten years, demand is great for bilingual teachers and teachers of color. The American Association of Colleges of Teacher Education reported that, in schools today, 87 percent of teachers are European American and a mere 7 percent of teachers are African American. Teachers clearly don't reflect the students they are teaching. T. Snyder (1988) reported in the *Digest of Education Statistics*, "Of the 51 million elementary and secondary students enrolled in American schools in 1997, approximately 35 percent were minorities." In a study conducted by the U.S. Department of Education, only 20 percent of public school teachers felt prepared to teach children from diverse cultures or children who are English language learners.

Unequal Outcomes

Life in the United States continues to be sharply divided along racial, cultural, social class, and gender lines. This is true in education as well. Data continues to show a different set of outcomes for children of color as compared to white children. Children of color score lower on standardized tests and have higher dropout rates. They are more likely than white children to be identified as having special needs, more often placed in noncollege tracks, less likely to be recommended for gifted and talented programs, and more likely to receive more and harsher discipline in school. If you doubt these statements, do a little research in your own school district or state. Investigate the graduation, dropout, and suspension rates of students by race. Find out how those rates have changed in the past ten or twenty years. The answers may surprise you.

Reasons for such unequal treatment and outcomes include the following:

- You can't teach someone whose identity you are trying to ignore or aren't willing to acknowledge.

- The classroom, the teaching-learning process, and the curriculum are oriented to European American or white students.

- Teachers assume children of color or children who are English language learners are inferior and, as a result, set lower expectations for these children.

- Children of color experience a lack of success in the early grades, which discourages them or alienates them from school.

Redefining Good Teaching

In response to the changing demographics in early childhood classrooms, we need a new definition of good teaching. The National Association for the Education of Young Children (NAEYC), the largest professional organization, has come to recognize the importance of addressing diversity in the preparation of teachers, as the following statements demonstrate:

> The face of America is rapidly changing. In three states including California, European Americans are no longer the majority group. U.S. babies born today will reach adulthood in a country in which no one ethnic group predominates. By the year 2005, children and adolescents of color will represent 40 percent of all U.S. school children. The largest proportion of individuals with disabilities is found in the preschool population. Thus, tomorrow's early childhood teachers must be prepared to serve and to value a far more diverse group of young children and families than at any time in the past. In addition, the profession needs to recruit many more early childhood professionals who share children's cultures and home languages (NAEYC 2001, 5).

> Candidates demonstrate the essential dispositions and skills to develop positive, respectful relationships with children whose cultures and languages may differ from their own, as well as with children who may have developmental delays, disabilities, or other learning challenges. In making the transition from family to a group context, very young children rely on continuity between the caregiving practices of family members and those used by professionals in the early childhood setting. Their feelings of safety and confidence depend on this continuity. Candidates know the cultural practices and contexts of the young children they teach and they adapt practices to be culturally sensitive. With older children, candidates continue to emphasize cultural sensitivity while also developing culturally relevant knowledge and skills in important academic domains (NAEYC 2001, 18).

> Before they come to school, all children learn and develop in their own unique and highly diverse linguistic, social, and cultural context. When previous learning and development are nurtured in early education programs, the overall benefits of early education are enhanced. Recognizing and using the child's and family's primary language ensures that early childhood education adds to and does not subtract from previous experiences at home and in the community.

In implementing effective approaches to teaching and learning, candidates demonstrate that they use linguistic and cultural diversity as resources, rather than seeing diversity as a deficit or problem (NAEYC 2001, 19).

Head Start, the largest federally funded early childhood program in the United States, has long served racially and culturally diverse populations. These programs revolve around the Head Start Performance Standards. The standards include principles for multicultural programming and addressing diversity in the classroom. The standards include teacher behaviors such as demonstrating respect for children's cultures, offering a classroom environment that naturally reflects the cultures of the children, promoting children's primary language while helping them acquire English, and avoiding stereotypic materials and activities.

In the past ten years, many states have begun efforts to increase the quality of child care through establishing standards for professional development. Core knowledge is often the foundation of these new professional development initiatives. Diversity is now an established element of the core knowledge in early childhood care and education.

Here is an example of indicators from the Core Competencies for Early Care and Educational Professionals (2001) used in Kansas and Missouri:

- Accepts cultural differences and the effects those differences may have on behavior and development.

- Creates environments and experiences that affirm and respect cultural/linguistic diversity.

- Uses materials that demonstrate acceptance of all children's gender, family, race, language, culture, and special needs.

- Offers learning opportunities reflecting the cultures represented in the community of the program.

- Designs learning opportunities reflective of cultures represented in the community of the program.

- Supports children's developing awareness of the individual as a member of a family and of an ethnic or social group and is sensitive to different cultural values and expectations.

- Accepts cultural differences that may affect children's ways of expressing themselves creatively.

- Works effectively with families from a variety of cultural, linguistic, and socioeconomic backgrounds.

Questions to Ponder

What are your dreams for society?

What impact do you want to have on children, families, and society?

What will happen if we continue to ignore racial and cultural diversity in our classrooms?

What will happen if we fail to restructure and update the curriculum?

What will happen if we don't revise the way we prepare teachers?

References

American Association of Colleges of Teacher Education (AACTE). 1999. *Teacher education pipeline: Schools, colleges, and departments of education.* Vol. 4. Washington, D.C.: American Association of Colleges of Teacher Education.

Chang, Hedy Nai-Lin, and Laura Sakai. 1993. *Affirming children's roots: Cultural and linguistic diversity in early care and education.* Oakland: California Tomorrow.

Gordon, Rebecca, Libero Della Piana, and Terry Keleher. 2000. Facing the consequences: An examination of racial discrimination in U.S. public schools. ERASE (Expose Racism and Advance School Excellence) Web site. <http://www.arc.org/erase/reports.html> (10 September 2001).

Haycock, Kati. 2001. Helping all students achieve: Closing the achievement gap. *Educational Leadership* 58, no. 6 (March 2001). <http://www.ascd.org/readingroom/edlead/0103/haycock.html> (July 24, 2002).

Kansas Stakeholders Advisory Committee for Early Childhood Education. 2001. Quality standards for early childhood education for children birth through eight in Kansas. <http://www.parsons.lsi.ukans.edu/kits/html/bestpractice/qs.html> (10 September 2000).

National Association for the Education of Young Children (NAEYC). 2001. NAEYC standards for early childhood professional preparation. Baccalaureate or Initial Licensure Level. <http://www.naeyc.org/profdev/prep_review/2001.pdf > (20 July 2002).

Northwest Regional Educational Laboratory. 1997. Closing The Achievement Gap Requires Multiple Solutions Equity Infoline. Portland, Oreg.: NWREL. <http://www.nwrel.org/cnorse/infoline/may97/article5.html> (24 July 2002).

OPEN Initiative. 2001. OPEN strategic plan: Creating a career development system for Missouri early childhood education professionals. Prepared by the University of Missouri, Columbia. <www.OPENInitiative.org> (10 September 2002).

Snyder, T. 1988. *Digest of education statistics.* Washington, D.C.: U.S. Department of Education.

U.S. Census Bureau. 2000. Coming to America: Profile of the nation's foreign born. 2000 Update. Census Brief (February). <http://www.census.gov/prod/2002pubs/cenbr01-1.pdf> (20 July 2002).

U.S. Census Bureau. 2000. Facts on the American Indian/Alaska Native population. <http://www.census.gov/pubinfo/www/aminhot1.html> (20 July 2002).

U.S. Census Bureau. 2000. Facts on the Asian/Pacific Islander population. <http://www.census.gov/pubinfo/www/hisphot1.html> (20 July 2002).

U.S. Census Bureau. 2000. Facts on the Black/African American population. <http://www.census.gov/pubinfo/www/afamhot1.html> (20 July 2002).

U.S. Census Bureau. 2000. Facts on the Hispanic/Latino population. <http://www.census.gov/pubinfo/www/hisphot1.html> (20 July 2002).

Yasin, Said. 1999. *The supply and demand of elementary and secondary school teachers in the United States.* Washington, D.C.: ERIC Clearinghouse of Teaching and Teacher Education.

Children and Prejudice

You've got to be taught to hate and fear
You've got to be taught from year to year
It's got to be drummed in your dear little ear
You've got to be carefully taught
You've got to be taught to be afraid
of people whose eyes are oddly made
and people whose skin is a different shade
You've got to be carefully taught
From the musical South Pacific.
Lyric by Oscar Hammerstein, II. 1949.

Is it hard for you to believe that preschoolers are prejudiced? If so, you aren't alone. Most teachers want to deny the slightest possibility of bias in young children. We think to ourselves, "These children are too young to even notice race much less understand racism." Or we say things such as, "Children don't notice differences, and besides, they like everyone they meet." There are many indications that young children are aware of differences and form strong attitudes toward themselves and others. This chapter challenges you to look at your assumptions about children's awareness of and attitudes toward human differences, and to think about prejudice in new ways.

Differences Children Notice

I wondered if the children in the child care center where I was working noticed differences among themselves or in the adults. The teachers weren't able to identify many comments from the children to suggest that they were aware of or interested in differences among people. In 1986, I conducted an informal poll of the parents in the center where I was working. Of the parents who completed the questionnaire, 83 percent confirmed that their children were aware of differences, and they described the specific physical attributes their children noticed. Louise Derman-Sparks, author of *Anti-Bias Curriculum,* reported similar results. Children ages two through five commented on and asked questions about the following:

People with disabilities. Wheelchairs, glasses, physical impairments, and use of special facilities

Gender differences. Male and female anatomy, and perceptions of what boys and girls can do (Some girls said things such as, "I can't be a doctor"; "I can't drive a tractor"; and, "I wish I could be a boy because boys can do things girls can't do.")

Physical differences. Skin color; facial features; and differences in hair color, texture, and style

Cultural differences. Different languages, foreign accents, diets, and celebrations

Family lifestyles. Who lives with and takes care of the child, what families do together, where they live, what pets they have, what rules and discipline they follow (Derman-Sparks, Higa, and Sparks 1980)

Once the results were in, staff had a better idea of what to listen for. As teacher awareness increased, we were able to identify more and more instances where children noticed physical differences and used stereotypes and social labels.

In another informal poll, teachers involved in the Culturally Relevant Anti-Bias (CRAB) Leadership Project listed the comments and questions they had heard that indicate young children are struggling with race (skin color and physical features), ethnicity, culture, class, physical ability, age, and sexual orientation. (The CRAB Project was a three-year project that took place from 1991 to 1994 in Seattle, New Orleans, and Minneapolis. You can find a complete account of the CRAB Project in *Future Vision, Present Work* published by Redleaf Press.) That information is summarized on the next page.

Children's Questions and Comments About Diversity

Gender	Race/Culture	Class	Disability	Age	Sexual Orientation
Am I a girl?	What's my color? (skin)	Is my dress pretty?	What's that? (pointing to a person in a wheelchair)	How old am I?	Are we gay?
Am I a boy?	What color are my eyes?	Is my shirt new?	Am I a handicapped?	How old are you?	What is he?
How do I know if I'm a girl?	When I get big, I'm going to have skin like yours.	Can I be your friend? (said to a child with a new toy)	Are my eyes going to get broken?	I'm three. (said as child introduces self)	What is she?
How do I know if I'm a boy?	You talk funny.	Look at that muddy new toy.	Deaf people can't have babies.	You're a baby.	She likes girls.
When I grow up I'm going to be a daddy.	Where do you come from?	She can't be my friend. She's got ugly clothes.	Blind people can't work.	When I grow up, I'm gonna do that.	He likes mommy.
You cut your hair. Now you got boy hair.	You eat that?	He can't be my friend. He's got dirty clothes.	She's weird.	That's a baby toy.	Do you have two moms?
He's not a boy. He's got an earring.	I'm glad I don't have to eat that yucky stuff.		He's not right.	No little kids allowed.	You can't have two dads.
That's a girl toy. That's a boy toy.	You're not an Indian. Where's your horse?		I'm not sitting next to him. He can't talk.		Do you have two dads?
You can't do that, you're a girl.	You can't play. You got brown skin.		I'll help her. She can't do it.		You can't have two moms.
You can't do that, you're a boy.	White girls go first.		We hate handicaps.		Well then, I have three moms.
Go away. No girls allowed.	You Chink! Get out of my way.				Well then, I have three dads.
Get out of here. No boys allowed.					Girls don't marry girls.
We don't like boys.					Boys don't marry boys.
We don't like girls.					I'm going to marry Cindy and there's nothing you can do about it.
					Boys can get married if they love each other.
					You fag.
					You queer.

Child Development

The field of child development formally began in the mid-1920s when such wealthy American families as the Carnegies donated large amounts of money to establish child development departments and child study stations in colleges and universities throughout the country. The first decade of formal research is known as the **child study movement.**

See glossary.

At this point, it is generally accepted that development is a continuous, interactive, and cumulative process. We measure this growth in children in terms of years, and it results in accomplishments such as learning to walk, talk, and think rationally. Each day individuals have experiences and are involved with the people and objects of our social world. We interact with and influence the world and others, and in turn, the world and its people affect us. These ongoing life experiences mesh with our age-related development, which results in an ever growing sense of self and understanding of the world. This is the nature of human development, and it serves to bring us to ever more complex and more integrated levels of functioning. At any given moment, we are the sum total of our development.

This developmental process can be seen in the progression of children's awareness of and attitude toward human differences. Though development involves the whole child, we often describe growth in terms of specific areas: physical, intellectual, social, and emotional development. Awareness and understanding of racial and cultural differences and the development of prejudice is influenced by growth and changes in each of these areas.

For example, in the early years, the development of self-concept and self-esteem play an important role in learning to recognize and accept others. In the preschool years, intellectual development brings the ability to notice how things are different and alike. This mindful attention to detail results in an increasing awareness of how people differ from one another. In the later preschool years and early elementary years, children begin to understand concepts of group membership and physical permanence.

Let's further explore children's awareness of attitudes toward race and culture at each stage of development.

Infants

The foundation of self-awareness is laid in the first years of life. Newborn babies notice color contrasts and love to look at human faces. Around four months, they can tell the difference between people who are familiar and people who are strangers, and they respond to and initiate more interaction with people they know. Around six months, babies begin to actively explore people and objects. They may grab your cheek, put their fingers in your mouth, or pull on your hair. This is their effort at trying to figure out "what's me and what's not me." In the development of a sense of self, babies progress from noticing human faces to distinguishing between familiar and unfamiliar people, to exploring individuals in order to gain a sense of themselves as individuals.

Infancy is also an important time in the development of feelings and trust in the world. Babies have feelings. They experience fear, anger, sadness, and joy. They learn which feelings are acceptable and which feelings to hide or deny based on how their parents and caregivers respond to them. Adults often deny their children's fear and anger. "There's nothing to be afraid of" is a common response to a child's fear. Older infants and toddlers are often abandoned (put in the crib and left alone) or punished for feeling angry. This lack of acceptance of normal human feelings paves the way for denying and hiding feelings of fear and anger about racial differences.

Erik Erikson (1963), one of the most important developmental theorists, described the significance of a sense of trust in infancy. Babies need adults and caregivers who will respond to their needs in a loving and timely fashion. By receiving warm, loving, and attentive care, babies learn that the world is a safe place and that people can be counted on and trusted. This is an important step toward believing people are basically good and to letting people into our lives.

Toddlers

Sometime between fifteen and eighteen months, the drive toward self-awareness reaches a high point when children can identify themselves as unique individuals. Now children can really take in all of the messages received about themselves and form a self-concept and self-esteem. Once children fully acquire this sense of self, they are capable of being shamed and of feeling ashamed. Shame is the label for feeling unworthy and defective, as if there is something wrong with me because of the way I look, act, think, and feel.

Toddlers are sensitive and "catch" feelings from adults. They pick up on how people feel and will use this information to guide their behavior. If the adult they are with walks into a room and is afraid, children will pick up that fear and act reserved and fearful themselves. If parents or caregivers are uncomfortable, wary, fearful, angry, or warm and accepting around people of other cultures, children will begin to "catch" these feelings and associate them with the situation at hand.

Imitative play emerges during the toddler stage. Children begin to act out simple adult behavior they have observed. Toddlers are most likely to imitate their parents. This comes from wanting to please the adults in their lives and to be "just like mommy" or "just like daddy." They begin to mimic behavior when they copy simple adult acts such as talking on the phone, washing dishes, and shaving. During these early years, imitative play becomes more elaborate, and it is common to see preschoolers acting out their home life in the dramatic play area of the classroom. In terms of racial awareness, young children may parrot or mimic their parent's biases in an effort to be like them.

Twos

The journey toward self-understanding continues as children gain language. Older toddlers and young twos begin using words such as "mine" and "me" to describe themselves. They use the word "you" to describe all others. As their sense of self grows stronger, they go through a period of wanting to be independent and in control of themselves. "No!" and "Me do it!" are the commands of a two-year-old. They need to act on and prove their independence, and children who are not allowed to do things for themselves risk feeling shame. Children who are shamed or develop a shame-based personality may need to put down others in order to convince themselves that they are worthy and acceptable.

Children at this age also begin to define themselves and others by physical characteristics such as skin color, hair color, and anatomy. They notice and are learning the names and location of their body parts. They can classify people by gender. Two-year-olds are learning the names of colors, and they can distinguish between black and white.

Two-year-olds may also start using social "labels" rather than skin color to describe another person. For example, when a two-and-a-half-year-old boy saw an African American man walking across the park he said, "There's a black boy." Later in the day I handed him an African American doll. I asked him, "What color is this doll's skin?" He answered, "Black." Then I asked, "If the doll's skin is black, what color is its hair?" He looked at the doll for a while and said, "His hair is black." I followed up with, "If its hair is black, then what color is its skin?" He looked again at the doll and got a puzzled look on his face. He looked up at me and then back at the doll. "His skin is brown," he answered. I affirmed, "Yes, the doll's skin is brown and its hair is black." In addition to learning racial labels, children at this age may begin to develop feelings of fear and show discomfort around unfamiliar physical attributes such as facial hair, glasses, skin colors different from their own, and disabilities.

Threes and Fours

Preschoolers get even better at noticing differences among people. They can name, identify, and match people according to their physical characteristics. By this age, European American children have developed a positive association with the color white and the racial label "white." In *Children and Prejudice,* Frances Aboud (1988) said that by age three, minority children are better at classifying faces by color. This seems to indicate that children are very aware of their skin color and that minority children have learned more about human diversity than European American children, who may believe everyone in the world is like them. Being part of the dominant culture means that many children have not had experience with or developed awareness of minority people living in a society.

Young children are naturally curious about the world, which is why the preschool years are often referred to as the question-asking stage. Preschoolers want to know about themselves and others. At age two their question was "What's that?" Now their question is "Why?" which demonstrates their developing interest in the origin and function of things. For example, a four-year-old may ask, "Where do people get their color? Why are her eyes like that? Am I yellow? What color is my blood?" It is important that young children receive honest, simple answers to their questions because they believe there is an explanation for everything. If they don't know the answer or aren't helped to think about it, they are likely to make up their own distorted answer.

Preschoolers do not understand that objects and people stay the same even though their physical appearance may change. As a result, it is common to hear a boy say, "I'm going to be a mommy when I grow up." Similarly, children may wonder out loud if they will have the same skin color when they grow up, or they may say they want physical features like someone else when they grow up. Children can be helped to understand that many of their features (such as their skin color, eye shape, and hair texture) are permanent by associating their physical identity with their biological parents.

Young children's thinking is very limited, distorted, and inconsistent, which makes them susceptible to believing stereotypes. For one, they base their thinking on how things look rather than on logical reasoning. They are also very limited in their understanding of time—the past and future have almost no meaning to preschoolers. If they see a Native American on horseback with bows and arrows on television, they may deny that their classmate is a Native American. They may also make false associations between events. For instance, a four-year-old European American child had an African American teacher. Whenever he saw a black woman walking down the street, he would say, "Look, there's my Wanda." Preschoolers focus on only one aspect of an object at a time. Usually it is a minor detail, and they totally miss the main characteristics or the main point of a story. The parents of a four-year-old came to the center to celebrate their daughter's birthday with her class. These parents recently emigrated from Poland and speak with an accent. In every other way, they look, dress, and act like European American parents. But one of the four-year-olds was afraid and wanted to avoid Katrina's parents because they talked funny.

Fives and Sixes

Children of this age are still asking questions and trying to make sense of the world. They continue to be interested in physical differences and can easily describe themselves in terms of their own physical features. They are more group-oriented and can begin to understand cultural identity. Fives and sixes will enjoy exploring the cultural heritages of their classmates. They can begin to identify stereotypes as they struggle to discriminate between real and pretend. I was reminded of how important the issue of "real and pretend" is to young children when I overheard a five-year-old boy repeatedly ask his father, "Dad, is that really real?"

Children at this age can be very rule bound and rigid in their behavior. They like to make rules and will get into conflicts of "fairness." Their understanding of gender and racial behavior may be very rigid and traditional. As a result, they may tend to choose friends of the same sex and the same race.

Fives and sixes use their increased language ability as their main way of showing aggression. Whereas preschoolers often use hitting to retrieve a toy or to keep a child out of their play, older children use their words to hurt others. They will use insults and call each other names as much as four-fifths of the time. This verbal aggression can be counteracted with discussions of "fair and unfair," as this is a moral concept they are able to understand.

Sevens to Nines

Between the ages of five and seven, children experience a major shift in their thinking. They finally understand that things stay the same even though they may change in appearance. Thus, children realize their gender and skin color will stay the same as they grow into adulthood.

Fully realizing that their culture comes from their family, they add the concept of group membership to their own identity and use it to distinguish themselves from others. Schoolagers can also consider more than one attribute at a time. This allows them to understand that they are a member of a family, an ethnic culture, a classroom, a religion, and a citizen of a town, state, and country.

Schoolagers are very interested in and aware of the world. They want to know what's going on now as well as what happened a long time ago. They can learn about important people and events that have shaped the world. In terms of emotional development, schoolagers understand the feelings of shame and pride. They are able to talk about and describe these feelings. They develop a true sense of empathy for others, being much more able to put themselves in someone else's shoes.

It is critical that we provide children with accurate information so their understanding does not stay like that of preschoolers—distorted and inaccurate. This happens all too often. For example, Marcy Hart, a Native American woman who speaks to groups of elementary school children, is often asked questions such as: "Do the soldiers have to guard the Indians?" "Do the Indians still live on reservations?" "Can they leave the reservation?" "What kind of food do Indians eat?" "Do they grow feathers?" "Do they know how to speak English?" "What kind of clothes do they wear?" "Do they have moms and dads?"

Research about Children's Awareness of Human Differences

The first documented research on the development of prejudice took place in the 1920s during the child study movement described above. Research on children's awareness of human differences and attitudes toward diversity has continued throughout the past eighty years. Because research findings are so remarkably consistent, we have a body of knowledge about the development of racial awareness and prejudice in young children. Unfortunately, this substantial body of research has been largely ignored. Few if any child development textbooks address the development of prejudice in children or cite this research. As a result, early childhood teachers don't learn about the development of prejudice in children as a part of their teacher preparation.

So what are these consistent research findings? Most of the studies involved showing children pictures of people and asking them questions about the photographs. Other studies used multicultural dolls and involved the observation of children's doll play. Over the decades, the results of these studies suggest that children notice skin color at an early age—as early as six months to be exact. Children as young as toddlers develop preferences associated with skin color. By age three or four, white children begin to form negative attitudes about people who are different from them, and they develop a fairly high level of rejection of other ethnic groups, which remains consistent until at least age seven. Children of color do not seem to develop strong rejecting attitudes toward white people until age seven. By age five, children correctly identify their own ethnicity. By age seven, children of color demonstrate attachment to their own ethnic group. White preschoolers show strong pro-white attitudes that remain constant throughout childhood.

One aspect of the research that has remained controversial and up for debate is that in many of the doll play studies, children of color preferred the white dolls rather than dolls that matched their own identity. Some early researchers interpreted this behavior to mean that children of color had low self-esteem. Alternative explanations are that the children of color were simply trying to please the white researchers or that the children had picked up societal messages that being white is better.

Here is a more detailed list of the research findings:

Stages of Racial Awareness and Prejudice

INFANTS: Self-awareness
- Recognize familiar people and show fear of strangers
- Recognize and actively explore faces to discern "what is me" and "what is not me"
- Developing a sense of trust in the world
- Experience and show fear and anger

TODDLERS: Identify self as an individual

- Experience and show shame
- Are sensitive and "catch" feelings from adults
- Begin to mimic adult behavior
- Ask "What's that?"

TWOS: Identify people with the words *me, mine,* and *you*

- Need independence and a sense of control
- Recognize physical characteristics
- Classify people by gender
- Learn names of colors
- Can tell the difference between black and white
- May begin to use social labels

THREES AND FOURS: Better at noticing differences among people

- Can identify and match people according to their physical characteristics
- Ask "why" questions
- No gender or ethnic constancy (Children don't know yet that attributes such as gender and skin color remain constant throughout a person's life.)
- Susceptible to believing stereotypes
- Make false associations and overgeneralize
- Mask fear of differences with avoidance, silliness

FIVES AND SIXES: Understand cultural identity and enjoy exploring cultural heritage of classmates

- Can identify stereotypes
- Explore real and pretend, fair and unfair
- Tend toward rigid thinking and behavior
- Show aggression through insults and name-calling

SEVENS TO NINES: Gender and racial constancy

- Understand group membership; form groups to distinguish self from others
- Can consider multiple attributes
- Aware of racism against own group
- Ask "What are you?"
- Want/need a wealth of accurate information
- Developing personal strength

NINES TO TWELVES: Interested in, and aware of, world events

- Interested in ancestry, history, geography
- Understand ashamed and proud
- Can put self in another's shoes
- Aware of cultural/political values
- Understand racism
- Can compare and contrast minority/majority perspective
- Can use skills to take social action

After age ten, racial attitudes tend to stay constant unless the child experiences a life-changing event. The research makes it clear that young children pick up prejudice and stereotypes about themselves and other people simply as a part of trying to make sense of their world. Without intervention, these misconceptions will not change. Let's look more closely at the nature of prejudice, stereotypes, and discriminatory behavior, and then examine how children's development makes them vulnerable to accepting societal stereotypes and prejudices without question.

What Is Prejudice?

Prejudice is simply *pre*-judging individuals based on attitudes and beliefs about an entire group of people. In other words, prejudice is judging people first without getting to know them. Prejudice is an attitude, a belief, or a state of mind. Unfortunately, prejudice is often irrational. It's rarely based on accurate information or real-life experience. Prejudiced attitudes or beliefs are very rigid ways of thinking. As a result, it is difficult to reduce or change them. People who have high levels of prejudice tend to reject evidence that contradicts their beliefs even though their beliefs are illogical. Anyone can be prejudiced—it transcends all racial and ethnic groups, gender, class, and ability.

The Root of Prejudice—Stereotypes

Stereotypes are at the root of prejudice and discriminatory behavior. **Stereotype** is another word for an overgeneralization or overly simplistic thought. Stereotypes are often based on misinformation, myths, and lies. Stereotypes

- Trigger the distorted thinking known as prejudice
- Cause us to pre-judge a person or an entire group of people without really knowing them
- Must be addressed in our attempts to prevent and reduce prejudice because they are rooted in the subconscious

Stereotypes can influence our behavior without our awareness. Real-life encounters with diversity can activate subconscious stereotypes, which in turn trigger corresponding emotions. Encounters can trigger stereotypes about a specific group of people and, though we might not be consciously aware of it, the stereotypic thinking can cause us to feel fear, anger, resentment, and distrust. Stereotypes and the feelings they trigger result in discriminatory behaviors. Young children are fed stereotypes through the media: the majority of their experience with people who are different from themselves comes from movies, videos, television, books, and toys.

Discrimination

Prejudice (stereotypes and the feelings they trigger) usually results in behavior known as discrimination. For example, a person who believes Latinos are lazy and feels anger, resentment, and distrust in their presence is likely to avoid contact with or ignore Latinos. If the individual is feeling particularly hostile or threatened, he or she may resort to more aggressive discriminatory behavior. Think of it as a simple mathematical equation:

Stereotypes $\rightarrow$ Prejudice. Prejudice $\rightarrow$ Feelings.
Prejudice + Feelings = Discriminatory Behavior.

Here are some common forms of passive and aggressive discrimination:

Passive Discrimination	*Aggressive Discrimination*
Ignoring	Name-calling
Avoidance	Teasing, taunting
Distancing	Rejecting, excluding
Silence	Threatening
	Physical aggression (hitting, beating, lynching)
	Destroying property

Forms of Discrimination

Passive/Verbal ⟵——————————————————————⟶ *Aggressive/Physical*

Talks about prejudice with like others	Ignores Avoids	Name-calling Teasing	Rejecting Excluding	Destroy property Physically hurt another for being different	Killing Genocide

I find it useful to think of discriminatory behavior as a continuum. The behavior moves from passive to aggressive and from verbal to physical.

Stereotypes, prejudice, and discrimination are intricately interwoven. They feed on each other. It's imperative that teachers understand the critical role stereotypes play in the development of prejudice and discriminatory behavior. This is why preventing and reducing prejudice is one of the core goals of culturally relevant/ anti-bias education. And that is why early childhood teachers must eliminate stereotypes from the classroom and the curriculum.

How Prejudice Progresses

You can now probably begin to see the strong connection between prejudice and normal developmental patterns. It is important to remember that these steps in development do not cause prejudice nor do they automatically lead to prejudice. In fact, gaining awareness, learning to identify and classify objects, and forming attitudes about things are positive signs of healthy growth and development. The dominant society and its prevailing values and norms provide the environment for developing prejudice. Children growing up in a racist society will very naturally learn to classify people the same way as the society-at-large classifies people. Children quickly learn which skin colors are good and which ones are bad, which ones are privileged and which ones are denied privileges.

Remember, children are not born prejudiced. Prejudice is learned. The developmental process is neutral, and children naturally come to recognize differences.

Because society is racist, children pick up the values and beliefs associated with the differences. Steps in the development of prejudice include the following:

Awareness. Being alert to, seeing, noticing, and understanding differences among people even though they may never have been described or talked about.

Identification. Naming, labeling, and classifying people based on physical characteristics that children notice. Verbal identification relieves the stress that comes from being aware of or confused by something that you can't describe or that no one else is talking about. Identification is the child's attempt to break the adult silence and make sense of the world.

Attitude. Thoughts and feelings that become an inclination or opinion toward another person and their way of living in the world.

Preference. Valuing, favoring, and giving priority to a physical attribute, a person, or lifestyle over another, usually based on similarities and differences.

Prejudice. Preconceived hostile attitude, opinion, feeling, or action against a person, race, or their way of being in the world without knowing them.

Noticing Differences

Infants enter this world alert and aware of their surroundings. As they grow, children notice more and more detail and use all of their senses to take in information from the world around them. Recently, I held a six-week-old infant who was acutely aware of the fact that I was not her mother. I didn't look the same. I didn't talk the same. I smelled different. I held her differently. She began reacting to all of these differences by crying. Because of her age, she didn't have the language ability to put these sensations and perceptions into thoughts or words to label and describe her experience.

As children grow, their perceptual abilities increase and their awareness becomes more and more refined. They naturally notice greater detail. By the age of four, children notice skin color, the shape of eyes, hair color, hair texture, body shape, the way people talk, and how people move their bodies. There is nothing wrong with developing a greater awareness of differences; it is a very positive and necessary skill.

Identifying and Classifying Attributes

Around age two, children learn to talk and begin using words to express themselves. Language allows them to name and identify all the people and things they've been watching, mouthing, and exploring since infancy. They can label physical characteristics with words: "I'm brown." "My hair is black." "I have blue eyes." That's identification. Two-year-olds can identify themselves, their own physical characteristics, and the physical attributes of others.

Preschoolers advance beyond identifying objects to sorting them into categories. This is **classification**. At first, their categories are very simple, as they can only consider one attribute at a time. Young preschoolers enjoy classifying things by color, shape, alike and not alike. Gradually, they learn to distinguish both people and things by their more subtle characteristics and differences. For example, a preschooler may say: "I live on a farm, you live in town." "I live upstairs, you live downstairs." "My hair is blond, your hair is brown." "My skin is white, your skin is brown."

Developing Attitudes and Preferences

The ability to identify and classify is accompanied by the acquisition of attitudes and preferences. Naming, recognizing, and classifying are mental activities that are influenced by cognitive development. An attitude about or a preference for or against something is a response based on a combination of feelings. For children, these feelings result from their efforts to get their needs met—the need to be happy, receive approval, and avoid fear—based on the society that surrounds them.

The development of a self-concept illustrates the progression from identification to preferences. Self-concept is the knowledge of who a child is as a person. Once she can identify herself, she begins the process of learning about who she is. As she gets to know herself from experiences in the world and with others, she forms attitudes about herself. She may, for example, acquire a positive attitude about her ability to learn and get along with others and form negative feelings about her body and athletic ability. These attitudes influence her behavior: she spends a lot of energy and time with friends, and she avoids sports. If she acts on these attitudes long enough, they will become preferences. When describing herself, she may say that she prefers socializing to working out at a gym.

Even very young children begin to make choices and show preferences for people and objects based on the external characteristics they can identify and the information they have received about those characteristics from social messages:

"I don't want the brown paper, I want the white paper." "I wish I were a boy because boys can be doctors." Children show preferences in who they choose as their friends and playmates. Preschoolers exclude playmates with statements such as, "You can't play because you have brown skin. You're dirty." Remember, these attitudes are influenced by the prevailing social attitudes and values as well as by the child's feelings.

Becoming Prejudiced

As people grow, attitudes and preferences become ingrained. As attitudes and preferences grow more rigid, they begin to resemble prejudice. We make choices without thinking about them, acting on an attitude or preference without considering the specific details of a situation. We judge people by their looks without getting to know them as individuals.

The prejudice we see in preschoolers is an emerging behavior pattern of consistently choosing one person over another without rational thinking or reasoning, and of automatically disliking people and things that are not familiar or are different.

As adults, we must be careful not to reward or reinforce children's discriminatory behavior. Rather, we want to help children examine their feelings and attitudes and challenge them to accept new information and a variety of people into their lives. These steps from basic awareness to attitudes and preferences outline normal development as it relates to prejudice. Prejudice is not an inevitable outcome of growth and development, but a hurtful, limiting, distorted behavior learned through experience in a racist society.

Why Children Are Pre-Prejudiced

There are many reasons why young children exhibit pre-prejudiced behavior. Some believe that children model or imitate others when they make discriminatory remarks. Others say that prejudiced behavior is reinforced through the child's environment. Perhaps children act out in discriminatory ways to relieve the anger and painful feelings that come from being humiliated by adults.

Today, immature thinking is the most widely accepted explanation for children's misconceptions. While young children create their own ideas, they are immature thinkers likely to confuse the facts and make false assumptions. Preschoolers are interested in knowing about other people, but they are not able to use logical thinking in their preferences for people.

The basis for adult thinking begins in early childhood as the child begins to make connections between themselves, their actions, and the environment. Children take all the information they receive and organize it their own way. They form ideas, concepts, and eventually an entire belief system. Then they construct ideas about themselves and others—ideas about age, gender, physical features, culture, disability, money, right and wrong, and fair and unfair.

Characteristics of Young Children's Thinking

Young children don't think like adults. Their reasoning is so different from adult thinking, that many adults find it difficult to understand young children. During these early years children are forming ideas about themselves and their world. Like building with blocks, they construct their belief system. As they master language, begin to express their beliefs, and act on their beliefs—we get a sense of what they know. Often we're caught off guard and very surprised by what they remember and what they think. It is important for all of us who work with young child to understand how young children think.

Children learn by exploring. Young children in a family child care center watch the provider diaper an African American baby and announce, "She's brown all over!" A preschool child peeks up the sleeve of an adult to see if her skin color goes all the way up her arm.

Children are naturally curious. They seem to be constantly asking questions. Their questions tend to follow a progression from "What's that?" to "Why?" to "How come?" to "Who are you?" to "Where do you come from?"

Children base their ideas on appearance. Young children are great at noticing details. They observe color, shape, size, and patterns. Children make judgments based on appearance and how things look to them. They say things such as, "You don't look like a girl 'cause you have boy hair." They assume taller children are older and shorter people are younger. A two-year-old European American boy thinks an African American man wearing earmuffs is a bear.

Children tend to overgeneralize. This is their attempt to form concepts. All men are assumed to be daddies. All women are assumed to be mommies. Teachers live at the child care center. "Indians" wear feathers.

Children's thinking is limited by centering. Children tend to focus on one aspect of a person or an object at a time and ignore all other features. A little girl refused to play with a classmate. She said that the other girl smelled bad when the teacher asked why. It turned out that this child didn't like the smell of the hair care products her classmate used.

Children base their ideas on their own experience. Seeing the world from your own perspective is called **egocentric thought.** Young white children are likely to believe that people of color are dirty and that if they take a bath their skin will turn white.

Children have limited information. Due to their limited experience, children may be missing information about their own and others' identities. Lack of information leaves them vulnerable to believing myths and stereotypes. If they don't have the information, they just make it up.

Children easily make false associations. Children have a tendency to equate two unrelated situations. For example, a young child who has seen cartoon Indians on television or has watched a lot of westerns may be afraid of a "real life" American Indian who comes to visit her classroom. She hides behind her teacher and asks, "Is he going to shoot us?"

Children are trying to understand changes. Children are trying to figure out things that change and things that stay the same. For instance, children are sometimes confused about whether or not their gender or physical features are permanent. A boy says, "When I grow up I'm going to be a mommy." An Asian American girl says to a European American child, "When I get big I'm going to have eyes like yours."

Children are magical thinkers. Dreams, dolls, stuffed animals, and cartoon characters are real to young children. When children tell us stories it is difficult to know if they are relating an actual experience, a dream, or a bit of fantasy.

The Adult's Role in Preventing and Reducing Prejudice

Unfortunately, many adults believe that children are color blind. And they falsely associate color blindness with innocence and awareness of human diversity with guilt. Because the research discussed in the first part of this chapter has been largely ignored, most teachers underestimate children's prejudice. The attitude becomes "if the children aren't talking about it, don't bring it up." Unfortunately, many schools don't address human diversity until the kids are involved in fights. By then it may be too late to reduce students' prejudices. Other teachers fear that talking about human diversity will encourage children to become prejudiced. Research by Aboud and Doyle (1996) strongly suggests that highly prejudiced children benefit from group discussions about human diversity. Exposure to other children's more tolerant attitudes helps the biased children recognize human similarities they hadn't considered. The discussions reduce their negative comments and result in an increase in positive comments about people who are different from themselves. Aboud and Doyle also found that the vast majority of children were eager to express their ideas and attitudes about human diversity.

There are many positive things adults can do to prevent and reduce prejudice in children. The following list was adapted from *Teaching Tolerance: Raising Open-Minded, Empathetic Children* by Sara Bullard (1996).

- Recognize children are not born prejudiced.

- Realize prejudice is based on stereotypes, irrational thinking, limited experience, and modeling.

- Recognize that prejudice can be prevented and reduced.

- Eliminate stereotypic materials and images from your environment. Carefully screen books and videos before using them with children.

- Use words of caring and tolerance daily: "Please." "Thank you." "Let's cooperate." "I like you. I'm so glad you're here."

- Encourage children to express their feelings.

- Expose children to human diversity. Help them recognize and celebrate human physical differences.

- Explore diversity in nature to teach that life comes in many forms and each life is dependent on others.

- Model comfortable, respectful, empathetic interactions with people who are different from you.

- Promote positive values. Use your favorite proverbs to help children think: "You can't judge a book by its cover." "To have a friend, be a friend." "We're all in the same boat."

- Use pretend play and storytelling to encourage children to take on new perspectives: I wonder what it would be like to live in the city? I wonder what it would be like to live on a farm? I wonder what it would be like to live on a reservation? What would we eat? What would we wear? What would we do? Who would be our friends?

- Discuss stereotypical messages on television, videos, books, toys, billboards, greeting cards, and holiday decorations.

- Help children recognize intolerant and unfair behavior such as name-calling, gossip, and rejection.

- Encourage empathy for others. Ask children, "What did you do today that made someone else feel good?" "What did you do today that made someone feel bad?"

Self-Reflection: Questions about Children's Development

Think about your own children, children you have known, and children in your class. For each question, identify the approximate age at which children first notice or think about the elements of human identity and diversity. Do not focus on when children have a complete and thorough understanding of the issue—these are life themes that we continue to explore throughout our lives.

Questions about Children's Development of Identity

When do children first recognize their own image?

When do children first become aware of their age?

When do children first become aware of their gender?

When do children first become aware of their physical features? (skin color, eye color, hair color, hair texture, shape of facial features, body size)

When do children first become aware of their economic status?

When do children first become aware of their culture/ethnicity?

When do children first become aware of their physical ability/disability?

When do children first become aware of their sexual orientation?

Questions about Children's Awareness of Human Diversity

When do children first recognize familiar people and strangers?

When do children first notice the age of other people?

When do children first notice the gender of other people?

When do children first become aware of other people's physical features? (skin color, eye color, hair color, hair texture, shape of facial features, body size)

When do children first become aware of other people's economic status?

When do children first become aware of other people's culture/ethnicity?

When do children first become aware of other people's physical ability/ disability?

When do children first become aware of other people's sexual orientation?

Questions about Children's Development of Prejudice

When do children first begin to comment on their own image?

When do children first begin to comment on the looks of others?

When do children begin to believe stereotypes?

When do children begin to avoid certain people?

When do children begin to call people names?

When do children begin to tease others?

When do children begin to exclude or reject other children from their play?

When do children begin to use fairness in their interaction with others?

As you are sure to recognize when you answer these questions from your own experience of young children, the idea that kids are too young to understand bias is a myth. Children are aware of differences, and they form strong attitudes toward themselves and others at an early age. By challenging our personal assumptions about children's awareness of and attitudes toward human differences, we can learn to think about prejudice in new ways. We can bring this new perspective into our classrooms by creating an environment in which prejudice holds no place.

Questions to Ponder

What physical characteristics do your students notice or talk about?

When did you first become aware of your racial and ethnic identity?

When did you become aware of other racial/ethnic groups?

How has growing up in American society influenced your awareness of and attitude toward people who are racially/ethnically different from you?

References

Aboud, Frances. 1988. *Children and prejudice.* New York: Basil Blackwell.

Aboud, Frances E., and Anna Beth Doyle. 1996. Does talk of race foster prejudice or tolerance in children? *Canadian Journal of Behavioural Sciences* volume 2, no. 28 (July) 161–70.

Brunson-Phillips, Carol. 1987. Foreword to *Alike and different: Exploring our humanity with young children.* Edited by Bonnie Neugebauer. Redmond, Wash.: Exchange Press.

Bullard, Sara. 1996. *Teaching tolerance: Raising open-minded, empathetic children.* New York: Doubleday.

Cronin, Sharon, Louise Derman-Sparks, Sharon Henry, Cirecie Olantunji, and Stacey York. 1998. *Future vision, present work.* St. Paul: Redleaf Press.

Davidson, Florence H., and Miriam M. Davidson. 1994. *Changing childhood prejudice: The caring work of the schools.* Westport, Conn.: Bergin and Garvey.

Derman-Sparks, Louise. 1989. *Anti-bias curriculum.* Washington, D.C.: NAEYC.

Derman-Sparks, Louise, Carol Tanaka Higa, and Bill Sparks. 1989. Children, race, and racism: How race awareness develops. *Interracial Books for Children Bulletin* 11, no. 3 and 4.

Edwards, Carolyn Pope. 1986. *Promoting social and moral development in young children: Creative approaches for the classroom.* New York: Teachers College Press.

Erikson, Erik. 1963. *Childhood and society.* New York: W. W. Norton & Co.

Hopson, Darlene Powell, and Derek S. Hopson. 1993. Raising the rainbow generation: Teaching your children to be successful in a multicultural society. New York: Fireside.

Mooney, Carol. 2000. *Theories of childhood: An introduction to Dewey, Montessori, Erikson, Piaget, and Vygotsky.* St Paul: Redleaf Press.

Ponterotto, Joseph G., and Paul B. Pederson. 1993. *Preventing prejudice: A guide for counselors and educators.* Newbury Park, Calif.: Sage.

Pulaski, Mary Ann Spenser. 1978. *Your baby's mind and how it grows.* New York: Harper and Row.

Seifert, Kelvin L., and Robert J. Hoffnug. 1987. *Child and adolescent development.* Boston: Houghton Mifflin.

Singer, Dorothy G., and Tracey A. Revenson. 1978. *A Piaget primer: How a child thinks.* New York: Plume Books.

Wardle, Francis. 1987. Building positive images: Interracial children and their families. In *Alike and different: Exploring our humanity with children.* Edited by Bonnie Neugebauer. Redmond, Wash.: Exchange Press Inc.

Racism

As early childhood educators we are skilled at understanding children from the developmental perspective. However, are early childhood professionals able to apply an ecological perspective—namely, can we recognize and analyze how the environment shapes children's development? As we saw in the previous chapter, the fields of early education and child development have long ignored the issues of race in the development of children. Few resources exist to help teachers minimize the impact racism has on their classrooms. And yet, racism is one environmental factor that influences children's development. In order to truly understand children's development and provide quality programs for them, early childhood educators need to understand the societal environment around children and how it affects them. This chapter examines race, racism, children's racial identity development, and how to create a nonracist classroom.

In order to look at children and development from an ecological perspective, we need some basic concepts. Let's begin by defining **socialization.** Socialization is the process through which children acquire the knowledge, skills, and behaviors that enable them to take their place in society. To socialize a child is to train the child to participate in society. A child who is un-socialized doesn't know how

See glossary.

to behave in public places, or acts in ways that are harmful or destructive to the social order.

Another important concept is **society.** Society refers to a nation of people with common systems, institutions, traditions, and patterns of relationships. A society is organized around and operates through systems. Some of the major systems in American society include the following:

- Government—federal, state, county, and city government
- Legal—federal, state, and local laws including those governing citizenship and immigration; the court system including sentencing guidelines, the death penalty
- Military—all the branches of the military, military spending, military activities at home and abroad
- Law enforcement—police, county sheriffs, state troopers, federal marshals, bureau of criminal apprehension, prisons
- Financial—stock market, banks, lending institutions
- Industrial—corporations, manufacturing, transportation, trade
- Communication—FCC, television, radio, newspapers, magazines and periodicals, book publishing
- Entertainment—media, movies, professional sports, recreation
- Social service—counseling, child care, nursing home care
- Education—public and private schools, colleges and universities, curriculum publishers, training institutions and professional organizations for teachers
- Health care—medical schools, pharmaceutical companies, insurance companies, hospitals, clinics, HMOs
- Housing—real estate agencies, mortgage companies, public housing, home builders, apartment management corporations, homeless shelters
- Agriculture—farms, food processing, food distributors, grocery stores
- Transportation—airlines, passenger trains, bus companies, public transportation, taxi companies, auto industry, auto dealerships, gasoline companies, auto insurance companies

These systems have been around in various forms since our nation's beginning. Each system provides a vital function in American society. Each system interacts with and is interdependent on the others. These systems are organized around key American ideals and principles.

The political ideology of democracy and the economic ideology of capitalism are carried out through our country's network of systems and institutions. These systems are also responsible for the production of goods and services and the distribution of these goods and service to American citizens.

Each system is made up of numerous institutions. The education system is made up of thousands of public and private nursery schools, elementary schools, middle schools, high schools, district school boards, state education agencies, and colleges and universities. As American citizens, we usually work in institutions, and we receive our services through institutions. While some institutions operate under federal or state regulations, most operate with a great deal of freedom. Institutions are free to determine the services they provide or the product they produce, their clients, their staffing criteria and hiring procedures, and their operating policies and procedures.

What Are Race and Racism?

The values, beliefs, and practices of the larger society affect how children develop. Racism is one social reality that must be examined in order to provide effective multicultural education. Racism is based on the ideology of race, so let's begin by defining race.

Race refers to a person's skin color, hair color and texture, and the shape and size of one's facial features. Katie Kissinger (1997) provides a simple, accurate explanation of skin color in her children's book *All the Colors We Are*. She explains that skin color is determined by the amount of melanin in a person's skin, which is a result of one's ancestry and their location to the sun. There is nothing magical about it. In and of itself, skin color has no bearing on any person's humanity.

Race is a very simple concept but people often confuse it with culture (what's on the inside of a person) and ethnicity (where someone is from geographically). The idea of "race" is just that: an idea. It doesn't have any basis in biological reality. There is only one human race. Race is a contrived social/political way to categorize people based on skin color, which doesn't represent any other underlying difference between people. In a society that categorizes people superficially by a made-up notion such as race, skin color falsely becomes the single most important factor in determining a person's value and worth.

Racism is many things. It is a system of domination and exploitation based on the idea of race. Racism has been around a long time and is alive and well today. It is perhaps the single most influential social force shaping American life. It is woven into the economic, political, and social fabric of our country. Here's a simple way to define racism: prejudice plus power. Institutions such as schools and child care centers have the collective power to enact and perpetuate racial prejudice in ways both overt and so subtle that often the people involved in these institutions don't even recognize what's happening.

We live under white racism in the United States. Racism is built into our society's systems and institutions. White people hold the economic, political, and social power by controlling and owning the major systems and the vast majority of institutions that make up American society. As a result, white people are in the position to determine how power, wealth, resources, goods, and services are distributed to all of America's citizens. Historically, white people created these systems and institutions (for example, the education system and schools) to serve themselves and to keep out people of color. Outright racial discrimination has been outlawed, but racism continues today in ways that are complex, subtle, and often invisible to the naked eye.

Look for racism in outcomes. For example, in your local school or district are the outcomes the same for white children and children of color in the following areas? If not, you can be sure that institutional racism is at work.

Test scores

Grade retention

Identification as having a special need

Selection for gifted and talented programs

Suspension rates

Graduation rates

Child Development Theories and Race

Our traditional ways of thinking about child development ignore race and the impact of racism on children's development. In preparing to teach a class on child development, I recently reviewed over ten basic child development textbooks. Only one cited research that considered the role of race and racism.

There are newer ways of understanding children's development. Rather than focusing on what's happening inside the child, ecological theories focus on the relationship between the child and his environment. This model examines the role neighborhood, schools, community, the media, and society in general play in shaping children's development.

Cynthia Garcia Coll (1996), challenges us to better understand the normal development of children of color. In order to do that, we need to pay greater attention to the social and political context in which children live. Coll and her colleagues said, "Segregation creates a complex web of factors that impact a child of color's development. Elements like substandard housing, inferior health care, run-down schools, and portrayal of people of color in the media create unique conditions that more directly influence individual developmental processes of children of color." In other words, in order to understand the development of children of color in the United States we must understand and look at how systemic racism, prejudice, and discrimination impact their development.

Is it difficult for you to look at child development from this perspective? Most of us have little or no prior experience looking at human development this way. We live in a society that highly values the individual, equality, and individual responsibility. We are taught to believe that everyone has an equal chance to reach his or her potential.

Given these conflicting views, let's see how traditional and ecological theories applied to the same situation might produce very different results. A Native American child attends a local public elementary school that is predominantly white. She is asked and agrees to perform a traditional jingle dance at a school assembly. She is very proud of her native ancestry, her jingle dress, and her dancing skills. After the assembly, children begin to tease her on the playground. They call her Jingles. This hurts her feelings and she asks them to stop. The teasing continues, so the girl tells the playground monitor. The monitor does nothing. She tells her teacher; her teacher tells her to use a problem-solving approach and talk to the kids who are calling her names. The name-calling continues. One day the girl gets mad and beats up one of the children who calls her names. The girl is sent to the principal's office. She is suspended from school for two days.

Traditional child development theories might lead us to believe that the children were unable to take another's perspective. They overgeneralized their thinking by focusing on the jingles and ignoring the purpose of the girl sharing her native dancing. The little girl is now experiencing mistrust of her school environment.

She is experiencing shame and doubt as a result of being teased. She is physically aggressive and lacks impulse control.

An ecological perspective would tell us that the child has a strong cultural identity, which is a source of personal strength. She was eager to share it with others as a way for her schoolmates to get to know another side of her, which is often hidden or ignored in the classroom. Systemic racism was present. The Native American child was used by the predominantly white school to "teach" white children about another race and culture. The child became a teaching object rather than a co-learner with her classmates. She experienced hostile prejudice in the form of teasing and name-calling. It felt to her like an attack on her core identity. The playground monitor and teacher ignored the name-calling and failed to protect the child. Ignorant of racism, prejudice, and cultural identity, the adults attached no special significance to the events. The child was left alone to stand up for herself. She used physical violence to counter the verbal abuse. The adults were unable to relate the fight to the assembly and subsequent name-calling incidents. So they treated it as an individual, isolated event. Racism was also present in the way the adults blamed the child of color and disciplined her. They excused the white children's behavior and they received no punishment.

As this example shows, interactions in the early childhood environment can be interpreted and acted upon in vastly different ways depending on the lens through which these exchanges are viewed. It is imperative that as early childhood professionals we take the time to identify what model or perspective is operating within our settings. We can then examine these assumptions in light of issues of racism and make needed changes.

Impact of Racism on Children's Development

Racism is a social condition that affects our personal lives, as well as the society at large. During childhood, it affects our social and emotional development. Without our even knowing it, racism shapes our personal and racial identity; and it shapes our experience in American society. Children learn social roles and become members of American society through the process known as socialization. Unfortunately, by growing up in America we have been socialized to take our place in a racist society. Joseph Barndt (1991), a well-known antiracism trainer from Chicago, strongly states it: "The primary thesis about racism is that we are all—people of color and white people alike—indoctrinated and socialized in such a way as to be made into 'prisoners of racism.'"

A simple classroom simulation exercise illustrates how systemic racism affects our behavior. Many people are familiar with the work of Jane Elliot in the 1960s. Elliot was a teacher from Iowa who implemented a two-day activity in which she divided her class into two groups: blue eyes and brown eyes. She established that the blue-eyed children were superior and gave them more power and privileges in the classroom. Elliott says:

> *"The results were almost immediate and overwhelming. The blue-eyed students delighted in their new status and adapted easily to a role of superiority and dominance. The brown-eyed students were docile in adapting to their new and inferior identity and subjugated role, accepting their new station in life with little resistance, and behaving accordingly. Even their test scores took an immediate plunge. The next day, the patterns were reversed. So also, and instantly, were the behavior patterns. This experiment has been repeated with both children and adults many times since 1968. Each time, it demonstrated how susceptible human beings are to indoctrination into superior and inferior roles"* (Peters 1987).

This is why Barndt calls racism *involuntary conditioning*.

Children also receive information about race through their social environment. This includes messages related to racial appearance, racial attitudes, and race relations. These messages comes from socializing agents such as parents, other adult family members, friends, child care, school, community (for example, churches or libraries), and the media (for example, books, television, videos, computer games). Over time, children internalize this information and use it to shape their world view.

The Development of Racial Identity

Janet Helms (1993), author of *Black and White Racial Identity*, defines racial identity as the "sense of group or collective identity based on one's perception that he or she shares a common racial heritage with a particular racial group." Racial identity refers to the level of commitment an individual has to his or her racial group including the extent to which people use their race as a reference that guides their thinking, feelings, and actions.

Since the seventies, researchers from the fields of child psychology and counseling psychology have developed a number of theories of identity development. Unfortunately, these models begin with adolescence or only refer to adult stages of racial identity. Clearly individuals don't enter high school without any sense of themselves as a racial being or any awareness of their race. So we don't have a complete model of racial identity development for children. Like prejudice, child development researchers have studied children's race awareness and racial attitudes for a long time. But we still have a very incomplete picture. The vast majority of studies related to racial identity development have focused on black and white children. The studies of white children have emphasized their awareness of attitudes toward other races but have not investigated how white children form their own racial identities. Only a few studies have focused on or included Hispanic, Asian, and Native American children. We need a lot more research in this area. Given that, here is a synopsis of research from 1929–1995.

WHITE CHILDREN

- Children as young as six months notice skin color.

- White children learn and use racial labels at an extremely young age, often even before they can classify alike and different.

- Preschool-age children can differentiate race on the basis of hair, physical features, and skin color.

- White children tend to prefer dolls of their own race, which is interpreted to mean that white children have very strong pro-white attitudes from an early age. Often these attitudes remain consistent throughout adulthood.

- White children's self-esteem seems to be associated with their race. In other words, they use race as one way to feel good about themselves.

- In doll play, white children associated *white* with good and *black* with bad.

- White children who watched a lot of television shared three common beliefs about race: black people are taking over the country, black people are given unfair advantages, and black people are associated with violence and crime.

- Preschool-age children of color who had been raised within their racial community and had little direct contact with whites preferred dolls that looked like themselves.

- Preschool-age children of color who had direct experience within the white community tended to prefer white dolls rather than dolls with brown skin.

- Children who had negative attitudes about their black racial identity tended to also have very negative attitudes toward white people.

- Children of color learn racial labels and use racial labels after they classify alike and different.

- By age five or six, children of color can correctly identify their own race.

- By age seven, children of color demonstrate more attachment to their own racial group. But unlike white children, their positive attitudes about their own race are not accompanied by negative attitudes toward other races.

When you think about the children you work with and the children you have known, you will recognize that identity development is a lifelong process. Who we think we are, how we feel about ourselves, and with whom we identify change throughout our lives. A lot of identity development happens in the early years, so we need to recognize and pay attention to these milestones.

Effects of Racism on White Children

Growing up in a segregated, racist society influences children's development. This is especially true in the areas of identity. It is important to realize that while racism limits all of us, it affects white children and children of color differently. The development of white children is influenced by racism in at least five ways:

- Denial of reality
- Rationalization
- Rigid thinking
- Superiority
- Fear and hatred

Denial of Reality

Children learn to see but not acknowledge the difference between people. This is because, time after time, children's honest questions and comments about people are met with responses meant to silences them: "Shhh." "Don't say that." "It's not nice to stare." "Don't be rude." "We don't talk about those things in public." When children sense adults' uneasiness with talking about physical differences and receive criticism when noting the differences, they gradually become silent. They stop asking about people and other races. On an individual level, the process allows white children to deny their own racial identity and it stunts their normal growth in terms of noticing, identifying, and classifying human differences. It also prevents them from exploring, understanding, and questioning the social treatment of people based on their skin color. White people, including children, are shielded from the effects of racism on people of color. This allows them to adopt society's denial of racism. White children learn: "We are all the same." "It doesn't matter what color you are." "We are all the same on the inside." But in the United States, the reality is that the color of your skin *does* matter. This whole process perpetuates the tradition in this country of ignoring and refusing to talk openly and honestly about race.

Rationalization

Sometime during their elementary school years, white children will likely learn how to justify the state of current and past race relations. Rationalization is a common defense mechanism in which individuals use elaborate explanations to justify their behavior. Children of color experience confusion about why they are called names and treated differently by their teachers. But a white child will likely be able to offer a clear and concise explanation. For example, an informal focus group was conducted with elementary-age children attending public schools in a major urban city. The children used the terms *race* and *prejudice* as they were discussing their cross-racial school experiences. One child offered an explanation saying, "Everyone's a little bit prejudiced. Everyone slips sometimes. Prejudice isn't just calling people names. Prejudice is not playing with a person from another race." On the surface, you might think to yourself, wow, this child gets it! Unfortunately, the use of appropriate terminology and detailed explanations did not reflect actual behavior. Later in the conversation, the same group of children were asked why they didn't play with children of color. The same child responded,

"We're accustomed to playing with our own." Another child offered, "When I go out to play, I don't look for someone who is another color." And a third child summed up the discussion, "I can't explain it, but it's just easier to play with your own." Even at an early age, racism is primarily experienced in white children's minds. It doesn't tear at their hearts and souls, the way it does children of color.

Rigid Thinking

When we raise children in a segregated, biased environment they grow up believing that their way of living in the world is the one and only right way. This is called **ethnocentrism,** or cultural racism. There is one correct way to be a family, one appropriate language to speak, one right religious faith to practice. This type of thinking closes off children from learning about and being able to live side by side with those who are racially and culturally different from them. In addition, this thinking produces judgmental attitudes, resulting in the stance that people who look different, live differently, speak differently, and practice different religions are not only wrong, they are bad.

This overly simplistic form of thinking is perpetuated and maintained by systems and institutions (such as education, child care, and health care) that were created by white people, to serve their own. These systems were designed to reflect the cultural orientation of European Americans. In addition, at the time that these systems were created, racism and segregation were legal. Thus by design, these systems set up the European American culture as the norm, and restricted access and relegated people of color to poorer service.

Superiority

Ideally, we hope that children experience an inner sense of goodness about themselves as worthwhile, capable, lovable human beings. Too often, children's inner sense of self is lacking. They try to protect themselves and build their sense of self by focusing on external factors such as what they have, what they look like, or what they can do. To a certain extent, white children's sense of self comes from believing that they are better than anyone else. According to Joseph Barndt (1991), as members of both the numerical majority and the socioeconomically and politically dominant group, white people have a sense of entitlement or superiority over people of color. As a result, we find white children who need to criticize, ridicule, and reject people of color in order to maintain their own sense of self-worth.

White children are at risk for internalizing society's false messages of superiority. As members of the racial group with social and political power, they are socialized to internalize entitlement. In one preschool classroom, two five-year-old girls (one white and one black) fought over who could be line leader. They went back and forth presenting all kinds of reasons why one or the other should go first. Finally, the white girl exclaimed, "White girls go first." This was her ace in the back pocket. At age five, she knew her race was her trump card and she knew how to use it for her advantage when her back was against the wall.

Fear and Hate

When children are raised in a society that is racist, children learn to hate and fear people who are different from them. This fear and hatred of others can also be seen in the irrational thinking of white people. One example of such irrational thinking is that if people of color gain power and privilege, white people will be dominated in the same way they have dominated people of color for the past four centuries. I remember showing a group of white preschool children photographs of all kinds of people. I asked them questions like, "Who do you see in the picture?" "What is this person doing?" "Could this person be your friend?" "Why or why not?" A boy looked at a photo of an African American man carrying a bag of groceries and said, "He stole those groceries." I asked him why he thought that and he responded, "Black men fight and steal." White children are socialized to fear people of color. The most feared and hated person in American society is the African American male. At a young age, children begin to associate aggression, danger, and anger with African American men.

Effects of Racism on Children of Color

Children of color who grow up in a racist, prejudiced society also show those influences, especially in the area of identity. But racism affects children of color differently than it does white children. The development of children of color is influenced by racism in several ways:

- Overidentification with white people
- Separation and alienation

- Confusion and bewilderment
- Rejection
- Shame
- Anger and rage

Overidentification with White People

This is often the first impact of racism on a child of color's social and emotional development. Toddlers may prefer caregivers or family friends who have a light complexion or light hair. Young preschoolers may prefer cartoon, movie, or storybook characters with light skin or light hair. As has already been noted, they may prefer white dolls to brown-skin dolls. Older preschoolers may try to identify with their lighter-skinned parent saying, "I'm more like Daddy because he has caramel skin, but I'm not like Mommy because she has chocolate skin." In addition, they may question why a family member has darker skin and express pleasure in having lighter skin than other family members. In some cases young children will outright deny that they have brown skin. In these instances, it is important to redirect children way from being interested in white skin and reinforce the beauty of their own brown skin and physical features. This can be done by pointing out the physical beauty of members of their own race.

Separation and Alienation

Children of color often find themselves in a no-man's-land. Because school devalues their race they may feel the need to distance themselves from their own people. At the same time, they don't feel that they fit in at school and they aren't willing to "act white" in order to fit in. As a result, they check out. Usually, we don't see children below third grade fully acting out of this dynamic. As early childhood educators, we need to be aware that it is present and fermenting within children. I was a foster parent in the early 1980s, and my foster son was Hmong. After living in our family for six months, he started to reject Hmong culture. He refused to look at Hmong folktales and refused to look at Hmong quilts and story clothes at art fairs. His pat answer was "Hmong, yuck." At the same time, he was experiencing alienation at school because he was behind in reading and math and his music teacher misinterpreted his wild enthusiasm for music. She assumed he was talking all the time and wiggling his body because he was disinterested. Nothing could have been farther from the truth. It was his favorite class.

Confusion and Bewilderment

Whereas racism is something that white children may think about, it attacks the hearts and souls of children of color. One workshop participant called it "soul murder." Children of color may be caught up in the pain of being undervalued, alienated, and rejected on a daily basis. This emotional turmoil makes it difficult for children of color to think clearly or critically about what's happening to them. Children of color may not understand why they are treated differently from white children or why they are denied opportunities offered to white children. For instance, when a group of Asian American children are asked why they are treated poorly, one child looks down at the floor in silence. Another child shrugs his shoulders and says, "Maybe they're mad about something else."

Rejection

Children of color will likely experience some form of rejection in their early years. They might be told by classmates on the playground to go away. Or perhaps they aren't invited to a classmate's birthday party or sleepover. They may experience rejection in the form of being ignored or passed over by the teacher during class discussions. They may receive more than their share of "dirty looks" or negative comments from teachers, bus drivers, playground leaders, and store clerks. These are the types of daily experiences that eventually cause children of color to feel unwanted, rejected, and alienated from mainstream society and its institutions such as child care programs, schools, libraries, and parks. An Asian American boy in the second grade was asked if America was his country. He put his head down and answered, "No, it will never be my country." He had already given up on the idea that he belonged. This is one of the reasons why so many communities of color have resorted to creating their own child care programs, charter schools, and after-school programs. They want their children to be in settings where they feel welcomed and affirmed for who they are.

Shame

During informal focus groups conducted with children of color, the children talked about their race and experiences of rejection. They said things like, "It makes me what to rip off my skin and jump into a new one." "Sometimes it makes me feel like I wished I'd never been born." One year a child development student at our college shared a particularly painful incident from her own childhood. She had dark skin and was teased constantly about the color of her skin. None of the adults in her life intervened. So one night she tried to make her skin lighter by taking a bath in bleach. She suffered chemical burns and was hospitalized. As a result she missed two weeks of school and begged her mom to not make her go back.

Recognize that this is a significantly different experience from that of white children. I've never heard of a white child saying, "I wish I'd never been born white," or "My white skin makes me want to rip it off and jump into a new one." Children of color are experiencing shame, whereas white children may experience guilt. Shame is the feeling that you are defective, unworthy, and unacceptable as a person. It's the feeling that there is something inherently wrong with you. Shame breeds hopelessness.

Society shames children of color through subtle indoctrination. Children receive these messages through the curriculum, children's books, television, movies, and videos. At some point, children of color come to believe the messages that tell them: you are inferior, you aren't good enough, you don't belong, you're never going to amount to anything, we don't want you here, you are a problem for us, you make our lives difficult and uncomfortable, go away. This is the effect on children of color growing up and living in a white racist society.

Anger and Rage

Anger and rage are common manifestations of shame. Children of color are likely to feel angry. Sometimes when anger is expressed by very young children, it's the anger of their parents that is being expressed. Once a child said, "I don't have to listen to no white teacher. My mama says all white people are the devil." One of the things white people are afraid of is the anger of people of color. So it's easy to get into patterns whereby children of color act out and display violent outbursts; and the white teaching staff overreact and overdiscipline the child, which multiplies the shame, humiliation, anger, and alienation. Rarely do we ever step back and look at racism as an underlying cause of violent behavior. Think back to the story I told earlier in this chapter of the Native American girl who performed a jingle dance in her elementary school assembly. She was pushed to anger and rage as a result of nothing being done about the name-calling. Finally, one day on the playground, the little girl "lost it" and beat up the white kid who was calling her names.

Interracial Children's Identity

Developing a sense of identity can be especially confusing to young children with a multiracial background. For example, a child in your classroom might be both Latino and Asian, or both white and black. Some children of color have been adopted into white families. Like all preschoolers, they are recognizing differences and developing classification skills. Questions such as "Who am I?" and "What am I?" are especially important to (and confusing for) them. Francis Wardle, executive director of the Center for the Study of Biracial Children, reminds us that interracial children are the sum total of their heritage. To ensure positive self-development, we as early childhood teachers must embrace, acknowledge, and celebrate all of the richness that interracial children bring to our classrooms. We do them an injustice when we try to put them into neat little categories. It is especially harmful to identify an interracial child by one race or associate the child only with the parent of color. We must help interracial children feel good about themselves, their physical features, and their families. Most of all, we must accept and recognize each interracial child as a unique individual.

Creating a Nonracist Classroom

Racism destroys all our humanity. The more I learn about systemic racism and the more I deal with my own racism, the less racism affects my teaching. Most of us are unaware of how racism affects us as teachers. We may unconsciously bring racism into the classroom. While we have good hearts and the best intentions, our unconscious racist behavior hurts all children. The more unaware and ignorant we are, the more we inadvertently perpetuate systemic racism in our classrooms. For many of us, this is an incredibly painful realization. Here are some things to think about in creating a nonracist classroom:

Check Your Racism at the Door

Racism plays itself out in common patterns. Low expectations of children, limited praise, harsher discipline, and failing to recognize children of color are some of the ways teachers perpetuate racism in a classroom. Read the descriptions below of these four behaviors and reflect on how you interact with and treat children of color in your classroom.

SET HIGH EXPECTATIONS FOR ALL CHILDREN

Don't automatically assume that children of color can't measure up to your normal developmental or academic standards. Racism traps teachers into thinking that children of color are mentally inferior, less gifted, and less inclined to work hard or put a lot of effort into school. Some white teachers translate their guilt about racism into feeling sorry for children of color. Don't fall into the pattern of underestimating children's potential simply because of their skin color. All children deserve to have teachers who expect and challenge them to be the brightest and do their best.

DELIVER EQUAL ATTENTION AND PRAISE

Racism can sneak its way into the classroom through the way we attend to children. All children want positive attention from their teachers. Attention and praise are powerful motivators for learning. Some children are better at getting it than others. We have the responsibility to make sure we give each child an equal amount of positive attention and praise. Watch yourself to see if you attend to white children more than children of color. When all the children have their hands up, who are you most likely to call on first? Second? Last? Who do you praise in your classroom? Do you praise white children more often than the children of color? Do you praise all your children for being smart, for being good thinkers? Don't limit your praise of children of color to qualities like being quiet, waiting for a turn, being polite, or having musical or athletic skill. Praise *all* children for their effort, hard work, and intelligence.

DISCIPLINE IN EQUAL MEASURE

In many schools children of color are disciplined more often and more harshly. Teachers are more likely to ignore the "mistaken" behavior of white children. White children are also more likely to get a second chance to turn their behavior around before experiencing a consequence or disciplinary action. Children of color are more likely to receive a "time out" as a first response from the teacher. Make sure that racism isn't triggering an unconscious fear, anger, or sense of aggression on your part. Create a simple chart that lists all the children in your class. Conduct a count of who you discipline and make note of how often and what the discipline was. Do you see any racial patterns?

Some teachers are so disgusted by, uncomfortable with, or afraid of children of color that they disengage from having a relationship with the child. A college student of mine recently labeled this behavior "power off." In this situation, the teacher lets the child do whatever he or she wants, acting as though the child were not present or not important enough to warrant his or her attention. Another form of "power off" is when the teacher allows a child to become invisible in the classroom. The child feels as though the teacher does not see him for who he really is. Often adults of color report that, as a child, they felt invisible to their teachers. See all your children as equally human. See each child as he or she is. Take time to get to know each child. Look into their hearts and souls. Discover and affirm each child's identity.

Create a Nonracist Classroom

Unfortunately, racism is present in many classrooms across the country. Fortunately, the classroom is a relatively small environment. As a teacher, you have a lot of control over that environment. In response to racism, the role of an early childhood educator is to create a nonracist classroom. Every child deserves the right to learn and grow in a safe and nurturing environment. Through conscious effort you can minimize the impact of racism on children's lives. Make a decision to stop perpetuating racism in your classroom. Implement the following strategies to create a racism-free learning environment for your children:

MAKE UNITY AND EQUALITY THE GOAL OF YOUR CLASSROOM
The classroom is a small enough setting in which to achieve a community where everyone feels that they belong, they are equals, and they are treated fairly. Welcome each child personally every day. Start off the morning by saying good morning to one another. Make morning circle time a community time. Facilitate group discussions in which everyone has an opportunity to express themselves and be heard without interruption. Use a "talking stick" or other tool to ensure that each child has an equal chance to talk. Sing and dance together, affirm one another, and celebrate each other's accomplishments. Plan activities, such as mural painting or rearranging the classroom, that require children to cooperate with one another to complete the task. Use a helper chart or a name basket to ensure that each child has an equal opportunity to be your special helper or lead the class.

LIVE BY THE GOLDEN RULE

Teach children the golden rule, "Do unto others as you would have them do to you." A preschool translation might be "Treat others as you would like them to treat you." Make a colorful sign with this saying and post it prominently in the group time area. Teach the saying to children. Talk about how they want others to treat them and how they don't want to be treated. Dictate their answers and post the lists in the classroom. Help the children take their answers and turn them into classroom rules to live by.

RESPECT YOURSELF AND OTHERS TOO

Help children learn the names of their classmates and require them to call one another by name. Don't allow children to refer to one another as you, him, her, or them. Teach children that it is not okay to call classmates names; name-calling, teasing, and rejecting behavior hurts people's feelings. Don't allow children to put themselves or anyone else down. Instill pride and dignity by encouraging children to walk tall with their heads held high and ask them to show you their "positive proud smile."

TEACH CHILDREN COPING SKILLS

Successfully negotiating life in a racist society requires special skills. Although it may take most of us a lifetime to learn these skills, many can be introduced to young children. We hope that parents and future teachers will continue to strengthen children's resilience in the face of racism. Children need persistence. We need to encourage children to keep going, especially when they get frustrated, want to give up, or say "I can't." Like the "Little Engine that Could," children need to learn how to tell themselves, "I think I can, I think I can." Children also need to respond to racism—dirty looks, name-calling, and exclusion can poison a child's soul. We want to minimize the amount of racism they internalize. Giving children options for responding lessens the likelihood that they will hold the pain silently inside their little bodies. One option is to let it go. Sometimes for your own survival, it is better to walk away from a racist and potentially dangerous situation. Help children learn how to recognize dangerous situations and how to let some things roll off their backs. Another appropriate response to a racist situation is to reject the rejection. Teach children how to stand up for themselves and others. Encourage children to be proud of themselves for using either response to a racist situation.

DEMYSTIFY SKIN COLOR

Racism is based on the false belief that skin color is the most important determinant of a person's ability and worth. By teaching children about melanin and where skin color comes from, we can take away some of the power society gives to skin color. Provide children with many opportunities to learn about and explore skin color. Read books about skin color, such as Katie Kissinger's *All the Colors We Are*. Set out skin-color crayons, markers, and paints and invite children to paint and draw using these materials. Challenge children to mix paint or homemade playdough that matches their skin color. These types of activities help children see that no one is "white" and very few people are "black." They discover that we are all shades of brown and that everyone has a little bit of all the colors in their skin.

PROVIDE POSITIVE CROSS-RACIAL EXPERIENCES

If your classroom is racially mixed, try dividing the class into small groups for certain activities. Make sure that each group is racially mixed so that children have an opportunity to work together with a child from another race. Another variation is to pair children with a partner who is racially different and give them a cooperative task to work on. These types of experiences will help children feel more comfortable working and playing with a child from another race, and help foster a sense of teamwork and affiliation with someone from another race. If your classroom is racially homogenous, try establishing a relationship with a class that is racially diverse. Take field trips to places where children will have first-hand encounters with people from other races, and invite visitors from other races into your classroom.

FOSTER SOCIAL AWARENESS AND ACTION

Help children learn to recognize fair and unfair situations related to race. Try reading books that contain name-calling, or create your own scenarios and act them out with puppets or dolls. Children can role play incidents from the classroom or their lives outside of the class. Reenactments or simulations of unfair situations are also powerful ways to help children learn to recognize and challenge unfair situations. Facilitate group discussions that give them opportunities to explore how they would feel and what they might do if they were mistreated because of their skin color. Take the next step by inviting children to take action. Action could be standing up for yourself and saying something such as, "I don't like it when you call me names." It could be learning how to stand up for another, such as when a kindergartener decided to get up from the lunch table with his friends and go eat with "the new boy with the dark skin." The new boy was eating at another table all by himself and the kindergartener was afraid that his friends would laugh at him, but he wanted the new boy to feel welcome and not lonely. These types of activities help children begin to see how race works in their lives. Finally, they help children think about how things could be different and this gives them hope for a better world.

INTEGRATE THE CURRICULUM

Help children respect and value all races by including the contributions of individuals from all races into the curriculum. Talk about Garrett Morgan (inventor of the stoplight) during a unit on transportation, George Washington Carver (an agricultural researcher who developed products from peanuts and sweet potatoes) during a unit on food, or Dr. Carlos Finley (identified the mosquito as the vector for the transmission of yellow fever and developed a cure) during a unit on bodies or health. In addition, integrate the history of people of color into the curriculum throughout the year. This will help children of color access the strength, courage, and determination of their families and ancestors. Highlight heroes and sheroes in the local racial communities to help children of color feel pride in and give them access to the strength of their communities.

Racism is one environmental factor that influences children's development, although the issues of race in the development of children has long been ignored. Racism poses some key questions that must be addressed by the child care field as a whole, but also by each individual child care professional. Can you recognize and understand how the environment shapes children's development in your classroom? How do external environmental factors such as racism affect the development of the children in your care? Teachers can be very influential in minimizing the impact racism has on their classrooms by examining race and racism, learning more about children's racial identity development, and taking steps to create a nonracist classroom. In the next chapter, we will examine the differences between children and teachers or parents and teachers that result from differences in culture.

Questions to Ponder

How do parents raise emotionally healthy children in a society in which children of color are devalued?

How does constant exposure to overt (open) or covert (concealed) racism affect children's development?

How is the deck is stacked against children of color? How is the deck stacked in favor of white children?

How do parents of color teach their children to survive growing up in a racist society?

To what extent is your program unintentionally creating a hostile environment for children of color?

Do teachers care as much about African American boys as white girls?

References

Barndt, Joseph. 1991. *Dismantling racism.* Minneapolis: Augsburg Press.

Coll, Cynthia Garcia, G. Lamberty, R. Jenkins, H.P. McAdoo, K.Crnick, B.H. Wask, and H.V. Garcia. 1996. An integrative model for the study of developmental competencies in minority children. *Child Development* 67 (October): 1891–1914.

Finkelstein, Neal W., and Ron Haskins. 1983. Kindergarten children prefer same-color peers. *Child Development* 54: 502–508.

Hale-Benson, Janice E. 1986. *Black children: Their roots, culture, and learning styles.* Baltimore: Johns Hopkins University Press.

Hatcher, Richard, and Barry Troyna. 1992. *Racism in children's lives: A study of mainly white primary schools.* New York: Routledge.

Helms, Janet E. 1993. *Black and white racial identity.* Westport, Conn.: Praeger.

Homes, Robyn M. 1995. *How young children perceive race.* Thousand Oaks, Calif.: Sage.

Jelloun, Tahar Ben. 1999. *Racism explained to my daughter.* New York: New Press.

Kissinger, Katie. 1997. *All the colors we are.* St. Paul: Redleaf Press.

Mathias, Barbara, and Mary Ann French. 1996. *Forty ways to raise a nonracist child.* New York: Harper Collins.

Peters, William. 1987. *A class divided then and now.* Expanded edition. New Haven, Conn.: Yale University Press.

Pine, Gerald J., and Asa G. Hilliard III. 1990. Rx for racism: Imperatives for America's schools. *Phi Delta Kappan* (April).

Reddy, Maureen T. 1994. *Crossing the color line: Race, parenting, and culture.* New Brunswick, N.J.: Rutgers University Press.

Wardle, Francis. 1987. Building positive images: Interracial children and their families. In *Alike and different: Exploring our humanity with children.* Edited by Bonnie Neugebauer. Redmond, Wash.: Exchange Press Inc.

Wright, Marguerite A. 1998. *I'm chocolate, you're vanilla: Raising healthy black and biracial children in a race-conscious world.* San Francisco: Jossey-Bass Publishers.

Culturally Responsive Care and Education

There is almost nothing that a person can do while interacting with children under three, while caring for a child under three, that is not cultural. Everything that one does is cultural.

Lily Wong Fillmore

Differences between children and teachers or parents and teachers often cause problems. Teachers must realize that these differences may be a result of culture. Culture influences how families raise children and how a child behaves, communicates, and learns. These behavior patterns and child-rearing practices reflect a specific culture's history, values, beliefs, and current situation. In order to provide good care and education for young children, teachers must make their work **culturally responsive**—the program must represent and support the home cultures of the families whose children attend.

See glossary.

This chapter will help you work successfully with children from diverse cultures by identifying ways in which culture and family patterns mold the children you serve. This chapter will provide you with some basic information about families and practical ideas for providing culturally responsive child care. As you read through this material, look inward and gain insight into your own culture. Reflect on your own family experiences. Think about how your orientation toward family may affect your work with children and families.

What Is Culture?

You may not be convinced that culture has a large influence on children in your classroom, much less your own teaching style. Let's begin by defining culture. Culture is things, customs, beliefs, and values. Culture can be thought of in terms of the concrete items and objects we see, hold, and use. Items such as clothing, artwork, food, and dance are tangible symbols of a person's culture. Culture is also experienced in how people live out their lives as well as what they believe and what values they hold dear. Family roles, childrearing patterns, communications styles, and holiday traditions are ways in which culture influences how we as individuals live our daily lives. People's goals in life and their beliefs about human nature and humanity are invisible but ever present aspects of culture. The chart on the next page suggests some of the aspects of life that are part of an individual's cultural experience:

Culture is a powerful force that shapes our lives. Culture is who we are on the inside. It is the set of values, beliefs, and behaviors shared by a group of people. Culture gives us roots. Cultural traditions give our lives meaning, stability, and security. Culture is dynamic and alive, and it changes slowly over time. Culture is transmitted through families from one generation to the next. That which is cultural, seems natural and normal.

Some people refer to culture as an iceberg. The cultural artifacts and behaviors make up the tip of the iceberg, or the 10 percent that is visible above the waterline. Cultural beliefs, which can often be learned by an outsider to the culture, are directly beneath the surface. Cultural values are deep and difficult to uncover and represent—such as the foundation of the iceberg, or the 90 percent that lies underneath the water.

Some individuals have recently embraced America as a country made up of many cultures, languages, and religions. This is often imagined as a tossed salad or a mosaic in which each part retains its own character, while adding to the whole. It is important to recognize, however, that the government's policy toward culture has been assimilation. The process of assimilation, represented by the familiar image of the "melting pot," involves stripping away one's own culture in order to create a new American culture. The melting pot is an image from steel-making, when ore is melted to burn off the impurities. The idea behind the melting pot is that if America as a nation is to be as strong as steel, culture must be removed in order to create a single unified American society, with no trace of the

Culture List

Things (cultural artifacts)	Customs or Traditions (how people live)	Values and Beliefs (deep invisible reasons behind the customs)
Clothing	Celebrations	Spirituality
Jewelry	Holidays	Role of people in the world
Food	Ceremonies	Role of children
Cooking and eating utensils	Communication style	Role of the environment in people's lives
Music and instruments	Ages and stages of development	Meaning of life
Dance	Family roles	
Language	Rites of passage	
Folk tales	Meal patterns	
Toys and games		
Coins		

Adapted from an activity in *Alerta: A Multicultural, Bilingual Approach to Teaching Young Children* by Leslie R. Williams and Yvonne De Gaetano, Menlo Park: Addison-Wesley, 1985.

original cultures. Because of white dominance in creating the systems of American society, the new "American" culture envisioned was also largely white and European. Do you see how assimilation (the melting pot) treats individual cultures as impurities to be burned away instead of as valuable and beautiful parts of a multicolored whole?

In defining what culture is, we can also look at what it is not. In reality, there is no agreed-upon American culture. Culture is not the same as citizenship. Many Americans, particularly European Americans, confuse culture with citizenship. Citizenship is what government you pledge allegiance to. Citizenship activities include things such as abiding by the laws, voting, contributing to the well-being of the community, demonstrating patriotism, and paying taxes. Look at the chart above showing the activities that reflect culture. Do you see how those are different from citizenship activities? Culture should not be seen as a threat to nationalism, patriotism, and cohesion. Likewise, promoting cultural identity does not promote separatism or result in the erosion of national unity.

Early Childhood Education Reflects a European American World View

Many European American ancestors gave up their cultural identity for white privilege. Most European Americans are unaware of their cultural traditions. Many European immigrants, like my grandfather, changed the spelling of their names so that they would sound more "American." The other side of my family has been in the United States for many generations. We are a mix of many European ethnicities. The result of this common pattern is that many European Americans don't experience culture as a core part of their identity, or pick and choose which parts of their culture to accept. Often they can't speak their ancestral languages and are monolingual. This doesn't mean that European Americans don't have culture. It does reflect two important facts: (1) the common elements of European American culture (such as values and communication style) dominate in the United States, and are often invisible to European Americans; and (2) the unique parts of different European cultures (such as languages and holiday rituals) have often been lost to individual European Americans through assimilation. These two somewhat contradictory facts—European American culture is omnipresent; European American culture is lost—make the concept of culture confusing. Uncovering European American cultural patterns, especially as they relate to child development and early childhood education may make more clear the concept of "culture" and the influence of European American culture on early childhood programs.

The field of early childhood care and education has been greatly influenced by European American culture. So understanding some of the common characteristics of European American culture can help teachers work more effectively with both European American children and children from other cultures. The chart on the next page shows some key traits of European American culture.

Culture Influences Childrearing Patterns

Culture influences childrearing and, as a result, people from different cultural backgrounds have differing ideas about what constitutes quality child care. According to Darla Miller (1989), the author of *First Steps Toward Cultural*

Characteristics of European American Culture

Communication	Greetings are brief, informal, and casual. People say, "Hi!" and call each other by first names. Communication is frank, candid, and explicit. "Say what you mean and mean what you say." Individuals communicate at arm's length from one another and look each other in the eye.
Time	Clock conscious. "Time is money." People are usually punctual and concerned with being on time. Five minutes late is late and fifteen minutes late is cause for concern.
Future-oriented	Emphasis on future rather than present. Tend to minimize the past. "The sun will come out tomorrow. Tomorrow will be a brighter day." This is evident in life insurance policies, retirement plans, and wills.
Youth-oriented	What's good for the child is good for the family. Elderly are seen as a burden or liability. Families use nursing homes to care for the elderly.
Family	Family is nuclear and mobile. Contracts and legal agreements define family relationships.
Eating habits	Eating is a necessity. Individuals may eat while doing other activities such as driving, working, or watching television. When families eat together, food is often served "family style." All family members sit down together. Food is placed in serving bowls and platters, which are passed from one member to the next, and people serve themselves.
Work	Strong work ethic. "Work and then play." Individuals are task-oriented, productive, and efficient. Individuals talk of working on relationships and working on their parenting skills. Prefer rewards based on individual achievement.
Thinking style	Logical sequential thinking. Knowledge is fixed and static. Value rational and objective thinking that can be proven scientifically or mathematically. Subjective or intuitive knowledge is not highly respected.
Learning style	People learn through exploration, problem solving, and interaction with objects. Value creative problem solving, seek creative solutions, continuous improvement, and progress.
Individualism	People are unique individuals, distinct from their family or culture. Individuals control their lives. Value personal freedom, personal choice, and autonomy.
Egalitarianism	There is a stated value of treating women and men the same. Children are given equal status with adults. Challenging authority is acceptable behavior.
Self-responsibility/ self-sufficiency	People are responsible for their own behavior and managing their own lives. Individuals should provide for their own basic needs and not rely on others. Needing help from others is viewed as being a burden or being weak.
Materialism	High value placed on things such as clothing, furniture, toys, and other consumer goods. Owning goods contributes to an individual's sense of self and status in the community.

Difference: Socialization in Infant/Toddler Day Care: "Methods of caring for and educating young children routinely expected by high-income families may shock and repel low-income families—and vice versa. Routines considered desirable by one group may be seen as inane by another. Guidance strategies believed in some cultural settings to be essential to healthy growth may be considered inhumane and destructive in others. What some consider to be essential experiences for effective early learning, others consider utter nonsense. Social workers, early childhood educators, and child care professionals have often felt the tension among these opposing views and have sometimes been snagged unknowingly by their own culturally biased assumptions."

In reality, culture influences how a parent responds to all elements of child-rearing, such as the following:

- Parent's age-related expectations of their children
- Interest in and concern over children acquiring skills by a certain age
- Attachment and separation
- Children's role and responsibility in the family
- Gender roles
- Diet and mealtime routines
- Sleep patterns and bedtime routines
- Medical care
- Discipline methods
- Children's play
- Children's learning styles
- Family's expectations of teachers and schools
- Selection and use of supplemental child care

As a teacher you have your own culturally based beliefs about how each of these childrearing issues should be handled in your classroom, as well as by parents at home. Sometimes we view our own style of childrearing as the normal or right way. Remember, each culture successfully raises new generations of children according to their own values and beliefs. We must be willing to look at the life experiences of the children and families in our care without placing judgment.

Early childhood programs institute policies and procedures that define a specific style of child care and education. A program can never be multicultural if its staff expects one style of child care to complement the endless variety of child-rearing patterns. Conflicts arise when programs rigidly follow one style. Parents and teachers may disagree about what's best for a child. You have probably observed or at least sensed these types of conflicts. For example, have you ever been frustrated by or found yourself wondering about the following:

- A child who refuses to play by himself and interrupts other children who are playing quietly and independently

- A child who has difficulty choosing an activity and prefers to cling to you, her teacher

- A child who asks for your help or attention by verbally teasing you

- A child who resists looking you in the eye when you are reprimanding him

- A child who has a high energy level and turns every activity into a large-motor experience

- A child who goes limp and becomes silent when you directly confront her behavior

- A baby who prefers to be held and gently rocked, and who cries loudly whenever you put him on the floor to play

- A three-year-old who drinks from a bottle and can't go to sleep without a pacifier in her mouth

- A child who comes to school every day in "party" clothes and his parents warn him to stay away from paint and other messy activities

- A parent who is very angry because her daughter comes home with a dirty face and sand in her hair

- A child who enjoys lively play with one or two playmates, but is silent and hangs back in group activities

A teacher may think she clashes with a child because of "personality" issues, when in fact it is a difference in culture.

On the following pages is a diverse list of culturally based family patterns, childrearing practices, and values—all of which may influence your classroom. Use this list to help you identify sources of conflict, recognize the child's experience, and understand the parent's perspective. The right-hand column offers suggestions for alternative caregiving and teaching practices and attitudes. Use this list to develop and institute culturally relevant care and education.

Culture and the Classroom

Cultural Pattern	Child's Experience	Caregiving and Teaching Strategy
FAMILY SYSTEM		
Highly mobile, nuclear	Child has little contact with extended family; friends take the place of extended family.	Sponsor family events to help families build support systems, encourage child's friendship that continue away from school.
Clan network in which family unit lives is in the same neighborhood or community	Child is used to a high level of activity within the home, with people coming and going (dropping by). Child may regularly eat or sleep in more than one household.	Child may become bored if there is little activity. Provide opportunities to move freely around room. Thrives on free choice play. Provide activities that encourage cooperation and sharing.
Extended family that lives together and shares resources	Child is involved in all activities and is used to a high level of cooperation and responsibility. Separating children can be seen as breaking up the family.	Child may try to watch out for younger brothers and sisters. Consider mixed age groups that allow siblings to stay together or allow child to "visit" sibling during the day. Provide activities that build cooperation and sharing. Understand that family may not need or attend family-oriented center events.
POWER STRUCTURE		
Democratic family with members sharing in decision making	Child is allowed/encouraged to negotiate, compromise.	Offer real choices to child; use problem-solving techniques.
One family member has the power and authority to make decisions	Child is expected to obey, follow commands, and respect adult authority.	Child may resist making activity choices and may be uncomfortable looking adults in the eye or calling them by name. Don't insist on eye contact; be aware child may need your help in making choices. If a concern exists, try to connect with the powerful family member.
WORK/EMPLOYMENT		
Career-oriented; job is very rewarding; parent brings work home and has few other interests	Parents want child to have similar opportunities to be creative and develop own interests; child relates to learning through play.	Provide meaningful choices and opportunities for creativity and self-expression.
Boring, monotonous job, or a job that requires little initiative or autonomy; personal fulfillment comes from recreation	Parents don't expect child to enjoy learning; model attitude of work now and play later; and may expect child to sit through long lessons.	Guide child in free play if he tends to become wild. Encourage and demonstrate short, quiet breaks from long lessons.

Culture and the Classroom, *continued*

Cultural Pattern	Child's Experience	Caregiving and Teaching Strategy
ATTITUDES TOWARD CHILD CARE		
Child care is a public place and the teacher should be respected	Child comes to school in dress clothes, is told to obey the teacher, and may not call teachers by their first names.	Provide smocks that actually cover and protect clothing; respect child's need to speak to you formally; consider adding a title (Ms., Mrs., Mr.) if you use your first name.
Child care is for the child, part of a modern extended family network	The child may come in worn, casual play clothes; the child and parent call teachers by their first names.	Don't be offended or judge the child based on her clothes; consider allowing the child to call you by your first name.
CHILD DEVELOPMENT		
Infancy equals the first twelve months of life	Child is breast-fed for the first six to twelve months; discipline begins with saying "no" and slapping the child's hand, and letting child cry after six months of age.	You may feel that the child's parent is pushing the child. Use active listening techniques and simple commands toward the end of the first year.
Infancy equals the first two years	Child is breast-fed for the first two to four years or is allowed to have a bottle for the first five years; toilet training is gradual; discipline begins at the end of this period; parent may not be concerned about developmental milestones.	Recognize that this child may have a difficult adjustment to child care due to grieving the perceived loss of mother. Find ways to hold and carry this child; do not force him to play alone for long periods.
Infancy equals the first five years of life	Child is breast-fed for the first two years; may spend all of waking hours with mother and may sleep with mother; few demands on child at this time; toilet training is gradual; child is not pushed to learn self-help skills.	Accept what may look like delayed separation anxiety, which may peak during preschool years and catch you off guard. Allow child to have transitional objects such as stuffed animals or blankets; push developmental information on parent only if you have a strong concern about delays.

Culture and the Classroom, *continued*

Cultural Pattern	Child's Experience	Caregiving and Teaching Strategy
SOCIAL EXPERIENCES		
Parents experience discrimination, lack of opportunities, violence, and police hostility	Child's demands are ignored or ridiculed as child is prepared to survive in a hostile environment, taught to tolerate unfairness, and conditioned not to expect too much.	Delay your response to a child; respect parent's need to keep child safe; and use firm discipline.
Parents experience privilege and many opportunities, and live in a safe environment	Child is given what she wants and is taught to expect that her needs will be met and that the world is a safe place.	Consider granting parent's request for individual treatment of child.
VALUES		
Strong, close-knit family	Child taught that the family comes before the individual; members are expected to sacrifice personal desire for the family.	Recognize child may be expected to miss school in order to take care of a family member.
Interpersonal relationships	Infant is usually in the company of others and is held most of the time, or passed from one person to the next; and child is people-oriented.	Find ways to hold and carry infant; provide lots of touching and caressing; play "people" games such as peek-a-boo; understand that child may be more interested in playmates than in manipulating toys and objects; use eye contact to guide child's behavior.
Independence	Infant only held for feeding, comforting, and moving from place to place; child sleeps alone for long periods of time; and child has own space and toys at home.	Recognize parent's fear that too much holding and cuddling will "spoil" the baby; allow infant to play on the floor and children to move independently around room; bring own toys from home and minimize sharing.
Interdependence	Child is raised to understand that being a member of a family involves relying on others to get his or her needs met; give and take relationships with siblings, parents, and extended family members. Child is fed when he or she is capable of feeding herself and carried when he or she is capable of walking.	Create situations where the child relies on you for assistance. Store toys in view but out of reach so that the child asks you to get them down, serve children their meals rather than having children serve themselves, pair up and encourage older children to help younger ones tie shoes or button coats.

Culture and the Classroom, *continued*

Cultural Pattern	Child's Experience	Caregiving and Teaching Strategy
VALUES, CONT.		
Present-time orientation	Child's lifestyle is very process-oriented with little emphasis on routines and eating or sleeping by the clock.	Offer flexibility in arrival and departure; avoid threats and bribes to get child to eat or nap.
Personal cleanliness	Infant may be spoon-fed, child's face is washed often, clothes are kept clean, and toilet training may begin after the first year.	Keep the child's face clean; avoid getting sand in the child's hair; put the child in clean clothes before going home from child care.
Honor, dignity, and pride	By their behavior and achievement, child upholds family honor; child is disciplined for rude behavior and poor manners.	Share child's achievements with parent; help child to learn manners; be sensitive to parent's need to maintain pride and dignity when confronting parent about child's negative behavior.
"Humanism"—emphasis on individual dignity, worth, and self-realization	Each child is accepted as an individual; child is not pushed to reach developmental milestones or learn self-help skills early; parent may trust individual teacher more than the program.	Avoid motivating child through competition; understand that the child may be more interested in friends or helping the teacher than in completing tasks; avoid misreading parent's acceptance of child's abilities as lack of interest.
"Personalism"—emphasis on, and orientation toward, close interpersonal relationships and friendships rather than outer achievements	The child is encouraged to be friendly, hospitable, charming, congenial, agreeable, open, and outgoing.	Encourage the child to be loyal and generous to classmates; don't be surprised if the child tries to be your "helper"; find ways for the child to help others in the classroom.
Modesty	Child taught to keep a low profile in public and discouraged from drawing attention to herself; it is not acceptable for child to ask for what she wants; there may be little public display of affection.	Respond to child's cries promptly; don't allow this child to become an invisible member of your class; this child may not ask much of you and easily can go unnoticed; avoid forcing the child to talk during group time.
Self-expression	Child taught to express personality through verbal communication; child is praised for speaking and listening well.	Look for child to enjoy group time and creative expression, and engage the adults in verbal interplay; try teaching through drama, stories, and song.

Culture and the Classroom, *continued*

Cultural Pattern	Child's Experience	Caregiving and Teaching Strategy
VALUES, CONT.		
Strong oral tradition	Culture passed down through storytelling, poetry, and song; adults guide child's behavior by telling a story with a moral.	Recognize teachable moments for telling a story to motivate or challenge the child's behavior; also, use lullabies and songs.
Expressing feelings is permitted	Child is allowed to cry, scream, and have temper tantrums; affection is often expressed among family members.	Accept child's crying while comforting the child; stay with child when he is having a temper tantrum.
Feelings should be hidden	Crying and screaming are discouraged, as are displays of affection.	Pick up infant as soon as she cries; try ignoring outbursts, or remove child from group to express feelings.
CHILD DISCIPLINE		
Clear, direct discipline	Child learns to respect authority, to do what he is told, and to come the first time he is called.	Child may ignore or not take positive discipline techniques seriously. Try using firm statements and commands, humor, gentle harassment, and animated gestures.
Motivate child toward inherent goodness	Child is given freedom to explore consequences; adults talk in quiet voices and warn child of possible embarrassment as a result of misbehavior.	Child may go limp or show other signs of passive resistance if you discipline him too strongly. Use natural consequences, ask rather than command, and talk softly.
Motivate child toward good behavior from inherent chaos or self-interest	Child is disciplined by scolding, threats, and promises.	Try modeling desired behavior using "if-then" statements: "If you put the toys away, then you can go outside"; praise good manners and polite behavior.
Harmony within family or with other people	Child is scolded, shamed, and humiliated for fighting or having temper tantrums.	Show disapproval through facial expression and body language; try talking to the child in a low, hushed voice; praise cooperation.
LEARNING STYLE		
Formal—learning takes place in a structured environment with clear, distinct roles	The child has been taught rules of appropriate social behavior such as addressing adults by a title, dressing appropriately when going out in public, and showing respect to adults and others.	Dress professionally; have children use a title when addressing you; provide a set daily schedule, a quiet learning environment, and less mobility; and make large group time more like a ceremony.

Culture and the Classroom, *continued*

Cultural Pattern	Child's Experience	Caregiving and Teaching Strategy
LEARNING STYLE, CONT.		
Novelty—learning is oriented toward the present, flexibility, creativity, and change	The child is encouraged to try anything once and is used to doing things on the spur of the moment; home may be a very dynamic, lively environment.	Use a variety of teaching methods; be creative and flexible; follow the child's lead and go with the unexpected; and avoid repetition.
Group orientation—learning is seen as a collaborative process in which everyone's input is necessary and valued	The child may be used to being in close physical proximity to others and doing things with siblings or as a family; sharing information may not be seen as "cheating," but as logical and helpful.	Create a warm, friendly classroom based on respect and cooperation; praise the group rather than individuals; and avoid individual reinforcements such as praise and sticker charts.
Visual—learning takes place primarily through sight; vision is used to take in information and feedback	The child likes to "see" the pictures in a book, have adults look at him or her when they are interacting, and notice visual details in an environment.	Demonstrate and model; use posters and illustrations to show children what to do.
Kinesthetic—learning takes place primarily through the child's active physical engagement with materials, and in motion	The child may need to move (jiggle, wiggle, fidget) to pay attention and process information and may need to demonstrate concepts with her body or gesture with her hands in order to convey information.	Make sure there is always space in the classroom where children can be active; give children sensory balls or worry stones to manipulate during large group or story times. If a child is having difficulty explaining herself in words, ask if she can show you with her body or demonstrate with her hands.
Relational—learning takes place through dialogue and interaction with others	The child is sensitive to the emotional experience associated with learning and needs harmony in the classroom in order to learn.	Pay attention to the emotional climate of the classroom; invite free communication, emotional expression, and simultaneous talk rather than alternating talk.
Independent—learning is easiest when working alone	The child enjoys playing alone for extended periods of time and making his own "projects."	Provide free choice time; allow children to work alone; praise self-motivation and completion of projects; invite the child to observe you, practice while you watch, and then continue to repeat the activity privately.

Culturally Inappropriate Programs

"Remember what happened to E.T. when he got too far from home? He lost his power over the world. And so it is with our children when their school settings are so different from home that they represent an alien culture to them. They too lose their power. But unlike E.T., our children cannot simply go home, for their homes are embedded in that alien culture" (Brunson-Phillips 1988). Cultural mismatches lead to academic failure. Research has linked academic failure of minority children to differences between the home and school. Often, classrooms are designed to meet the needs of European American children. As a result, the classroom fails to validate the home culture or life experience of children who are not European American. Many current efforts are designed to improve school achievement through positive interaction between the home and school. Research suggests that learning style is related to the primary caregiver's child-rearing practices.

Culturally inappropriate programs

- Fail to promote children's cognitive and social growth
- Disrespect children's life experience and turn children off from learning
- Make children feel rejected and cause children to reject school
- Cause children to feel unappreciated and misunderstood
- Weaken children's connection to their family and home culture and cause children to lose their sense of identity
- Increase the likelihood children will reject their home culture and rebel from their family

Cultural behaviors can be similar to one another, different but complementary, or different and contradictory. Dichotomous (all or nothing) thinking is not very helpful when thinking about culturally related behavior. I find it much more useful to think about a continuum of behaviors.

What Is Culturally Relevant Education?

"Work to consciously establish a program approach which both assists children to function in their own cultural community and builds their competence in the culture of the larger society" (Brunson-Phillips 1988). Culturally responsive care honors and meets the needs of today's changing families. In a culturally responsive program, children maintain their personal power and sense of identity. The child's family is supported and enhanced. Children don't experience daily conflict or confusion. The purpose of child care is to foster children's healthy identity development as a member of a family and a cultural community. Culturally responsive programs share three important components:

- Curriculum is based on children's daily lives
- Activities incorporate children's home language
- Activities encourage children to learn about their family and home culture

How can you help children feel at home in your classroom? Culturally competent teachers and caregivers demonstrate the following qualities:

- Deep sense of respect
- Awareness of own culture
- Ability to maintain cultural integrity
- Knowledge of other cultural practices
- Understanding of the history of cultures in the United States
- Ability to get accurate information about the families and cultures
- Ability to avoid assumptions
- Belief that other perspectives are equally valid
- Skills needed to critique existing knowledge base and practices
- Ability to take another perspective
- Open, willing, and able to adapt and try new behaviors
- Good problem-solving skills
- Ability to tolerate ambiguity, conflict, and change

What makes cross-cultural work difficult? We learn the rules and expectations for behavior within our home culture by age five. We tend to think that our own culture's patterns are the norm. We may not have a lot of cross-cultural experiences. It is hard for adults to learn new cultural patterns. Our values are cultural and may conflict with those of other cultures. Our own culturally based perspective makes it difficult to accurately interpret other cultures.

You can get to know yourself as a cultural being by answering these questions:

What is your cultural identity?

Where did your family originate?

When did your family immigrate to the United States? Why did they come here?

Where did your family first settle in the United States?

What are some of the values, beliefs, and behaviors associated with your cultural heritage?

What are some traditional foods that are served in your family?

What are some words of wisdom that your elders passed on to you?

What are the childrearing patterns in your family?

When do you say "no" to a child?

How are children disciplined in your family?

When does a baby become a child?

What are some childrearing practices that shock or appall you?

Who would you ask or where would you go for parenting advice?

How does your culture influence your caregiving style?

How does your culture influence your teaching style?

What do you need in order to become culturally competent?

What Do You Need to Work Effectively with Other Cultures?

Sometimes teachers think they need to know everything about a culture before they can work effectively with children and families from that culture. Some teachers feel they need to have all the power and be the expert in the parent-teacher relationship. Sometimes we get trapped into acting on our own assumptions. We may lack communication skills, or we may not be used to reflecting on our practices, or it may be hard for us to step back and take other perspectives.

A number of steps can be taken to help teachers work effectively with children from cultures other than their own. Here are some suggestions:

- Become culturally competent (see pp. 107–108).
- Get to know families and identify their strengths.
- Build partnerships with parents.
- Interact with children in culturally congruent ways.
- Provide culturally consistent care.
- Work to reduce cultural conflicts between home and school.
- Differentiate problem behavior from a culturally different pattern of behavior.
- Incorporate children's home language into the classroom.
- Help children develop strong cultural identities.
- Invite families to share their culture with the school.
- Recognize the contributions of children's home culture.
- Strengthen families by connecting them to the neighborhood and community.
- Participate in community cultural events.

Our teaching and caregiving practices must go beyond our own cultural orientations. We must be fully aware that cultural differences between children and teachers or parents and teachers often cause problems for children. Some of these problems, such as feelings of alienation and isolation, can be extremely hurtful and result in very negative consequences for the child. Culturally responsive care evolves from teachers realizing that differences may be a result of culture—in other words, how families raise children and how a child behaves and learns. You can work successfully with children from diverse cultures by identifying the behavior patterns and childrearing practices that reflect a specific culture's history, values, beliefs, and current situation.

All too often, children who speak a language other than English do not receive developmentally appropriate language instruction and, as a result, are less likely to succeed in school. In the next chapter, we'll look at how children acquire a second language and classroom strategies you can use to support second language learners.

Questions to Ponder

1. Try to uncover your own culturally-based values, beliefs, and behaviors. Ask yourself these questions:

- What were some words of wisdom, sayings, or advice that your parents or grandparents passed on to you?
- What are some childrearing practices of others that shock, appall, or frighten you?
- To whom or where would you go for advice about children or parenting?

2. How can you develop the sensitivity and perspective that will enable you to provide culturally responsive care and education that honors and meets the needs of today's changing families?

3. In your experience, how have cultural differences created challenges in the classroom? How did you resolve or manage those differences? Would you do it differently now?

4. Use the form on the following pages to help you think about diversifying your caregiving routines and practices.

What if?

(From *Developing Roots & Wings*, 1992, Redleaf Press)

This activity allows you to think about diversifying caregiving routines and procedures. Read through the list and do the following:

- Circle those practices that would be the easiest to change.
- Put a star next to those practices that you could never do.
- Underline those practices that would be possible, but difficult to change.

1. What would happen if we considered different family systems in the design of an early childhood program?

- What if we created mixed-age groups?
- What if we allowed siblings to stay together during the day?
- What if we allowed a child to visit his baby sister?

2. What would happen if we respected the power structure of various families?

- What if we allowed children to participate in making the classroom rules?
- What if we invited a child's mother and grandmother to the parent/teacher conference?

3. What would happen if we respected how parent's work and social status influences their parenting?

- What if we allowed children to move around more or to be more physically active during free choice play?
- What if we included some product-oriented activities in the curriculum?
- What if we granted a given parent's request that their child not go outside today?

4. What would happen if we considered parents' attitudes toward teachers?

- What if the children were to call me by my first name?
- What if the children were to use a title of respect to identify me?

What if? *continued*

5. What would happen if we recognized that child development theories and developmentally appropriate practices are culturally based?

- What if we held a baby instead of putting her on the floor?
- What if we allowed babies to fall asleep in the middle of the hubbub of other children, instead of in a separate "crib room"?
- What if we let them sleep where they were, instead of in a crib or on a mat?
- What if we allowed parents to decide when their child is ready to be toilet trained?
- What if we allowed toddlers to have bottles, pacifiers, or blankets?

6. What would happen if we incorporated values from different cultures into our program?

- What if we played touching and "people" games with babies instead of encouraging them to play with toys and objects?
- What if we allowed children to bring toys from home?
- What if we didn't make children share?
- What if we didn't make all children be here by 9:00 A.M.?
- What if we washed children's faces, combed their hair, and tucked in their shirts toward the end of the day?

7. What would happen if we modeled different styles of communication?

- What if we casually told stories throughout the day to make a point or teach a concept?
- What if we allowed children to show their anger?

8. What if we recognized that parents' discipline methods are part of their culture?

- What if we tried humor and gentle harassment with some children?
- What if we lowered our voice and talked very softly when disciplining some children?
- What if we used if/then statements with some children?

What if? *continued*

Add your own what-ifs.

References

Brunson-Phillips, Carol. 1988. Nurturing diversity for today's children and tomorrow's leaders. *Young Children* (January): 42–47.

Brunson-Phillips, Carol. 1998. Preparing teachers to use their voices for change. *Young Children* 53 (3): 55–60.

Center for Child and Family Studies, Far West Laboratory for Educational Research and Development and the California State Department of Education. *Infant/toddler caregiving: A guide to culturally sensitive care.* 1993. The Program for Infant/Toddler Caregivers. Sacramento: Center for Child and Family Studies, Far West Laboratory for Educational Research and Development and the California State Department of Education.

Chang, Hedy Nai-Lin. 1993. *Affirming children's roots: Cultural and linguistic diversity in early care and education.* San Francisco: California Tomorrow.

Chang, Hedy Nai-Lin, Amy Muckelroy, and Dora Pulido-Tobiassen. 1996. *Looking in, looking out: Redefining child care and early education in a diverse society.* San Francisco: California Tomorrow.

Comer, James P., M.D., and Alvin F. Poussaint, M.D. 1975. *Black child care: How to bring up a healthy black child in America: A guide to emotional and psychological development.* New York: Simon and Schuster.

Far West Laboratory in collaboration with California Department of Education, producers. 1992. *Essential connections: Ten keys to culturally sensitive child care.* Sacramento: California Department of Education.

Gonzalez-Mena, Janet. *Multicultural issues in child care.* 1993. Mountain View, Calif.: Mayfield Publishing Company.

Hale, Janice. 1991. The transmission of cultural values to young African American children. *Young Children* (September).

Hale, Janice E. 1994. *Unbank the fire.* Baltimore: The Johns Hopkins University Press.

Harkness, Sara, and Charles M. Super, eds. 1996. *Parents' cultural belief systems: Their origins, expressions, and consequences.* New York: The Guilford Press.

Hildebrand, Verna, Lillian A. Phenice, Mary M. Gray, and Rebecca P. Hines. 1996. *Knowing and serving diverse families.* Englewood Cliffs, N.J.: Merrill Prentice-Hall, Inc.

Hopson, Darlene Powell, and Derek S. Hopson. 1991. *Different and wonderful: Raising black children in a race-conscious society.* New York: Prentice Hall Press.

Hyun, Eunsook. 1998. Making sense of developmentally and culturally appropriate practice (DCAP) in early childhood education. New York: Peter Lang.

Ingoldsby, Bron B, and Suzanna Smith, eds. 1995. *Families in multicultural perspective*. New York: The Guilford Press.

McAdoo, Harriette Pipes, and John Lewis McAdoo, eds. 1985. *Black children: Social, educational, and parental environments*. Newbury Park, Calif.: Sage Publications.

McAdoo, Harriette Pipes, ed. 1993. *Family ethnicity: Strength in diversity*. Newbury Park, Calif.: Sage Publications.

Miller, Darla. 1989. *First steps toward cultural difference: Socialization in infant/ toddler day care*. Washington, D.C.: Child Welfare League of America, Inc.

Nieto, Sonia. 1999. *Affirming diversity: The sociopolitical context of multicultural education*. 2d ed. Reading, Mass.: Addison-Wesley.

Shade, Barbara J., Mary Oberg, and Cynthia A. Kelly. 1997. *Creating culturally responsive classrooms*. Washington, D.C.: American Psychological Association.

Slonim, Maureen B. 1991. *Children, culture, and ethnicity: Evaluating and understanding the impact*. New York: Garland Publishing.

Spector, Rachel E. 1985. *Cultural diversity in health and illness*. 4th ed. Norwalk, Conn.: Appleton-Century-Crofts.

Sue, Derald Wing, and David Sue. 1990. *Counseling the culturally different: Theory and practice*. 2d ed. New York: John Wiley and Sons.

Trawick-Smith, Jeffrey. 1999. *Early childhood development: A multicultural perspective*. 2d ed. Saddle River, N.J.: Prentice Hall.

Williams, Leslie R., and Yvonne De Gaetano. 1985. *Alerta: A multicultural, bilingual approach to teaching young children*. Menlo Park, Calif.: Addison-Wesley.

York, Stacey. 1992. *Discovering Roots & Wings*. St. Paul: Redleaf Press.

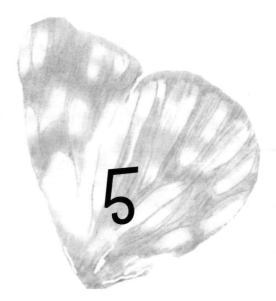

5

People can't learn from each other if they don't speak the same language.
Charles Fillmore

Bilingual Education

Seventy percent of the world's population speaks more than one language. In other words, only thirty percent of the people in the world are monolingual. Second language learners are one of the fastest-growing populations in early childhood classrooms. It seems that every classroom I visit has at least one child who does not speak English and a few children whose parents speak more than one language. Often, second language learners attend early childhood programs in which no adults speak their language. In most cases, the program and teaching staff have little knowledge of how children learn a second language and no training in how to foster the development of a second language. Most children who speak a language other than English do not receive developmentally appropriate instruction and, as a result, are less likely to succeed in school. This chapter explores how children acquire a second language, bilingual education approaches, and classroom strategies you can use to support second language learners.

Language as a Tool for Development

Language is the communication tool we use to organize and express our thoughts, experiences, feelings, wants, and needs. Children naturally learn a language through interaction with their family, friends, and community. By age five or six, most children are able to speak clearly and accurately, according to the rules of their home language. Language is important in all aspects of the development of the child.

Language is critical to social relationships. Home language is important to children for many reasons. Socially, it enables the child to communicate and learn from his or her parents, grandparents, extended family, and community. The loss of the home language often negatively impacts the parent-child relationship, particularly during adolescence.

Language is an important element of culture. Individuals who speak the language of their home culture find it gives them a sense of identity and strengthens their connection to their culture. Vocabulary, phrases, intonation, and even gestures combine to express cultural values and beliefs. Language conveys the unique nuances of a culture. This is why it's often difficult to translate ideas and meanings across languages. Language is critical for maintaining cultures, and so the United Nations Declaration of Human Rights recognizes language as a basic human right. People have the right to speak, read, and write in their home language. No one has the right to outlaw or take someone's language. When a child loses her home language, she loses a part of her cultural identity.

Language is connected to cognitive development. Language development affects children's ability to process information, memory, and experiences. Children learn to think in their home language. Loss of the language has a negative effect on their cognitive functioning. We see children's academic skills drop when they are required to replace their home language with English. Actually, children learn English (or any second language) better when they have a strong foundation in their home language. When children are introduced to a second language after they've acquired their first language, they are building on cognitive structures and thinking process that are intertwined with the first language. So it's very important to continue to strengthen and expand the child's first language since it is so closely tied to their cognitive functioning.

Language is political. Though all languages are equally valid, within each country certain languages carry more social-political power and prestige.

Historically, when countries were invaded and colonized, the native people were often not allowed to use their home language(s). Usually the language of the ruling culture was established as the norm and all residents were required by law to speak that culture's language. Today, some countries embrace multiple languages while others attempt to enact a one-country, one-language policy. You may be surprised to find out that the United States does not have an official language, a deliberate decision on the part of the founders.

How Do Children Learn Languages?

Children typically pass through similar stages of language development, regardless of which language they are learning. During the first four months of life, infants recognize different voices. Cooing describes the first sounds they make, which are the vowel sounds of the language. Next comes babbling. Babbling is a combination of consonant and vowel sounds such as *ba, ba, ba,* or *da, da, da.* At one year, children attend to people who speak their home language and ignore people who speak a different language. Usually children speak their first words between the first and second year. Once they begin speaking simple words, their vocabulary grows rapidly. Children begin to combine two or three words into abbreviated sentences. This is called **telegraphic speech.** "Me cookie" and "Go bye-bye" are examples of telegraphic speech. Usually by age three, children have internalized the sound systems (phonics) of their home language(s). By age five, most children have developed basic interpersonal communication skills.

See glossary.

Bilingual Language Development

Not all children are bilingual from birth. Many different situations lead to bilingual language development in children:

Immigration. Families leave their home country and resettle in another country. Children of immigrants usually acquire their first language at home, from their family. They acquire the second language from interaction with people and programs (such as schools) in their new country. Often, a family's home language is lost by the fourth generation.

Migration. Families temporarily leave their home country with plans to return to their country of origin. These families may feel that it is very important to maintain their home language.

Close contact. Children growing up in border states, such as southern Texas, may have a lot of contact with people who speak another language (in the case of Texas, this would be Spanish). Children learn both the language of their family and the community to achieve a broader range of communication.

Schooling. Despite the fact that the United States does not have an official language, most school districts set policy and practice as if English were the official language of the United States. But children who attend public schools in large urban schools districts may have an opportunity to attend a language immersion program, thus learning a second language at school.

Bilingual families. Some children learn two or more languages naturally by growing up in a bilingual family. Their parents may speak two languages or one parent speaks one language and the other parent speaks a different language. Families differ greatly in the strategies they use to help their children learn both languages. Some families adopt a one-parent, one-language approach. One parent speaks one language in their interaction with the child, and the other parent speaks the other. In families in which both parents speak the same home language, they may speak the home language only within the home and speak English in their interactions outside the home. In other families, the adults use both languages indiscriminately. This is often the least successful approach.

Bilingual children's language development follows the same progression as that of monolingual children. Some additional milestones are found between age five and six when children use language in the appropriate social context—for example, a bilingual child will speak English to people who only speak English and their home language to people who speak their home language.

Patton Tabors (1998), research associate and instructor at the Harvard Graduate School of Education, observed and audio tape-recorded preschool children who were acquiring a second language in an early childhood classroom. She found that children who attend an early childhood program and for whom English is a second language, pass through a developmental sequence in learning a second language. She identified four specific steps. As children pass through these stages they will continue to operate out of the previous stages, except for one—they will stop using their home language with people who don't speak it. According to Tabors, the stages of learning a second language are the following:

SPEAK HOME LANGUAGE

Children at this stage use their home language to communicate with others who speak their home language, as well as with those who only speak English. At this early stage, they may not realize that people are speaking a different language from their own.

Your role: introduce the concept of different languages; help children listen; and use gestures and nonverbal language to communicate.

NONVERBAL PERIOD

Children at this stage stop communicating with words. They realize that the adults and children in the classroom don't understand them. They continue to use their home language with their family and others who speak their home language. Tabors says children at this stage resort to "crying, whimpering, whining, pointing, and miming." At the same time, they are carefully watching, listening, and collecting knowledge of this new second language.

Your role: speak simple words and phrases in the child's home language; invite parents to participate in the classroom; and incorporate music, audio books, and other teaching materials in the child's home language.

TELEGRAPHIC SPEECH

Telegraphic speech is the use of simple one- and two-word utterances. Examples include words such as *hi, bye, okay, no,* and *mine.* Children at this stage also name familiar objects, count numbers out loud, and say the alphabet.

Your role: help the child expand his or her vocabulary; label the classroom in the child's home language and English; and introduce basic vocabulary in English and the child's home language so children can hear the different sounds and meanings.

PRODUCTIVE LANGUAGE

The child begins to combine the one-word utterances with simple phrases to form sentences. Expect the child to make grammatical mistakes because he is now creating original sentences rather than repeating words and phrases from memory.

Your role: give children opportunities to use language; ask children to respond verbally as a way to check for comprehension; and increase the complexity of your language with children.

Although language development follows similar paths in bilingual and monolingual children, interesting differences appear when three- to six-year-old bilingual and monolingual children are compared to one another. A bilingual five-year-old child's ability to match a language to the appropriate context represents a higher level of social cognition than that of a monolingual child of the same age. Monolingual children tend to have larger vocabularies while bilingual children tend to use more words and concepts in their storytelling. This supports other research that suggests that people who are bilingual are more flexible and creative in their thinking and use of language.

CODE SWITCHING

It is very common for bilingual children to blend their two languages. For example, young children may speak a sentence of English that includes a word or two of Spanish. Older children and adults switch phrases, sentences, and entire conversations. This is called **code switching.** Code switching—the art of adjusting one's language to the setting, culture, or community—is a very sophisticated language skill that plays an important role in communicating and maintaining one's cultural identity. Code switching enables a person to clarify one's thoughts or express oneself more precisely.

Code switching often confuses monolingual teachers. They may mistakenly think that it is a sign of poor language skills or that the child doesn't possess a large vocabulary in either language. Teachers may also assume that the child is confused, or that she can't keep the two languages straight or forgets whom she is talking to.

"Teachers frequently ask if code switching should be allowed in the classroom. There is no doubt that teachers should accept children's language and speech patterns, including code switching. And there are times when code switching by a bilingual teacher has been found to be a particularly effective strategy for teaching since it can help in establishing positive interpersonal relationships with children" (Genishi 1978; Tikunoff and Vasquez-Faria 1983).

Teachers can use children's books to encourage and model code switching. Here are some books that incorporate code switching into the text:

Dumpling Soup, by Jama Kim Rattigan. 1993. Boston: Little, Brown.
Pablo's Tree, by Pat Mora. 1994. New York: Macmillan Publishing
    Company.

Tomás and the Library Lady, by Pat Mora. 1997. New York: Alfred A. Knopf.

Neeny Coming, Neeny Going, by Karen English. 1996. Mahwah, N.J.: BridgeWater.

Pedrito's Day, by Louis Garay. 1997. New York: Orchard.

Ali: Child of the Desert, by Jonathon London. 1997. New York: Lothrop, Lee & Shepard.

Moma Povi and the Pot of Rice, by Sylvia Rosa-Casanova. 1997. New York: Atheneum.

Abuela, by Arthur Dorros. 1991. New York: Penguin Books.

COMMON MISPERCEPTIONS

There are many false notions about second language learning. For instance, young children do not learn another language more easily than adults. Research shows that adults consistently outperform children in all areas of second language learning except in the area of pronunciation. It seems that young children are great mimics, less inhibited, and more playful in their approach to speaking a second language. There is no proof to suggest that young children learn faster; actually adolescents learn second languages faster than young children. Children don't have the same analytic skills that adolescents and adults have. It is more difficult for them to perceive subtle similarities and differences between languages.

People are often concerned that children who speak another language won't learn English. In fact, children living in the United States are exposed to English on television, at school, and out in the community. They are much more likely to lose their home language than fail to learn English. Furthermore, children with a strong foundation in their home language will achieve greater success in learning a second language. Likewise, children who don't have a strong foundation in their home language will have difficulty developing cognitively in either of their languages.

Another myth—that introducing a second language slows language development—is also untrue. During the process of learning to speak English, children may go through a period where they are not proficient in either English or their home language. Their home language skills decline because they are less exposed to it and are using it less. Their English skills are developing, but not meeting age-level expectations. This is a temporary phase. In time these children will function on par with their peers in both their home language and English.

Learning a second language is highly dependent on having a high skill level in the first language. James Cummins (1999), one of the most important researchers in the area of bilingualism, defines bilingual competence as having two components. First, children need such basic interpersonal communication skills as vocabulary, pronunciation, grammar, and fluency. Second, children need to achieve what Cummins calls "Cognitive Academic Language Proficiency." This level of language development goes beyond interpersonal communication skills. It is the ability to read, write, do math, and explore new subjects in their home language. Cognitive Academic Language Proficiency includes the cognitively demanding tasks children must perform apart from the spoken language.

Too often teachers only look at speaking skills. Once second language learners speak English, it is often assumed that they are bilingual or no longer need bilingual education. Once children have achieved basic speaking and listening skills, however, it doesn't mean that they have mastered the deep cognitive levels of a language that allow them to take in new information and construct new knowledge using it. Until they do (which can take five to seven years of learning the new language), they still need to receive content instruction in their first language.

Bilingual Education: History and Myths

Bilingualism is the ability to speak, read, and write in more than one language. It is a concept that is difficult to define because rarely does someone achieve the ability to speak, read, and write two languages with 100 percent accuracy. Bilingualism is not necessarily the goal of **bilingual education.** Bilingual education has been defined by Lourdes Diaz Soto (1991), professor of education at Pennsylvania State University, as "an educational program for language minority students, in which instruction is provided in the children's primary language while the child acquires sufficient English skills to function academically."

Bilingual education has been debated since public schools began in the United States. Ohio legalized German-English instruction in 1839, and Louisiana enacted French-English instruction in 1847. Later in the nineteenth century, the trend reversed toward English-only instruction. German Americans in Wisconsin and Illinois filed some of the first lawsuits in the country in the 1880s, because the public and private schools adopted an English-only policy. As a result, school districts in Texas, St. Louis, Indianapolis, Milwaukee, and Cincinnati operated German-

English programs. Public schools around the country offered instruction in a variety of languages including Dutch, Swedish, Norwegian, Polish, Italian, and Czech.

Bilingual education continues to be a hot topic—only the language in question has changed. Often the debate over bilingual education and the selection of approaches to bilingual education are based on social/political ideals rather than educational research. For instance, many believe that all people living in the United States should speak English. Some believe that using tax dollars to support bilingual education in the public schools is a waste of money.

Parents also have differing opinions about bilingual education. Parents of English-speaking children may see bilingual education as a waste of time or a way of watering down the curriculum at their children's expense. Some non-English-speaking families also may not support bilingual education. They may have enrolled their child in an early childhood program to learn English. As a result, they may not support incorporating their child's home language into the classroom. Other families may see maintaining the child's home language as their responsibility, and not the school's or the teacher's. They may use their own cultural community by enrolling their child in separate language or cultural classes apart from child care or public school.

Approaches to Bilingual Education

There are many different approaches to bilingual education. Each approach falls into one of two categories: either *additive* or *subtractive*. Additive approaches seek to *add* a second language (usually English) while continuing to support the child's home language. These approaches seek to strengthen or complement the child's cognitive, language, and social development by supporting the first language. Subtractive approaches seek to teach English to children who speak a language other than English without supporting the home language, thereby replacing the home language with English. These approaches shift children away from the home language, so that it is *subtracted* from their language abilities. The result is a weakening of the child's cognitive, language, and social abilities. Given these two broad categories, let's take a look at the major bilingual education models implemented in classrooms today.

> *Submersion approach.* This model is a "sink or swim" approach that offers no support or additional assistance to children whose home language is other than English. The children are placed in an English-speaking classroom;

all instruction, classroom routines, and social interactions take place in English. The goal of this approach is assimilation. This model is considered subtractive, because children usually lose their home language. The result is often poorer cognitive functioning, social marginalization, and higher dropout rates.

Immersion approach. This model comes from Canada where it was used to teach French to English-speaking children. Here in the United States it is most often used to teach English-speaking children another language such as Spanish or French. For example, school districts may operate a Spanish immersion school. In an immersion model, attention is paid to teaching content such as math, social studies, and science in both languages, and making sure that children master content in whatever language is most comfortable for them. The outcome for native English speakers is that they become bilingual and biliterate in two languages. This approach is different from a submersion approach, where content is only provided in English, and the language learning is assumed to go in one direction only. In a submersion approach, the goal is for the children whose home language is not English to learn English. In an immersion approach, the goal is for all the children to learn both (or in some cases, all three) languages. In addition, children whose first language is English are in no danger of losing their home language or culture as a result of being immersed in a second language. English surrounds them at home, on television, and in the wider community, and is the language of power in the United States. The opposite is true for children whose first language is not English.

Pullout approach. This approach pulls children out of the mainstream classroom to attend an ESL class. This approach, also considered both assimilationist and subtractive, often results in children falling behind in other subject areas when they miss crucial class time to work on their English skills.

Transitional approach. This approach attempts to teach children English as quickly as possible so that they can participate in English-only (mainstream) classrooms. Initially, children are taught in their home language and receive instruction in English as a second language. Second language learners may be integrated with native English-speaking children for some subjects such as physical education, art, or music, which would be taught in English. Once children are able to pass a test, they are placed in English-only classrooms. The federal government recommends that children receive three years of transitional instruction, but studies from the field suggest that children actually need five to seven years of instruction in their home language in order to achieve the same outcomes as native English-speaking children.

Maintenance approach. This additive approach promotes the development of both the child's home language and English skills. Children in maintenance bilingual programs receive both content instruction and language arts instruction (reading, writing, and speaking) in their home language, as well as instruction in English as a Second Language (ESL). This strategy enhances the child's native language and allows learners to gain concepts in the native language while introducing ESL. Children are usually served by additional "pull out" English as a Second Language (ESL) instruction from teachers trained in ESL methods. As a result, children become literate in both their home language and English without losing ground in other content areas while they are learning English.

Dual language approach. This model is a two-way approach that addresses both English-speaking children and children learning English as a second language. Classes are taught in one language for part of the day and in a second language for the other half of the day. Or, classes are taught by a team of teachers with one teacher using English and the second teacher using the other language. The end result is that both groups of children are bilingual and biliterate. An evaluation of Head Start classrooms showed this approach to have the most positive outcomes for children. This approach is clearly related to the "immersion" approach discussed above, and also promotes positive attitudes toward both languages and cultures. A recent curriculum book, *Kaleidoscope: A Multicultural Approach for the Primary School Classroom* (De Gaetano, Williams, and Volk 1998) uses this dual language approach. Since it is the most successful approach in terms of outcomes for children, let's explore this approach a little further.

DUAL APPROACH TEACHING STRATEGIES

There are at least six different teaching strategies used in a dual language approach. A given classroom may use just one of these techniques, or a combination of several of them.

Translation. An adult translates everything that is said in this classroom.

Preview-Review. Each activity begins with an introduction in the child's home language. The activity proceeds in English and concludes in the child's home language.

Alternating days. One day the class is taught in the child's home language and the next day the class is taught in English.

Second language instruction. In small groups, children who don't speak the first language receive instruction in that language. In another small group, children who don't speak the second language, receive instruction in the second language.

Concurrent. The teacher shifts back and forth between the two languages throughout the day as needed.

Sister classrooms. One class and their teacher speak English. Another class and their teacher speak another language, such as Spanish. At specific times each day, the teachers swap classes, offering instruction in the second language. In addition, the two classes play together and work on projects together at designated times (De Gaetano, Williams, and Volk 1998).

Second Language Learners in Early Childhood Classrooms

Unlike public schools, child care centers, preschools, and family child care homes are not required to provide ESL or bilingual services to children and families. Historically, these programs have served relatively few second language learners at any one time. As a result, very few programs have policies or procedures for serving families and children who don't speak English or are bilingual.

Patton Tabors, author of *One Child, Two Languages: A Guide for Preschool Educators of Children Learning English as a Second Language,* found that young second language learners were most often enrolled in one of three types of early childhood programs: first language classrooms, bilingual classrooms, and English-speaking classrooms.

First language classrooms. The teachers are native speakers of the child's first language. All of the adult-child and child-child interaction is in the first language, which helps children develop their first language. Lily Wong Fillmore, professor of education at the University of California, Berkeley, and an acknowledged expert in the area of bilingualism and biculturalism, is one proponent of this type of program because young children are developmentally at risk for losing their first language and this type of setting helps children maintain their first language.

Bilingual classrooms. These classrooms usually include a mix of different first languages. English-speaking staff and children can also be included in a bilingual classroom. The two key elements are that there is at least one staff member in the classroom who speaks the child's home language and that there is a clear plan for using both English and the children's home language throughout the day. The outcome of this type of classroom is that children maintain and improve their first language skills and also learn English.

English language classrooms. The most common early childhood setting is the English language classroom. Children whose home language is not English are placed in classrooms in which all instruction and interactions between adults and children are in English. The class may include other children who speak the same language, presenting the opportunity for child-child interaction in the children's first language. But by and large the outcome is learning English with little or no development in the first language.

Let's take a look at a common scenario: A child who speaks a language other than English, attends an early childhood program in which no other adults or children speak the home language of the child. The program has no plan to care for children who do not speak English. The curriculum does not incorporate the child's home language or home culture. The child is pushed to learn English and attempts are made to resocialize the child away from the home culture and family. The teachers encourage the child to replace culturally based values, beliefs, behavior, and language with European American culture. The teachers are uncomfortable with the fact that the child does not speak English and the other children ignore, pull away, or refuse to interact with the child because of the language difference. When the child attempts to communicate, the teacher misreads or ignores the child's signals. Interactions between the child and teacher are rare, brief, and unnatural. Teachers and the other children may become frustrated in trying to establish and maintain relationships and the child may be isolated, withdrawn, or invisible within the classroom. Other children may ignore the child or treat him or her like a baby.

The child experiences high levels of stress in the classroom and as a result loses the ability to communicate when angry, scared, excited, or self-conscious. The child "freezes" when asked to stand up and speak at group time.

What impact do you think this experience will have on the child's cognitive, language, and social development? How do you think this will affect the child's success in school, and eventually in life? Remember, this experience is common to most preschool-age children in the United States who do not speak English as their first language.

Serving Second Language Learners

Ideally, young children would attend programs in which their teacher or primary caregiver and some of the children speak the child's home language and share the child's home culture. Given the cultural and linguistic diversity in many communities, this is not always possible. However, early childhood programs can support second language learners in many ways. Programs should base their practices on the assumption that bilingualism is an asset that should be fostered. In early childhood, the emphasis of bilingual education should be to establish a solid base for speaking, reading, and writing in the child's home language. The following strategies for supporting second language learners are based on recent research and best practices from the field of bilingual education.

Parents

- Encourage parents to speak to the child in their home language and continue using their language at home.

- Find a way to communicate with the child's parents. Begin with orientation. If the family does not speak any English, you may need to use a translator.

- Use a parent questionnaire like the one in chapter 6 to help you get to know the family.

- Discuss home language and culture at parent conferences. With the parent, set goals related to home language and learning English.

- Introduce families who speak the same language to one another. Form support networks among families from the same culture.

- Invite the child's parents to volunteer in the classroom. Ask them or community members in to tell stories in children's home languages. Ask parents to share their favorite songs, rhymes, and games with the class.

Adult-Child Communication

- Communicate a positive, supportive attitude. Use a pleasant speaking style. Keep your body relaxed and smile often. Use gestures and body language to convey what you mean. Avoid derogatory comments, looks, or jokes that could make children embarrassed of their home language.

- Listen to children, and don't dominate the conversation.

- Encourage and positively reinforce children's attempts to use their home language or English in the classroom.

- Offer gentle correction. Don't be afraid to correct a child's language. Do so by correctly rephrasing or expanding the child's speech.

- Adjust your communication. Think about how you would speak to a preverbal child. Use short, simple, and clear sentences. Repeat phrases. Use your voice, facial expressions, and body language to communicate nonverbally. Emphasize and repeat the important words. When giving instructions, ask children to paraphrase what you said to them in order to make sure they understand what you said. Avoid slang. Ask simple yes or no questions.

- Learn how to correctly pronounce the child's name. Require all adults in the program to correctly pronounce the child's name. Teach the other children in the class how to pronounce the child's name.

Child-Child Relationships

- Help English-speaking children understand the second language learner's speech and behavior.

- Use bilingual buddies. Pair the child with another child who speaks the same language (this is especially helpful if the buddy is a little older or more fluent in English). The buddy can tutor the child in their home language.

- Don't allow English-speaking children to mimic, tease, or ignore second language learners.

- Try using persona dolls or role-playing activities to address these behaviors. *Kids Like Us* by Trisha Whitney (Redleaf Press, 1999) is a good resource to help you foster respect among children.

Daily Routine

- Establish and follow a daily routine. A consistent routine promotes a sense of security. A regular routine also allows second language learners to become part of the group more easily, because they can get a sense of the daily schedule.

- Make a photographic wall chart of the daily routine. Include a photograph of children at that time of the day, a drawing of the clock's position, and a written label in English and the child's home language.

Classroom

- Create a language-rich environment. Include language-rich activities such as dramatic play, telephone or walkie-talkie play, puppetry, opportunities for child-child conversations, story time, and field trips.

- Provide areas and opportunities for private play. All children need time away from the group, and this is even more important for children who are second language learners. Think of how stressful it would be to spend three to eight hours a day with ten to thirty people who don't speak your language. A large refrigerator box can easily become a private space. A small table with one chair and a special manipulative or an individual sand tray in the corner of the room provides relief from the pressure and demands of communicating in a language other than your own.

- Add bilingual signs and labels to the classroom. Consistently use the same color for each language. For example, write English labels in blue, Spanish labels in red, and Chinese labels in green. Use the same color system for flash cards and translating books.

- Add tape-recorded stories from children's home cultures and in children's home languages to the book or listening area.

- Display bilingual children's books in the book area. Here are some examples:

  Walk About: Life in an Ahtna Athabaskan Village, by John Smelcer and Tricia Wilson. Illustrated by Robert Jordan (Ahtna Heritage Foundation, 1998)
  The Park Bench, by Fumiko Takeshita (Kane/Miller Book Publishers, 1989)
  A Is for Asia, by Cynthia Chin-Lee (Orchard, 1997)
  ¡Fiesta! by Ginger Fogelson Guy (Greenwillow, 1996)

Free Play

- Provide play-by-play commentary during free play time.

- Work individually with second language learners.

- Establish a buddy system. Tabors suggests pairing an outgoing, friendly English-speaking child with a child who is learning English as a second language. This is especially important during free play and outside play when second language children are more likely to be isolated or excluded from English-speaking children's play.

Small Group Time

- Implement small group times. This makes it easier for second language learning children to focus, listen, and communicate without being too distracted or overwhelmed by the large group.

- Introduce new concepts in the child's home language.

- Avoid drills and rigid teaching methods.

- Use levels of representation to introduce a concept, project, or unit. Begin with real objects. Second, introduce replicas or models. Third, relate the real objects to photographs or realistic drawings. At this point, children may want to draw or make three-dimensional models of the object. Last, introduce and relate the written word in both English and the child's home language to the object. This way you will embed new vocabulary into a meaningful context.

Large Group Time

- Plan seating arrangements. Structure the seating arrangements at circle time, small group time, or meal times to pair English-speaking children with children who are learning English.

- Modify your teaching techniques. Minimize lecturing. Use objects, models, and pictures along with words. Use songs with body movements. Use books that are predictable or have a lot of repetition.

- Sing the same songs consistently at circle time so that non-English-speaking children have an easier time catching on and joining in the singing.

- Incorporate the children's home languages into common circle time activities. For instance, count out loud to ten or twenty in English and another language, recite the alphabet in English and another language, learn the names of the colors and days of the week in children's home languages. Translate simple songs, or the chorus of favorite songs into the home languages of the children in your class. Read books that include words or phrases in the child's home language or read the English version and the version in the child's home language side by side at circle time.

- Sing songs, and use finger plays and rhymes from children's home cultures and in their home languages.

Curriculum

- Present new information in context. Relate new information to children's life experience and what they already know. Choose curriculum themes and materials that relate to their lives and cultures. Introduce new vocabulary within the context of a curriculum project or unit theme.

Assessment

- Incorporate home language into your observation and assessment. Assess children's English abilities, abilities in their home languages, and their cultural communication patterns. Examine all elements of a child's communication. What language does the child speak at home? What language does the child speak with other children? What language does the child speak at school? Does the child use a dialect? Does the child speak with a strong accent? How does the child use body language and gestures to communicate? What type of eye contact does the child use when communicating? How much personal space does the child use when communicating?

- Assess children's bilingual development by asking these questions:

  Language development. To what extent has the child maintained or lost the home language? To what extent has the child acquired or maintained the second language?

  Language acquisition. Were the languages acquired at the same time or was one acquired after the other?

  Language competence. How proficient is the child in the home language? How proficient is the child in the second language?

  Language use. When, in what contexts, and with whom does the child use the home language? When, in what contexts, and with whom does the child use the second language?

  Linguistics. Does the child code switch? Does the child mix words or phrases from one language when speaking another language? Does the child use the accent or grammar of one language when speaking another language? Does the child follow the spelling rules of one language when writing words in another language?

  Attitude. What is the child's attitude toward the home language? What is the child's attitude toward learning English?

  Pressure. What pressure does the child put on herself to use the home language? What pressure does the child put on herself to use the second language? What external pressures are on the child regarding language use?

Circumstances. What are the circumstances surrounding the child's use of two languages?

Culture. To what extent is the child familiar with the home culture? To what extent is the child familiar with European American culture?

Staffing and Staff Development

- Hire or request a bilingual co-teacher or assistant teacher. The coworker can translate classroom labels, clarify instruction, work with the child individually, translate teaching materials, and provide cultural information to help you work effectively with the child and his family.

- Collaborate with the ESL teachers if you are in a public school. Provide them with class rules, daily routine, goals for the year, and lists of interest areas and basic classroom materials so the ESL teacher can learn more about the language that is used in your classroom.

- Learn some simple words in the child's home language—for example, *hello* or *good morning, good-bye, mom, eat* or *hungry, bathroom* or *potty, stop, play.* Learn how to sing one of the child's favorite songs in her home language. Incorporate the child's home language into daily activities such as greeting, calendar time, transitions, group singing, and story time.

Language learning is interwoven with social, cognitive, and language development. Second language learning is integrally connected to the child's home culture and future academic success. A culturally responsive and developmentally appropriate classroom will help children become bilingual. Bilingual education is a rapidly growing aspect of teaching. It should now be a part of every teacher education program. Teachers entering the field should understand the role of home language in a child's development and the process of acquiring a second language, be familiar with the major theorists, be able to function in at least one other language, and know how to assist second language learners.

In the next chapter, we'll explore how families, neighborhoods, and communities in which we work, including the social, political, and historical environment, affect provision of culturally relevant anti-bias care and education.

Questions to Ponder

How do I convey a positive, respectful, and supportive attitude toward children's home languages?

How do I respond to children when they initiate contact with me in their home language?

How do I encourage children and parents to use their home language?

What are the ways I use home language in my interactions with children?

How do I create opportunities for children to use home languages in our daily activities?

What classroom materials are in the children's home languages?

How do I work with parents to develop a plan for implementing their home language?

References

Chang, Hedy. 1996. Many languages, many cultures. *Scholastic Early Childhood Education Today* (November/December).

Crawford, James. 1998. Language politics in the U.S.A.: The paradox of bilingual education. *Social Justice* 25, no. 3 (Fall).

Crowell, Caryl Gottlieb. 1998. Talking about books: Celebrating linguistic diversity. *Language Arts* 75, no. 3 (March).

Cummins, James. 1999. Putting language proficiency in its place: Responding to critiques of the conversational/academic language distinction. Published online at <http://www.iteachilearn.com/cummins/index.html>

De Gaetano, Yvonne, Leslie Williams, and Dinah Volk. 1997. *Kaleidoscope: A multicultural approach for the primary school classroom.* Upper Saddle River, N.J.: Pearson.

Feinberg, Rosa Castro, and Consuelo Conde Marencia. 1998. Bilingual education: An overview. *Social Education* 62, no. 7 (November/December).

Fillmore, Charles J. 1997. A linguist looks at the ebonics debate. *TESOL Matters* 17, no. 1 (February/March).

Fillmore, Lily Wong. 1992. Quoted in *Essential connections: Ten keys to culturally sensitive child care.* Far West Laboratory in collaboration with California Department of Education, producers. Sacramento: California Department of Education.

Genishi, C. 1978. Language use in a kindergarten program for maintenance of bilingualism. In *Bilingual education,* edited by H. La Fontaine, B. Persky, and H. Golubchick. Wayne, N.Y.: Avery.

Kagan, Sharon L., and Eugine E. Garcia. 1991. Educating culturally and linguistically diverse preschoolers: Moving the agenda. *Early Childhood Research Quarterly* 6: 427–443.

McLaughlin, Barry. 1995. Fostering second language development in young children: Principles and practices. *Educational Practice Report* 14. Washington, D.C.: National Clearinghouse Bilingual Education.

Nissani, Helen. 1990. Early childhood programs for language minority children. *Occasional Papers in Bilingual Education,* no. 2 (Summer).

Roberts, Cheryl. 1995. Bilingual education program models: A framework for understanding. *Bilingual Research Journal* 19, no. 3 and 4 (Summer/Fall).

Scholastic. Diversity, children, communication, and culture. *Scholastic Early Childhood Education Today* (November/December).

Soto, Lourdes Diaz. 1991. Understanding bilingual/bicultural young children. *Young Children* (January).

Tabors, Patton O. 1997. *One child, two languages: A guide for early childhood educators of children learning English as a second language.* Baltimore: Paul H. Brookes Publishing.

Tabors, Patton O. 1998. What early childhood educators need to know: Developing effective programs for linguistically and culturally diverse families. *Young Children* (November).

Tikunoff, William J. 1982. *Descriptive study of significant bilingual instructional features.* San Francisco: Far West Laboratory for Educational Research and Development.

Tikunoff, William J., and José A. Vasquez-Faria. 1983. Components of effective instruction for LEP students. In *Teaching in successful bilingual instructional settings,* edited by William J. Tikunoff. San Francisco: Far West Laboratory for Education Research and Development.

Humankind has not woven the web of life.
We are but one thread within it.
Whatever we do to the web, we do to ourselves.
All things are bound together.
All things connect.
Chief Seattle

Family, Culture, and Community

Culturally relevant and anti-bias education requires us to understand the families, the culture of child care programs, and communities in which we live and work. The community context consists of the geographic region; type of community; and the community economy, diversity, history, events, and issues. The child care program and family culture includes the diversity of the families served and program mission as well as race, culture, home language, economic class, religion, and sexual orientation.

Culturally relevant and anti-bias education reflects the children, families, and community. As a result, an early childhood program in a Baptist church in Chicago should differ from a Head Start program on the Navajo reservation. The program of a downtown child care center will differ from that of a family child care provider in a small rural community. An early childhood program operated by the Urban League will differ from a public school early childhood program. The context shapes both the *how* and *what* of an early childhood program. It shapes how we work with families, how we provide child care, and how we teach. It also informs what we teach—the content of the curriculum. This chapter will help you identify and learn more about the context in which you work. We will also look at practical strategies for working with families to provide culturally relevant and anti-bias education.

Communities

Your work with children takes place in a specific community, located in a specific geographic region. The programs we create and the curriculum we design must reflect the families, cultures, and communities we serve. Yet communities are dynamic. They change constantly. The mix of diversity in your classroom may differ greatly from one year to the next. As a teacher, you need tools to identify and analyze the diversity of the families, the children in your child care program, and the community in which you work.

Begin by immersing yourself in the community. Julie Bisson (1997), author of *Celebrate! An Anti-Bias Guide to Enjoying Holidays in Early Childhood Programs*, reminds us that it is important to spend time in the community. She suggests that teachers "Participate in everyday activities in the neighborhoods where the children and families live. Shop at a local store, visit a park, eat at a restaurant, or go to the post office." In addition, pick up a neighborhood newspaper, watch a local cable television program, and attend community events. Talk with parents, elders, and community leaders about the community. Learn about the history of the community. Sometimes the community name alone can hold significance to diversity work. Don't you wonder what the story is behind city names like White Settlement, Inkster, and Savage?

Try asking these questions as a way of getting to know the community in which you work:

What's the name of the community in which I work? How did it get its name?

Where is the community located?

How would I describe this community to an outsider?

What is the history of this community?

How is the community changing? How has it changed in the last five years?

How do people make a living in this community?

What are the natural resources in this community?

What do people do for recreation in this community?

What community issues are parents and children concerned about?

What are the threats to people's health and well-being in our community?

What is the racial and cultural composition of our community?

What are the prevailing stereotypes in our community?

What are the conflicts, controversies, or ongoing tensions in our
community?

What do children need to know to be safe and competent in our
community?

Here's another activity for learning about your community—create a diversity
portrait of your community. Cover the top of a table with a large piece of butcher
paper. Set out felt-tip pens and, with a few other teachers and/or parents,
attempt to draw a map of your town. Be as detailed as possible. Include all the
kinds of diversity in your community. For example, if families are segregated by
economic class, race, or culture, show that on your map. What are the cultural,
educational, human service, health, and advocacy agencies serving families with
young children? Where are they located in the community? Where are the government agencies, police, and fire departments? Where are the businesses and
places of employment? What and where are the elements that weaken the community? What and where is the life of the community? As you look at the map,
ask yourself who is supporting the community and who has turned its back on
the community? (This activity is adapted from the Big Foot exercise by the
People's Institute in New Orleans, Louisiana.)

Culture

The culture of the staff and the culture of the families contribute to the context
in which you teach. Chances are some of the children and families in your classroom come from cultures other than your own. You took an important first step
when you identified the cultures in the previous exercises. I've presented workshops in which I've asked participants to name the cultures represented in their
class and they cannot. I've heard answers such as "children at risk," or "some
kind of oriental," or "a mix of something." It's distressing to think that many
teachers haven't taken the time to really reflect on the children in their care.

As a teacher of young children, begin thinking about program design by learning about the cultures of the children in your class. Carol Brunson-Phillips (1992),
executive director of the Council for Early Childhood Professional Recognition,
states that it is every provider's responsibility to get their hands on some good
information about the family's culture and then bring that information back to

the family. Ask them, "I read this about your cultural group, is this true for your family? Is this information helpful in working with you and your child?" You can also learn about the cultures in your classroom by attending workshops, cultural events in the community, reading novels by authors from that culture, or watching movies about that culture by filmmakers from the culture.

A few years ago, I worked with early childhood educators in a predominantly Latino community. The Latino teachers told me a story about a European American coworker. The coworker didn't attend the workshop because, after all, she worked with Latino children and families, what would she need to know? Recently, this teacher brought a book about dogs to work and was reading it in the staff lounge on her breaks. She was in the process of selecting a new dog for a family pet. She was reading about all the different breeds, their temperaments, and the care requirements. She also asked all the other teachers what type of dog they had and what their experience had been like. The Latino teachers were incensed, and rightly so. This teacher was willing to put time, energy, and effort into learning all about dogs. But she was not the least bit interested in learning about the culture of the children with whom she worked.

Many books on culturally relevant and anti-bias education include thumbnail sketches of the major cultural groups in the United States today. I have made a conscious decision not to include these types of descriptions for three reasons. First, as a European American woman, I do not have the right to speak on behalf of other cultural groups. Second, culture is too complex to be adequately described in a page or less. Third, condensing cultural information would likely result in both my stereotyping and the reader (you!) stereotyping the children and families you serve.

Don't forget that the most important way of finding out about the cultures represented by the children and families in your program is to talk with parents. Find out their expectations for their child in your program. Above all, involve parents in your classroom. This will help you recognize and respect children and their family's cultural beliefs and rules for behavior.

Families

Is a family a mommy at home with the baby and a daddy at work? Is it grandmas, grandpas, aunts, and uncles? Does the family celebrate holidays, graduations, funerals, weddings, and births? Government defines family for the census, and dictionaries have their own definition for family. In terms of culturally relevant and anti-bias education for young children, it is important to realize that your own definition of family relates to your culture, economic class, and life experience. For this discussion we will define family as a group of people with a long-term commitment to one another who share living space and the tasks involved in maintaining the group.

The traditional or nuclear family is actually the white, middle-class, European American model of family. When European Americans think of family they often imagine a two-parent family with two children, a boy and a girl. This family owns their own home, two cars, and a dog. The father works full-time outside the home to support the family. The mother stays home to raise the children and provide them with wonderful experiences and nutritious meals. Focusing on this image makes many European Americans feel warm, safe, and secure. In reality, 86 percent of families living in the United States fall outside of these traditional family patterns. Other kinds of families include single-parent families, dual career families, families with gay or lesbian parents, blended families, and families that live communally. To see the unique characteristics and strengths of all families, early childhood professionals need to look beyond the idea of the traditional family as the one right, correct, or normal family model.

Families Transmit Culture

Families pass their culture on to their children by socializing their children to become members and participate in a particular culture. Although the family lives in the United States, it may function within a subculture based on its ethnicity, economic class, religion, or sexual orientation. Children are first socialized into their particular subculture so that the child's first experience with the values, beliefs, and ways of the European American culture often come with participation in child care or an early childhood education program.

Cultural values change over time. A family's cultural values may change from one generation to the next depending on how long the family has lived in the United States. A refugee family struggling to adapt to an entirely different culture will find strength and support from the familiarity of their home language and traditional practices. A second-generation family may be bilingual, functioning successfully in the mainstream society while continuing to live out its cultural practices at home. Often the ability to read, write, and speak the home language is lost by the third generation, but strong evidence suggests that cultural values, cultural identification, lifestyle, and behavior are retained through the fourth and even fifth generation after immigration.

Families also differ in their desire to become like the traditional American family. Families who are in this country for a brief period of time because of schooling or a work opportunity may want their children to "experience" American life and learn some English, but do not want their children to lose their home language and customs. Other families may be quite new to the United States but plan to stay here permanently. They may want their children to learn English quickly and to actively participate in "American" holidays and celebrations. They may be concerned that an accent will cause their children to stand out and be rejected by other children. Families may also see learning English and assimilating as the door to opportunity and security for their children. In recent years many families have come to this country as refugees. They have been forced to leave behind their homeland, lifestyle, and extended family. While they may want to learn English and how to live in this country, their own traditions and language provide a great feeling of security as they go through a time of many changes.

Here is a simple way to begin thinking about the families within your program. Create a diversity chart. On a large piece of chart paper list your answers to the following:

What is the racial mix of the families participating in your program?

What is the cultural mix of the families participating in your program?

What languages are spoken by the families in your program?

What family styles are represented in your program? (For example, single, blended, foster, gay/lesbian, extended)

What is the socioeconomic mix of the families participating your program?

What disabilities are represented by the families participating in your program?

Review and analyze the list. To what extent do the families in your program reflect the larger community? To what extent does the staff reflect the families in your program? To what extent does the program (caregiving methods, classroom materials, curriculum, and teaching methods) reflect the families in your program? Answering this set of questions can give you some ideas of where your program is serving families well, and where you might start to make changes.

Early Childhood Programs as Extended Family

When working with young children, we cannot separate the child from the family. Early childhood teachers must broaden the vision of their mission to encompass serving families, not just children. Teachers in high-quality programs realize this, and they seek to foster the child's developmental education while at the same time supporting parents in creating a healthy, satisfying family life.

Often families reach out to child care and early childhood education programs to supplement the care and education received from the family. In this sense, early childhood programs come to resemble an extended family. Early childhood programs become part of the extended family network by accepting all types of families, establishing respectful parent-teacher relationships, including parents in all aspects of the program, and engaging in problem solving to manage cultural clashes.

When families participate in early childhood programs, they open up their family system to include other adults in the care and teaching of their youngest members, the children. In this way, early childhood programs are like extended families, and they share in the responsibility for encouraging both cultural identity and acceptance of human diversity. As an extended family member, programs must provide care and education in a way that complements each family that they serve.

As early childhood educators, we talk about individualizing curriculum and the importance of matching activities and experiences to the needs, interests, and the abilities of each child. This is individualized planning at the activity level. How can we individualize service to families at all levels of the program? How can an early childhood program meet the wants and needs of each family? One way to make sure that your program meets families' needs is to get to know each family, provide ongoing communication, involve parents in the program, and engage in problem solving when conflicts arise.

Get to Know Your Families

Enrollment is the perfect time to establish a relationship with the parents and children. It is very important that staff make parents feel welcome and accepted. A personal relationship with parents gives a much stronger message than the written information in the program flyer or parent handbook. This is the time to tap into parents' knowledge of their children and to ask them to share information about their family's beliefs and practices. Inform parents of the center's commitment to a culturally relevant and anti-bias program. Reiterate that commitment by stating the center's culturally relevant and anti-bias policy in the center's brochure and parent handbook. Conclude the intake meeting by inviting the parents to participate and share their family's traditions, home language, and holidays with their child's class.

Enrollment forms can be used to collect information about a family's culture and its influence on parenting and family life. Some people may feel that asking such questions is invading the privacy of others. The truth is that parents who are asked these questions usually feel valued and can be confident that the center staff won't overlook or forget this important information when it is included on the enrollment forms. In addition, teachers need complete and accurate information if they are to meet the individual needs of each child. Use this information gathered on the enrollment forms to individualize caregiving styles and routines and to plan curriculum activities, celebrations, and family events. Respecting and including cultural information in the daily program tells families that you respect them and will help them preserve their home language, cultural values, and traditions. Here are some questions to include in your enrollment forms or in the intake interview.

Sample Enrollment Form Questions

FAMILY STRUCTURE

Who lives in your household? Please name them.

Who else has cared for your child?

What type of residence do you live in?

FAMILY CULTURE

What is your family's ethnic or cultural background?

How do you identify yourself?

What languages are spoken in your household? With your extended family?

How comfortable are you speaking and reading English?

What traditions, objects, or foods symbolize your family?

Why are these things important? What values or history do they represent?

What is your current religious affiliation or background?

What values do you want us to teach to your children?

How can we validate and support your family's lifestyle here at the center?

What songs, rhymes, chants, stories, or toys could we include that would represent and support your home culture?

What heroes and/or celebrations could we include that would represent and support your home culture?

Does your family celebrate birthdays? If so how?

Would you be willing to come and share your home culture with your child's class?

PARENTING

Describe your child's eating schedule.

How are meals served in your family?

What foods does your child like?

    Dislike?

What words does your child use for urination? Bowel movement?

Describe your child's sleeping and napping schedule.

How do you put your child to sleep?

Does your child share a bedroom? If so, with whom?

Does your child sleep in the same bed as someone else? If so, with whom?

How does your child relax or soothe herself?

What are your child's favorite activities?

How do you discipline your child?

How do you handle the following situations?

    Toilet training

    Sharing

    Messy play

    Gender roles

    Racial concerns

Who does your child play with at home?

What are your child's responsibilities at home?

What are the rules in your home?

Is there anything else you would like to tell us about your child?

Home Visits

Home visits help teachers get to know children and their families in more personal ways. They also offer opportunities to meet other family members and increase your understanding of how the family lives. Visits should be brief, lasting no more than thirty minutes, and should be arranged ahead of time with the child's parent(s). As a teacher, keep in mind that some families may view home visits with caution and concern, especially if they have experienced negative visits from social workers, child protection workers, or other human service workers.

Ongoing Communication

Once a parent-teacher relationship has been established, it is crucial that teachers maintain open communication with parents. Staff need to talk with parents as often as possible, not just when a child is sick or having a particularly difficult day. Realize that some parents may be shy, timid, or just not accustomed to asking questions of their child's teacher. Teachers can develop a warm, friendly, outgoing manner that will help parents feel accepted, valued, and welcome. Try staffing each room with at least two adults during arrival and departure so that one adult is free to greet and talk with parents. Use tools such as a notebook with dividers so that each child has a section. Use the notebook like a daily log, writing brief descriptions of each child's day. Encourage parents to write back in response or use the notebook for requests or to update you on family matters. Some teachers use little notepads and attach them to children's backpacks. This works well if your program provides transportation and you don't get a chance to see parents on a daily basis.

Because of complex schedules and multiple responsibilities, it may be difficult for staff to talk with each parent on a daily basis. Centers can send information home to keep parents informed of program activities. Bulletin boards can be used to inform parents of the classroom activities as well as multicultural events in the community. Newsletters can feature articles about different families at the center, how to strengthen children's cultural identity, children's developing awareness of diversity, ideas for multicultural activities to do at home, and highlights from multicultural activities that have recently taken place at the center.

Parent involvement enhances a center's efforts to provide culturally relevant and anti-bias education. The child experiences greater continuity between home and school when parents are involved. Parents can have input in many ways. They can participate on decision-making committees and advisory boards. For instance, they can participate on a personnel committee to see that hiring practices work toward staffing that reflects the diversity of the children served. They can help with recruiting applicants and formulating interview questions. Parents can also participate in the classroom. They can share their home culture, home language, hobbies, careers, as well as assist with field trips and special events. Parents can also help behind the scenes by translating children's books, making bulletin board displays, or making teaching materials.

Holidays and Celebrations

Many holidays and celebrations have cultural or religious roots. They express the values, beliefs, and practices of a particular group of people. Celebrating cultural holidays helps strengthen cultural connections and family ties. Sometimes holidays commemorate significant historical events or people. Holidays and celebrations may seem like a good way to begin culturally relevant and anti-bias education. In fact, there is a lot of disagreement surrounding holidays. One holiday can mean different things to different groups of people. Thanksgiving is often a time of celebration for European Americans. Yet it is a day of mourning for many in the Native American community.

Because of these kinds of differences, families should play an integral role in setting a holiday policy. Parents can form a holiday/celebration committee to decide which holidays will be celebrated at the center and how they will be celebrated. The following key questions need to be answered: What is the purpose of observing holidays and other celebrations in our program? What role will holidays have in our curriculum? How will we decide which holidays to celebrate? How will we celebrate holidays in the classroom? The committee may decide to send out a questionnaire to poll all of the families. Julie Bisson includes an excellent sample family questionnaire about holidays in her book *Celebrate! An Anti-Bias Guide to Enjoying Holidays in Early Childhood Programs.*

Parents may also enjoy planning and participating in celebrations, such as the observance of Dr. Martin Luther King Jr.'s birthday, Cinco de Mayo, or the Hmong New Year. Parent involvement in holidays and celebrations promotes a stronger home-school connection because parents feel like their culture and family are recognized by and are included in the program. Often parents are the best source of holiday activity ideas and resource materials. Parents can visit the classroom and share how they celebrate a particular holiday in their home. They can bring artifacts and photographs to show the children. This is also the most developmentally appropriate and culturally relevant approach because it connects holidays and celebrations to the daily lives of real people. Bisson (1997) offers some additional suggestions for involving parents in holidays and celebrations:

- Encourage families to share information about their holidays and how they celebrate.

- Ask for ideas about what activities would be appropriate to provide for children.

- Welcome family members who would like to come in and lead an activity, such as cooking a holiday dish with the children or helping to decorate the classroom.

- Request materials that you can use as sources for classroom activities such as recipes, music tapes, or written words to special holiday songs.

- Invite families to loan materials to the program for sharing during circle time. Decorations, children's books, holiday cards, candleholders, and other holiday-related items from families enrich your classroom celebrations.

- Communicate to families ahead of time about what you are planning to do in the classroom, so parents or guardians can let you know if they have anything to contribute or any concerns.

When Families Don't Observe Holidays

What can you do when families don't celebrate a particular holiday? Holidays and the decision to celebrate them or not brings up strong feelings for both teachers and parents. I've known many teachers who became outraged with Jehovah's Witness families whose children could not participate in the class holiday and birthday celebrations. They couldn't understand why the family had to have its child in the program and why they as teachers should be responsible for figuring out what to do with one child during events planned for the entire class. In situations such as this, it's important not to lapse into blaming or punishing the child or the family for their cultural or religious beliefs. For example, many Jehovah's Witness families don't perceive their children as missing out because they don't celebrate birthdays or other holidays. Often Jehovah's Witness communities are tight-knit and have many community celebrations, parties, and sleepovers that are not tied to birthdays or holidays. They may feel sorry for children who don't live in such a warm, connected community of families! Many Jehovah's Witness families keep their children at home because of potential conflicts around holidays, but many others have few choices. Whatever decision a program makes about how to handle this delicate issue, it should be made with respect for all the families.

Parent Support and Education

Become knowledgeable about your local community resources, especially culturally specific resources—high-quality programs that place families first can serve as a community resource for parents. Create a community resource file and connect families to resources and services in the community. A parent resource center could be established with multicultural books, cassette tapes, and CDs for parents to borrow. Programs can also offer a parent support group to help parents explore their own cultural identity and attitudes toward human diversity. Offer workshops that help parents raise children in a diverse society. You might include topics such as the following:

- Culture and parenting
- How to help your child become bilingual
- Racial and cultural identity
- Preventing prejudice and bias

Managing Cultural Conflicts

When I was a director of a white, suburban, middle-class child care center, I enrolled a rather large three-year-old boy whose family had just come from Israel to spend one year in the United States. The little boy arrived for his first day of school complete with a baby bottle full of chocolate milk in one hand and a pacifier in the other. The teaching staff was appalled by such parenting practices, and the teachers of the three-year-olds were bound and determined to stick to their rule of no bottles and no pacifiers. After all, this was a preschool room, not a toddler room. The little boy screamed, kicked, and cried as soon as he entered the room.

He did this every day, all day for almost a month. He became the topic of conversation in the staff lounge, the center kitchen, the playground, and the hallway.

Every staff person had a different complaint about this child. He cried too much. He was too immature. He was spoiled. He wasn't ready for child care. His parents were lazy because they hadn't weaned him from the bottle or pacifier. His parents were spoiling him. His parents must be ignorant—didn't they know about baby bottle syndrome? One teacher was afraid that soon all of the three-year-olds would be begging for—no, demanding—their own bottles of chocolate milk. The more staff complained, the less interested they became in a solution. They thought this little boy was bad and that his parents were bad. It was a negative situation and they wanted me to ask the boy to leave the program. It was very hard for the staff to recognize that the conflict came from a cultural difference in child raising. The boy's parents were competent parents from a different culture than the staff—they had different beliefs, behaviors, and values about bringing up their child. This didn't mean that they were wrong. In this case, the staff's own culturally based beliefs, behaviors, and values about child raising got in the way of their clear vision of this child and his family.

From the training I do today, I know that this happens all of the time. Cultural clashes occur in early childhood programs. While we cannot solve every disagreement, we can use a problem-solving approach to manage the situation. In dealing with cultural dilemmas such as this, I offer these suggestions:

ANALYZE THE SITUATION AND IDENTIFY WAYS IN WHICH YOU MAY BE INVOLVED IN A CULTURAL DILEMMA

Ask yourself, "What is the child's experience at home?" and "How is the child's experience related to a cultural practice or value?" In this case, the teachers and parents had different goals for the child based on cultural beliefs about child development, specifically, when is a baby a baby and when is a child a child. From the parent's perspective, their son was still a baby. From the teacher's culturally based perspective, he was a preschooler.

DON'T BLAME THE CHILD

The child is not bad, evil, spoiled, or developmentally delayed. Contrary to how it may seem, the child is not out to get you. The child may be acting in a culturally appropriate way. The little boy in my story was an absolute delight to his parents.

GET INFORMATION

Go to the child's file and read through the enrollment forms. Call the parent and set up a time to talk. Find out what the behavior means to the parent, what the parent would do in this situation, and what has been done in the past.

REALIZE THAT THE CHILD IS COPING IN THE BEST WAY HE KNOWS

He is responding to a new situation in the ways he knows how. His only expectation is to receive care that is similar to what he had known his whole life. These big changes are scary, frustrating, and angering. The boy in our story found himself separated from his parents and in the company of people who spoke a different language. He was totally overwhelmed. That bottle was his only form of security.

RESPOND TO THE CHILD AND PARENT AS INDIVIDUALS

Culturally relevant caregiving and education means the willingness to bend, change, and revise in order to meet individual needs. It may mean breaking the rules, making exceptions to the rules, or changing the rules in order to provide complementary care and culturally appropriate education. For example, if a baby's family carries him in a sling, hold the infant more than you usually might. Serve meals to a child who is accustomed to being served by adults. Use drills and direct teaching methods with a child whose family culture calls for learning through brief, highly charged encounters.

High-quality early childhood programs are an integral part of the community. In order to serve our community, we have to get to know it and establish a sense of accountability to it. Programs designed around the local community and cultures naturally become contextually relevant. This is very different from a program that is "out of context" or unlike the surrounding community. High-quality programs also work hand in hand with the families they serve. They strive to form culturally sensitive relationships and involve parents in all levels of the program. A high level of community and family involvement leads to a culturally relevant and anti-bias curriculum that feels natural.

Questions to Ponder

Alone or with a group, answer each of the following questions in an attempt to identify your own culturally based beliefs, behaviors, and values.

What are traditional foods that you or someone else in your family prepares?

What celebrations, ceremonies, rituals, or holidays do you celebrate with your family?

What were some words of wisdom, sayings, or advice that your parents or grandparents passed on to you?

How do adults and children interact with one another?

What are some examples of acceptable child behavior?

When would you say "no" to a child or discipline a child?

What are some examples of acceptable discipline for a child?

When does a baby become a child?

What are some childrearing practices of others that are shocking, appalling, or frightening to you?

To whom/where would you go for advice about children or parenting?

Who/where would you go to for help with a family problem?

Review your answers. What is the purpose of these practices or beliefs? In other words, what are the underlying values?

References

Bisson, Julie. 1997. Celebrate! *An anti-bias guide to enjoying holidays in early childhood programs.* St. Paul: Redleaf Press.

Brunson-Phillips, Carol. 1992. *Essential connections: Ten keys to culturally sensitive child care.* Far West Laboratory in collaboration with the California Department of Education, producers. Sacramento: California Department of Education.

McGoldrick, Monica, John Pearce, and Joseph Giordono, eds. 1982. *Ethnicity and family therapy.* New York: Guilford Press.

Whitney, Trisha. 1999. *Kids like us: Using persona dolls in the classroom.* St. Paul: Redleaf Press.

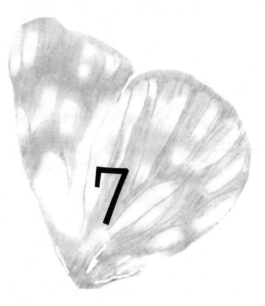

Multicultural Education

The education of our young people must begin where they are, using their knowledge, experiences, cultures and languages as the basis for their learning.
Sonia Nieto, University of Massachusetts—
Amherst, School of Education

Ask five people to define **multicultural education** and you're sure to get five different answers. Multicultural education can be confusing because it means different things to different people; it is complicated by many definitions, a variety of approaches, and a number of terms that describe its many aspects. This chapter will help you sort out things by examining the nature of multicultural education, listing its goals, and explaining the basic approaches. Let's begin the journey into the world of multicultural education by asking some basic questions.

See glossary.

What Is Multicultural Education?

Multicultural education is many different things:

- A field of study (In its own right, multicultural education is an entire area of specialization within various fields such as education, counseling psychology, and public health.)
- A way to reform schools

- An umbrella term for many different curriculum models that try to incorporate culture or diversity into the curriculum

- A factor at all levels of education (Individuals and institutions serving children from prekindergarten through graduate school are involved in multicultural education. Today multicultural education occurs with children, adult learners, parents, and in the workplace. Multicultural education has been and continues to be a major educational reform movement in the Western world in countries such as the United States, Canada, United Kingdom, Netherlands, Australia, and New Zealand.)

Here are some definitions of multicultural education from some of the leaders in the field:

AN AFFIRMATION OF PLURALISM

Multicultural education challenges and rejects racism and other forms of discrimination in schools and society and accepts and affirms the pluralism (ethnic, racial, linguistic, religious, economic, and gender, among others) that students, their communities, and teachers represent. Multicultural education permeates the curriculum and instructional strategies used in schools, as well as the interactions among teachers, students, and parents, and the very way that schools think about the nature of teaching and learning. Because it uses critical pedagogy as its underlying philosophy and focuses on knowledge, reflection, and action (praxis) as the basis for social change, multicultural education furthers the democratic principles of social justice. As Christine Bennett, author of *Comprehensive Multicultural Education* (1999, p. 11) puts it,

> *Multicultural education in the United States is an approach to teaching and learning that is based upon democratic values and beliefs, and affirms cultural pluralism within culturally diverse societies and an interdependent world. It is based on the assumption that the primary goal of public education is to foster the intellectual, social, and personal development of virtually all students to their highest potential.*

AN EXTENSION OF DEMOCRACY

Multicultural education seeks to extend the ideals that were meant only for an elite few to all people. Multiculturalism consists of the values and beliefs inherent in a democracy: the promotion of human rights and privileges, the sharing of power, and equal participation in all social contexts. James Banks, a distinguished professor and author on the subject of multiculturalism, has written much about the connection between multicultural education and democracy. For example,

> *The goal of multicultural education is an education for freedom . . . Multicultural education should help students to develop the knowledge, attitudes, and skills to participate in a democratic and free society.. . . Multicultural education promotes the freedom, abilities and skills to cross ethnic and cultural boundaries to participation in other cultures and groups* (quoted in Lockwood 1992, p. 23).

> *Multicultural education is an education for freedom . . . that is essential in today's ethnically polarized and troubled world* (1991/1992, p. 32).

> *To fully participate in our democratic society, these students and all students need the skills a multicultural education can give them to understand others and to thrive in a rapidly changing, diverse world* (1991, p. 35).

A COMPREHENSIVE APPROACH TO SCHOOL REFORM

Banks and others also define multiethnic education as a reform movement designed to make major changes in the education of children and youths. Advocates of multiethnic education believe that many school practices related to race and ethnicity are harmful to students and reinforce ethnic stereotypes and discriminatory practices in Western societies. Multiethnic education includes but is much more comprehensive than ethnic studies or curriculum reform related to ethnicity. Multiethnic education is concerned with changing the total school environment so that students from all ethnic groups will experience equal educational opportunities. Educators must reform their total educational environments in order to implement multiethnic education. Here's how James Banks and Cherry McGee Banks (1997) put it in *Multicultural Education: Issues and Perspectives*:

> *Multicultural education is at least three things: an idea or concept, an educational reform movement, and a process.*

> • *It incorporates the idea that all students, regardless of their gender, social, ethnic, racial or cultural characteristics, should have an equal opportunity to learn in school.*

- *It is a reform movement designed to make some major changes in schools and other educational institutions so that students from all social classes, gender, racial, and cultural groups will have an equal opportunity to learn.*

- *It is an ongoing process whose goals, which include educational equality and improving academic achievement, will never be realized because they are ideals toward which human beings work but never attain.*

Sonia Nieto (1996), another respected thinker in the field of education, says it this way:

> *Multicultural education, defined in a sociopolitical context, is a process of comprehensive school reform and basic education for all students. It challenges and rejects racism and other forms of discrimination in schools and society and accepts and affirms the pluralism (ethnic, linguistic, religious, economic, and gender, among others) that students, their communities, and teachers represent. Multicultural education permeates the curriculum and instructional strategies used in schools, as well as the interactions among teachers, students, and parents, and the very way that schools conceptualize the nature of teaching and learning. Because it uses critical pedagogy as its underlying philosophy and focuses on knowledge, reflection, and action (praxis) as the basis for social change, multicultural education promotes the democratic principles of social justice.*
>
> *The seven basic characteristics of multicultural education in this definition are*
> - *Multicultural education is antiracist education.*
> - *Multicultural education is basic education.*
> - *Multicultural education is important for all students.*
> - *Multicultural education is pervasive.*
> - *Multicultural education is education for social justice.*
> - *Multicultural education is a process.*
> - *Multicultural education is critical pedagogy.*

Multicultural education is far reaching and multifaceted. Multicultural education attempts to address educational inequality that results from racism. We can identify key traits that best define multicultural education by saying that it attempts to do the following:

- Minimize and heal damage to children's sense of self that results from racism

- Minimize the development of prejudice and increase children's ability to function cross-culturally

- Foster children's cultural identity and home language

- Teach children knowledge, attitudes, and skills that will help them fully function in a free and democratic society, which includes ensuring that all children develop strong skills in the basic subjects of reading, writing, math, science, and social science

- Teach children to learn how to think critically to recognize discrimination and injustice and work together to challenge injustice

Early Childhood Multicultural Education

Multicultural education grew out of the civil rights movement. But it wasn't until the 1980s that early childhood educators began to examine what multicultural education means for our field. In the early 1980s, several key books were published that shaped the thinking about multicultural education: *Diversity in the Classroom,* by Francis Kendall; *Teaching and Learning in a Diverse World,* by Patricia Ramsey; *Alerta: A Multicultural, Bilingual Approach to Teaching Young Children,* by Leslie Williams and Yvonne De Gaetano; and *Black Children: Their Roots, Culture, and Learning Styles,* by Janice Hale Benson. The 1989 publication of *Anti-Bias Curriculum: Tools for Empowering Young Children,* by Louise Derman-Sparks and the ABC Task Force, launched a movement toward multicultural or anti-bias education within early childhood education.

In early childhood settings, multicultural education begins with knowing, respecting, and setting high expectations for each child in your classroom. It involves working with parents and adapting caregiving practices to complement the style and form of caregiving used within the child's family. Multicultural education also includes teaching children about their own culture—their ethnic heritage. It involves incorporating children's home languages into the daily life of the classroom. It also means exposing children to other cultures and helping them be comfortable with and respect all the ways people differ from each other. It is teaching children how to relate to one another and how to play fair. Multicultural education encourages children to notice and think about unfairness and challenges them to do something about the unfairness toward people in their world.

Multicultural education is more than teaching information directly. It means providing a classroom that includes materials depicting people from many different places doing many different things. It's creating and maintaining an environment that says everyone is welcome here. It is also encouraging children to act, think, and talk like members of their own culture. Multicultural education means helping children to like themselves just the way they are. It's encouraging children to actively explore a variety of materials and exposing them to experiences that might not be part of their daily life experience.

What Multicultural Education Is . . . and Is Not

I hope that multicultural education is becoming clearer in your mind. Because of its complexity and controversial nature, multicultural education is often misinterpreted and misrepresented in both schools and the media. On the next page is a simple chart outlining what multicultural education is and is not.

Why Is Multicultural Education Important?

The Center Accreditation Project has identified multicultural education as one component of a quality early childhood program. As early childhood teachers, we know that quality programs produce positive outcomes for children, families, and society as a whole. Yet many of us still do not understand why multicultural education is so important in the early years. Multicultural education

- Encourages a true sense of self
- Promotes healthy development
- Prepares children for the future
- Prevents isolation
- Discourages denial and fear of differences

Let's look at each of these, one at a time.

ENCOURAGING A TRUE SENSE OF SELF

Multicultural education is important for young children because they deserve to be in programs where it is safe for them to be who they are. Children deserve to know the truth about themselves, the real world, and the people in it. Children have the right to feel proud of themselves, to learn to be courageous, and to not feel like victims. Children are entitled to their cultural heritage, a strong positive cultural identity, and a home language.

Multicultural Education Is . . .

A moral conviction to help all children reach their fullest potential

A way to achieve fairness and equity in child care and educational settings

An education reform movement that is almost fifty years old

For all children

A way to embrace and equally value cultural diversity within the United States

Opening children's minds to diversity and helping to think critically about injustice

Relevant to all age levels and all areas of the curriculum

A way to embrace universal rights and wrongs while respecting differences

An intentional, sustained effort

A lifelong journey that begins with knowing yourself as a cultural being

Multicultural Education Is Not . . .

Political correctness

A way to solve all of society's problems

A trend or a fad

Only for children of color

White bashing or a rejection of Western/European American culture and tradition

Ignoring or devaluing differences

Simply one aspect of social studies, children's literature, and the arts

The idea that anything goes and everything is relative

A one-time event such as a culture fair, one thematic curriculum unit, or an annual celebration

Something teachers and administrators can "learn" in a one-time workshop

PROMOTING HEALTHY DEVELOPMENT

Early childhood teachers know that these years are an important time for children's growth and development. During this time, children acquire a self-concept, build their self-esteem, learn how to make friends, become aware of family and community, learn to use words to express themselves, have strong feelings and fears, use magical (and often distorted) thinking, and tend to believe everything they see and hear. This is the time to prevent or minimize prejudice and help children learn to function successfully and cooperatively in a culturally diverse society and world. Racism inhibits all of our development. Multicultural education offers children an opportunity for "corrective development." Cireci Olatunji (1998, p. 106) used the term "corrective development" to describe the process and setting needed to correct children's false ideas about themselves and others that they may have internalized from growing up in a racist society.

PREPARING CHILDREN FOR THE FUTURE

Multicultural education is important because teachers must prepare children to live both in today's very diverse country and global marketplace as well as to live in the future. Today, the United States is the most diverse and most international country in the world and over time is becoming even more diverse. By the year 2020, children of color will make up 46 percent of the school-age children in the United States. The children in our classrooms will need cross-cultural skills and will probably need to be bilingual if they are to fully participate in the future workforce.

PREVENTING ISOLATION

When I taught in and directed suburban and rural programs, I often wondered if multicultural education was relevant because all of the children in my program seemed the same. Since then, I've learned that multicultural education is just as important in an all–European American program or an all-Latino program as it is in a multiracial program.

Growing up in a community where everyone is the same can give children the false impression that everyone everywhere is alike. Children in monocultural communities and monocultural early childhood programs can grow up not knowing about other cultures, without developing a sensitivity to the life experiences of others, and without ever thinking about people of other cultures. Unfortunately, these children don't know that their country and the world are made up of many communities that are very different from their own. Excluding multicultural education from the early childhood curriculum is to risk isolating children from the rest of the world.

DISCOURAGING DENIAL AND FEAR OF DIFFERENCES

Children in monocultural environments risk growing up denying or being afraid of the differences among people. It's common to hear teachers in rural or suburban programs say, "I never knew there were differences." "My family never talked about them." "In a small town it's different because everyone is the same and everyone is accepted."

An early childhood program that doesn't provide multicultural education encourages denial and teaches children a narrow view of the world. Teaching as if there was only one perspective that really matters promotes the idea that other ways of being in the world are somehow deficient, inadequate, or even wrong.

European American children need to understand and accept that there are other perspectives and other ways of being in the world.

When I lived in a small town people noticed and talked about differences. Sometimes it was just gossip, but other times the differences were used to put someone down or make us feel superior. People talked about what church you attended, what side of the railroad tracks you lived on, what crop you farmed, where you bought your seed, where you worked, what kind of truck you drove, what make of farm machinery you used, where you went on vacation, who was married and who was single, who stayed in town and who left. To teach multicultural education in classes where everyone seems the same, begin with the differences at hand. Even programs in which everyone seems to be the same can emphasize differences among the children such as hair color, family size, where they live, and where their parent(s) work.

Types of Multicultural Education

Now that we've defined multicultural education, let's think about how it gets implemented in the classroom. Christine Sleeter and Carl Grant, researchers in multicultural education, studied sixty books and hundreds of articles about multicultural education in kindergarten through twelfth grade in the United States. They identified five main approaches to multicultural education. Other researchers (Louise Derman-Sparks and James Banks, for example) have identified different numbers of approaches. From my perspective, there are at least six different approaches to multicultural education and they vary greatly. It's important to be familiar with them and understand the differences so you can recognize what approach is being used in your program, and whether or not it is likely to meet your goals. The approaches include the following:

- Human relations
- Single-group studies
- Multicultural education
- Anti-bias education
- Culturally specific education
- Culturally relevant anti-bias education

Though many aspects of each approach are effective and helpful, most fall short of being truly all-encompassing multicultural approaches that also embrace anti-bias principles. For instance, the human relations approach naively assumes all people are treated equally, perpetuates white superiority, and ignores human diversity.

The second approach, single-group studies, is also known as the "tourist" approach, and has been around the longest. Many adults today can remember a "multicultural" curriculum from their childhoods that studied "Christmas around the World" for example. Most commercial curriculum materials reflect this method. According to Louise Derman-Sparks (1989), a "tourist" approach "teaches simplistic generalizations about other people, that leads to stereotyping rather than to understanding of differences."

The multicultural approach does a wonderful job of introducing children to diversity but doesn't help children learn how to stand up to bias, and the anti-bias approach, in its original form, ignored children's cultural identity. Think of your program and your curriculum as you examine each approach below.

Human Relations

This approach focuses on teaching children how to make and maintain good relationships with children of different ethnic groups. The human relations approach emphasizes the development of a positive self-concept and skills in forming and maintaining friendships. It focuses on the importance of appreciating each other, talking to one another, and learning how to get along with one another. Children learn about similarities and differences, and that name-calling hurts people's feelings. Teachers who implement this approach aren't thinking about curriculum in terms of culture and race. By default, the classroom is centered around European American values, beliefs, and practices because European Americans are inadvertently held up as the norm, or standard, of humanity. This approach also denies racial and cultural differences and that's why Louise Derman-Sparks has termed it the *dominant culture* or *color-blind approach*.

The human relations approach can be summarized this way:

Goals. Self-awareness; positive self-esteem; communication skills; and social skills

Themes. I'm me and I'm special; let's be friends; alike and different; and living with others

Activities. Feelings games; group discussions; painting self portraits; cooperative play; and games with partners

Single-Group Studies

This approach is based on the belief that knowing oneself is the beginning of understanding and accepting others. Single-group studies are especially popular at the college level with departments and entire degree programs such as African American studies, Latin American studies, Scandinavian studies, and women's studies. The goals of single-group studies are to teach appreciation of one's own culture, to raise cultural awareness, and to encourage individuals to take action on behalf of their people. The curriculum includes learning about the historical influences, cultural patterns, and current issues that influence or affect the culture.

In early childhood, this approach is sometimes called the "Four Fs" approach (food, festivals, folk tales, and fun). In an early childhood setting, children would learn about another culture. It may be a culture that is represented in the classroom or community or it may be a culture with which children have no experience.

Unfortunately, many European American programs and multiracial programs have turned this model into another form of classroom entertainment. Consequently, children learn about cultures through units or themes that focus on one group of people at a time, for example, Hawaii Week, Africa Week, Mexico Week, and Indian Week. Louise Derman-Sparks calls this method the "tourist" approach because it's like taking a short trip. For a brief period of time the class goes sight-seeing, trying out and enjoying the food, the folk costumes, exotic dances, and music of each culture. At the end of the week the class leaves the country and the topic is dropped until the same time next year. The tourist approach does little to meet the goals of multicultural education. It can hinder children by reinforcing the idea that people who are different from them lived a long time ago and all they do is wear funny clothes, eat weird food, and dance. In other words, this approach with young children often teaches stereotypes, which we know leads to prejudice.

The single-group study approach can be summarized this way:

Goals. Global awareness; appreciate other cultures; and learn about other cultures

Sample unit themes. Mexico; Japan; African American Week; it's a small world

Activities. Culture fairs; cultural festivals; ethnic food; folk tales; folk
music; folk dance; ethnic costumes; cultural artifacts; maps and globes;
and holidays

Multicultural Education

This approach advocates that America is like a "tossed salad" and that the
strength of our society comes from diversity. Multicultural education provides
children with the message that it is all right to be different, differences are good,
and people deserve to choose how they want to live. This approach also affirms
equality: people deserve the same opportunities regardless of gender, race, class,
religion, age, ability, or sexual orientation. Programs using this approach are
nondiscriminatory and show respect for children's families, home life, and learning style. Children learn about the contributions and traits of the cultures represented in their classroom or community. They may also be encouraged to use
more than one language. The classroom materials and bulletin boards reflect all
types of diversity. Units on boys and girls, families, bodies, and celebrations are
examples of themes that affirm diversity.

The multicultural approach can be summarized this way:

Goals. Recognize and respect human similarities and differences, and
develop skills for living in a diverse society

Sample unit themes. Alike and different; clothes; foods; and families

Activities. Paint with skin-color paints; play a guessing game by describing
a classmate's physical characteristics; sort people by alike and different;
and read a story in two or more languages

Anti-Bias Education

This approach focuses on changing inequality and the sources of stereotypes. Anti-
bias education prepares people to change the social structures that perpetuate
injustice. Whereas the other approaches assume that changing people's attitudes
will eventually change the social structure, an anti-bias approach is built on the
belief that if the structures change, people's attitudes will change. As a result, students are taught to take action against the inequalities present in society.

Anti-bias classrooms attempt to model democracy. Teachers include children in
decision making and any changes such as rearranging the room. Children make
choices, are encouraged to act on their choices, and are given opportunities to

work cooperatively. They are taught skills in individual and group problem solving and critical thinking, and they are provided with experiences in taking social action. Louise Derman-Sparks (1989) shows this approach through an example from a preschool classroom. A boy's father had difficulty visiting his son's class because he was handicapped. The school provided no handicap parking spaces, so the class made a handicap parking space in the school parking lot. This shows how the curriculum is based on and emerges from the daily lives of the children, incidents that take place in the classroom, and current world events.

The anti-bias approach can be summarized this way:

Goals. Foster self-identity; foster comfortable, empathetic interaction with diverse people; foster critical thinking about bias; stand up for oneself and others in the face of bias

Sample unit themes. Racial differences and racial biases; gender differences and gender biases; social class differences and class biases; disabilities and bias against people with disabilities; age differences and age biases; and sexual orientation and bias against gays and lesbians

Activities. Wash baby dolls to learn about skin color; solve problems related to discriminatory behavior using persona dolls; introduce a classroom visitor to help children learn about a disability; reading and rewriting a stereotypic book; celebrate a holiday honoring a civil rights leader or event; as a class, take action against an unfair issue

Culturally Specific Approach

Many urban schools districts have launched culturally specific programs in recent years. In my community, the public schools offer an Afrocentric academy, a Native American school, and a Latino charter school. Culturally specific approaches are designed to meet the developmental and educational needs of children from a specific cultural group. Cultural communities become frustrated with the continually high levels of academic failure within mainstream programs and these program's inability to meet their children's needs. In order to inspire academic achievement and increase children's cultural identities, culturally based organizations have started child care programs, preschools, and elementary schools designed specifically to serve children from that culture.

The culturally specific approach can be summarized this way:

Goals. Inspire student achievement; increase children's cultural identity; maintain the community's cultural integrity; provide children with cultural role models

Curriculum components. Incorporate cultural values and beliefs into the daily life of the school; incorporate culturally based learning styles into teaching methods; provide cultural studies; build strong ties between the school and the cultural community

Activities. Learn how to speak, read, and write native languages; learn about cultural heritage; recognize the accomplishments and contributions of their people; study an accurate version of United States history

Culturally Relevant and Anti-Bias Education

Culturally relevant, anti-bias education is the most current term for a comprehensive approach to multicultural education in early childhood settings. The term originated with Sharon Cronin, faculty member at Pacific Oaks College Northwest in Seattle. Sharon was one of the site coordinators in a large Anti-Bias Leadership Project (the CRAB Leadership Project) funded by the Kellogg Foundation and directed by Louise Derman-Sparks. The project is discussed in *Future Vision, Present Work* (1998). Here is the description of the origins of the name "culturally relevant, anti-bias" or "CRAB":

> *Sharon Cronin suggested that the name should be changed to acknowledge the long history of work by people of color in establishing a decisive voice as to how their children are cared for and taught. She proposed adding the term "cultural relevancy" to the project's title to clarify the fundamental connection between the concept of providing programs for children of color that support and reflect their home culture (thus, "culturally relevant" environments) and the anti-bias goals as they were originally formulated (1998, p. 22).*

As the name implies, culturally relevant/anti-bias education begins with providing care and education that includes the following:

- Caregiving practices that complement the parent's style of caring for their children

- Classroom environments that reflect the children's home cultures, use teaching strategies that are common within the children's home cultures, incorporate the child's home language into the life of the classroom, and implement activities that help each child learn more and gain greater appreciation of her home culture

- An anti-bias approach that helps children learn about human diversity, gain respect and appreciation for diversity, learn to recognize and resist stereotypes and unfair behavior, and learn to work with others to stand up for oneself or to challenge bias; anti-bias education is implemented through classroom materials and planned activities

Curriculum Goals

Ideally, curriculum goals and objectives of early childhood education are based on child development principles. Previous chapters described the importance of culture, prejudice, and racism to children's development. From a developmental perspective, we know that it is important to promote children's cultural identity, strengthen their connection to their home culture, and strengthen their home language. We also know that children are developing prejudice. As teachers, we can work to reduce children's prejudice by helping them recognize stereotypes and learn to resist name-calling and teasing others who are different from them. We know that racism destroys our humanity. As teachers we can work to minimize the negative impact of racism on children's lives.

Child development knowledge is translated into educational practice through goals and objectives. Goals are broad, sweeping statements that describe our hopes and dreams for children. They are the principles on which a curriculum is based. The following four goals translate our knowledge of culture, prejudice, and racism into positive outcomes for children. They were originally published in *Anti-Bias Curriculum: Tools for Empowering Young Children* and have been refined by Dr. Carol Brunson Day and others participating in the many anti-bias leadership initiatives coordinated by Louise Derman-Sparks. Notice how the goals match the developmental issues that lay the foundation of culturally relevant/anti-bias education.

Developmental Issue	Corresponding Educational Goal
Culture	To develop positive, knowledgeable, and confident self-identity within a cultural context.
Prejudice	To demonstrate comfortable, empathetic interaction with diversity among people.
Prejudice and Racism	To think critically about bias.
Racism	To stand up for oneself and others in the face of bias.

Curriculum Objectives

It's difficult to plan curriculum based on goal statements because they are so general. Objectives are used in conjunction with goal statements to connect child development and educational practices. Each of the goals described above is accompanied by a set of objectives. Objectives are specific statements with a narrow focus, written in behavioral terms. Objectives describe what the child will know, feel, or do. Here is a complete list of the goals and objectives of a culturally relevant/anti-bias curriculum.

Goal 1: Develop a positive, knowledgeable, and confident self-identity within a cultural context.

OBJECTIVES

Recognize one's own physical features

Recognize one's own language

Recognize one's own dress

Recognize one's own diet and style of eating

Recognize one's own family

Recognize and identify the meaning of one's own name

Identify one's own culture, cultural traditions, and customs

Appreciate one's own cultural heritage

Understand the concept of homelands

Use one's home language in public

Demonstrate positive sense of self-worth

Recognize one's own beauty

Demonstrate dignity and pride

Demonstrate feeling of being special and unique

Describe self using positive language

Demonstrate self-acceptance of one's cultural identity

Demonstrate self-acceptance of one's physical features

Begin to understand racial constancy

Identify with one's own culture

Recognize one's family celebrations

Share one's family celebrations with others

Experience a connection between families and schools

Experience a sense of belonging in the classroom

Talk about one's home life with others

Experience high expectations of oneself

Demonstrate sense of determination

Participate in a positive, supportive group

Recognize role models within own culture

Demonstrate belief in oneself

Identify own skills and abilities

Recognize one's own value and contribution to the group

Goal 2: Demonstrate comfortable, empathetic interaction with diversity among people.

OBJECTIVES

Accept others who are different from oneself

Appreciate physical characteristics of others

Explore similarities and differences in positive ways

Recognize human similarities/differences and develop positive attitudes toward them

Recognize that people have the same basic needs

Recognize that people do things in different ways and have different lifestyles

Recognize that human differences make people unique and special

Recognize that our community is made up of many different types of people

Identify some of the cultural groups that make up American society

Recognize one's own culture within American society

Understand that all people deserve respect

Show respect for all people

Experience positive relationships with people who are different from oneself

Increase one's willingness to interact with diverse groups of people

Show empathy for others

Explore the cultures of the other children in the class

Notice another's point of view

Pronounce the names of one's classmates correctly

Experience human diversity in various ways

Show increasing comfort with human diversity

Experience cross-cultural relationships

Attend community cultural events

Meet leaders from diverse cultural groups

Recognize the contributions from all cultural groups

Goal 3: Think critically about bias.

OBJECTIVES

Recognize a stereotype

Describe and define *stereotype*

Compare *real* and *pretend*

Recognize prejudice

Recognize that some people are afraid of others

Recognize that some people have misconceptions about others

Recognize that some people treat others unfairly because of differences

Accept that unfair treatment because of differences is wrong

Compare *respectful* and *disrespectful* behaviors

Compare *fair* and *unfair* behaviors

Recognize unfair behavior when it occurs

Recognize that name-calling and teasing hurts others

Resist name-calling and teasing

Recognize those who are left out and those who are included

Recognize that rejecting others hurts them

Identify ways to avoid rejecting others

Explore why people are discriminated against

Identify the importance of doing something about discrimination

Identify ways to respond to discrimination

Put oneself in another person's situation

Practice thinking before acting

Recognize the concept of *human rights*

Show concern about people's welfare

Show concern for people in our community

Clarify one's misconceptions about human diversity

Receive simple, truthful information about human diversity

Recognize the importance of not making judgments based on appearance

Recognize that people within a group are not all alike

Think for oneself

Distinguish right from wrong

Goal 4: Stand up for oneself and others in the face of bias.

OBJECTIVES

Practice standing up for oneself

Practice standing up for another person

Contribute positively to the classroom and to the community

Recognize that people can work together to help each other

Cooperate with others

Practice conflict-resolution skills

Participate in group problem solving

Take personal responsibility in social situations

Relate values and principle to action

Feel responsibility to oneself and to one's family, culture, and community

Seek adult assistance for and protection from mistreatment

Participate as a group member and in group decision making

Generate solutions to problems

Experience democratic conflict resolution

Work cooperatively with others

Choosing an Approach

Given all this information, how can you choose the best approach to use in your own classroom? Two of the approaches we discussed, the single-group studies approach and the human relations approach, are incompatible with early childhood education. The single-group studies approach (also called the "tourist" approach) is inappropriate for early childhood settings because it perpetuates white superiority. Unfortunately, it continues to be the most popular approach in early childhood programs. It's been around the longest, and most commercial curriculum materials reflect this method. Teachers have invested a lot of time and money in building resources that support this approach. As a result, they are often very resistant to examining other methods or restructuring their curriculum. Until recently, teacher education programs either excluded multicultural education from the curriculum or promoted the single-group studies approach. As a result, many early childhood teachers aren't aware of how damaging a single-group studies or the "tourist" approach can be. According to Louise Derman-Sparks (1989), a "tourist" approach "teaches simplistic generalization about other people, that leads to stereotyping rather than to understanding of differences."

On the other hand, the human relations approach is no more appropriate. Gloria Boutte (1999) describes the possible consequences of a human relations approach for children. "They miss out on valuable pieces about other world views and do not understand the ultimate connectedness that humans share. When white children are exposed to a curriculum that constantly validates their culture and invalidates other cultures (often subtly and unintentionally), superiority over other races is encouraged. When confronted with issues of diversity, later in life, whites who have not learned to appreciate diversity may be less empathetic, respectful, and sensitive to the needs of other cultural groups. This hampers effective relationships with others and the opportunity to work and live together in harmony."

As a guideline, Sleeter and Grant (1988) say you can combine two approaches and still give adequate attention to the goals and methods of each approach. For example, you might combine the human relations approach with the multicultural approach. This may be the place to start, since many early childhood programs already do a good job of emphasizing self-esteem and socialization. This book is written from a culturally relevant, anti-bias perspective, though it focuses on racism and not on other oppressions. Clearly, it's my perspective that the culturally relevant, anti-bias perspective is best for children. It's also the hardest to implement well, so it may make sense to ease into it by beginning with another, less comprehensive approach.

By now you are probably developing your own definition of multicultural education. I hope that reading about different approaches has you thinking about your own group of children, activities you've tried in the past, and possibilities for the future. Perhaps now you can see how culturally relevant/anti-bias emerged as the most current and comprehensive approach to multicultural education in early childhood settings. Use the list of goals in this chapter as a starting point for implementing culturally relevant and anti-bias education in your program.

Questions to Ponder

How would you define multicultural education?

Why is multicultural education important to you?

Which of the approaches to multicultural education fits with your beliefs?

Which of the approaches best matches what is currently taking place in your classroom?

What changes can be made to improve multicultural and anti-bias education in your classroom?

References

Banks, J. A. 1988. *Multiethnic education: Theory and practice.* 2d ed. Boston: Allyn and Bacon.

Banks, J. A. 1991. *Teaching strategies for ethnic studies.* 5th ed. Boston: Allyn and Bacon.

Banks, J. A. 1991/1992. Multicultural education: For freedom's sake. *Educational Leadership* 49, no. 4 (December/January) 32–36.

Banks, J. A. 1992. It's up to us. *Teaching Tolerance* (Fall) 20–23.

Banks, J. A., and C. A. McGee Banks. 1991. *Multicultural education: Issues and perspectives.* Boston: Allyn and Bacon.

Bennett, Christine I. 1999. *Comprehensive multicultural education: Theory and practice.* Needham Heights, Mass.: Allyn and Bacon.

Boutte, Gloria. 1999. *Multicultural education: Raising consciousness.* Belmont, Calif.: Wadsworth.

Cronin, Sharon, Louise Derman-Sparks, Sharon Henry, Cirecie Olatunji, and Stacey York. 1998. *Future vision, present work.* St. Paul: Redleaf Press.

Derman-Sparks, Louise. 1989. *Anti-bias curriculum.* Washington, D.C.: NAEYC.

Grant, Carl A., and Christine E. Sleeter. 1989. *Turning on learning: Five approaches for multicultural teaching plans for race, class, gender, and disability.* Columbus, Ohio: Merrill.

Hernandez, Hilda. 1989. *Multicultural education: A teacher's guide to content and process.* Columbus, Ohio: Merrill.

Lockwood, A. T. 1992. Education for freedom. *Focus in Change* 7: 23–29.

Nieto, Sonia. 1996. *Affirming diversity: The sociopolitical context of multicultural education.* 2d ed. White Plains, N.Y.: Longman Publishers.

Sleeter, Christine E., and Carl A. Grant. 1988. An analysis of multicultural education in the U.S.A. Harvard Educational Review 57: 421–444.

Sleeter, Christine E., and Carl A. Grant. 1988. *Making choices for multicultural education.* Columbus, Ohio: Merrill.

Williams, Leslie R., and Yvonne De Gaetano. 1985. *Alerta: A multicultural, bilingual approach to teaching young children.* Menlo Park, Calif.: Addison-Wesley.

A Culturally Relevant, Anti-Bias Classroom

The quickest and easiest way to add or improve culturally relevant and anti-bias education is to improve the classroom—it's easier to change things than it is to change people. Working on the classroom first allows you to roll up your sleeves and dig in right away. So jump into culturally relevant and anti-bias education and get started with the classroom.

At some level, most early childhood teachers already know that starting with the room arrangement is a good idea. Ask a teacher what she does for culturally relevant and anti-bias education. Most often the answer is: "The center has a set of multiethnic dolls that we rotate from room to room. Our director bought each classroom a few books and a poster. I put the things out but now I don't know what to do next." Although many programs and teachers begin in the right place, they don't go far enough to realize their goals. Because they aren't sure if the few materials are making an impact on the children and they don't have any more money in the equipment budget, they stop. Not knowing what else to do, they become stuck and bewildered.

This chapter will help you go beyond buying a few dolls and posters. It includes many ideas for teaching through interest areas, criteria for evaluating books and materials, suggestions for making your own visual displays, and a long list of sources for culturally relevant and anti-bias materials. Let's begin with a brief discussion about how room arrangement relates to program goals and the importance of classrooms in facilitating developmentally appropriate education for young children.

Classrooms Affect Behavior, Attitudes, and Learning

Classroom environments give children and parents strong messages. The arrangement of equipment and the display of materials affect children's behavior, attitudes, and learning. For example, open classrooms with toy shelves flush against the walls encourage running and rough-housing. Piling different kinds of toys onto one set of shelves gives children the message that it's acceptable to combine toys and to replace them in any order. Creating separate play areas helps children focus their attention and fosters social interaction with others. Labeling the areas and shelves helps children learn identification, matching, and classification concepts. Setting out certain types of toys and materials gently directs children's play.

So think of the classroom environment as your assistant teacher. Make the environment work for you, not against you. Use the classroom to reinforce your educational goals for the children. The following are specific ways in which you can establish and maintain a culturally relevant and anti-bias program in your classroom setting.

Arrange the Classroom into Interest Areas

Physical space and room arrangement influence the length of activities, the number of choices available to children at any one time, and the presentation of activities. By looking at a classroom, you can tell what and how children are taught. Room arrangement silently communicates a program's philosophy toward early childhood education. It says, "This is how we believe children learn, and this is what we want children to learn." There are three basic principles underlying the organization and arrangement of an early childhood classroom:

1. Children learn through play and should spend much of their day engaged in free choice play where they can move around the room, make choices about their activities, and freely explore the people and materials that interest them.

2. Toys, books, and other learning materials should be organized into at least five clearly defined interest areas and displayed neatly on low, open shelves so that children can tell what their choices are and select their materials without relying on adult assistance.

3. As teachers, we present the curriculum through free play, small group activities, and large group time. We strengthen learning through play by carefully selecting materials, arranging materials on the shelves, rotating materials regularly, and changing the bulletin boards and visual displays.

Establish an Educational Orientation

We are professionals in the field of education, not the entertainment industry. Too many classrooms today are filled with cartoon characters. Walls are covered with murals depicting the antics of popular cartoon animal characters. Classrooms and groups of children are identified by cartoon mascots. At educational conferences, teachers swarm display booths that sell paraphernalia with cartoon characters such as stickers, pencils, erasers, bulletin board kits, flannelboard kits, decorated attendance charts, and calendars. The end result is classrooms that look like fantasy world flea markets rather than learning environments.

To top it off, these cartoon-decorated materials often contain illustrations of human beings that are stereotypic. Some de-emphasize human facial features through simple line art with a color wash to vary the skin tones. Others are caricatures, making individuals look silly or grotesque through exaggerated physical features. These types of "educational" materials distort children's understanding of people and human diversity.

Children are bombarded with stereotypical images through the media. The classroom should be a place where children can learn simple, accurate information about people and the world around them. So select bulletin board materials, posters, calendars, and teaching materials that are reality based and have educational value. Look for materials that use bright, colorful, contemporary photographs that realistically portray the world. Replace the cartoon animals with photographs of actual animals, the cartoon forests and castles with posters of actual environments and buildings. Replace the cartoon people with posters and photographs of actual people. Look for the most realistic version available when purchasing dramatic play equipment, dolls, blocks, play people, and art supplies that include skin colors.

Welcome Every Child

Too many children go through school never seeing themselves reflected in their teachers, the classroom, or the textbooks. Think for a moment about your own experience. What is it like for you to go into a new environment for the first time? What is it like when you walk through the door and realize that everyone else is from another race or culture? Everyone is dressed differently from you. Everyone else speaks differently from you. The leader smiles and gestures to you to come in. Everyone else looks at you, wondering who you are and why you are here. They may try to make you feel welcome. You certainly feel out of place. That's how educational settings feel for many, many children.

As a teacher, I cannot reflect the identities of all the children in my classroom. In fact, I may not even reflect the identities of the majority of children in my room. The children who do look like me, will likely feel comfortable. I look like their mom and other adults in their lives. My language, dress, and mannerisms are familiar. Our shared identity also helps them to believe that they can and will be successful learners in my classroom. What about the children who are racially, culturally, and linguistically different from me? Is there anything, anywhere in the school entryway, halls, or my classroom that tells these children, "You belong here—you will achieve academic success here"?

This is why it is critical that classrooms reflect every child and every family in that room. In order to do that, you have to get to know the children and their families. You must know their identities. You can't simply guess. I've heard teachers say, "Oh, I think they are some kind of oriental, I'm not sure." If in fact the child is Asian, there is a difference between Japanese, Chinese, Vietnamese, Korean, and Hmong cultures. Get to know the children so that you can respectfully and accurately reflect them, their families, and their lifestyles in the classroom.

Here's a list of materials to add to your classroom environment to strengthen children's connection to their families and home cultures:

Photographs of the children in your class

Photographs of the children with their families

Photographs and posters of important people from the children's home cultures

Photographs and posters of children's homelands (especially important for immigrant, refugee, and first-generation Americans)

Classroom labels and alphabet and number charts in children's home languages

Art and fabric from children's home cultures

Dolls, puppets, and block play figures representing the identities of the children in your class

Music and books with audiotapes from children's home cultures

Books in which the main character shares your children's identities

Games from the children's home cultures

Pretend food, eating, and cooking utensils from the child's home culture

Computer with Internet access to connect to culturally related Web sites

Promote Positive Attitudes toward Diversity

The classroom conveys attitudes to the children and parents by what is included in the room and what is left out. Omissions can be just as destructive as stereotypes and inaccurate information. Leaving culturally relevant and anti-bias education out of the curriculum gives children and families the message that it isn't important: "You don't need to know this . . . This doesn't relate to your life . . . You are too young to learn about this." It is our job as early childhood teachers to make sure that the classroom includes all kinds of people doing all sorts of things and living out their daily lives in many different ways. This may be done through many visual images such as pictures or representations in the form of artwork and objects from daily life. Remember that displaying just one or two pictures is **tokenism.** It gives children the message, "Yes, these people are out there in the world somewhere, but you don't have to take them seriously."

See glossary.

Careful selection and display of all materials can "normalize diversity." For example, if you are learning about shells, display many different types of shells. If you are learning about the color red, create a display of many different red objects in many different shades. Use the classroom environment to give children the message that diversity is good and it's a normal part of everyday life.

Instead of displaying just one or two pictures or cultural items, create displays with variety. Actually count all the bulletin board illustrations and posters in the classroom. Out of those, how many reflect non-white people? A classroom contains six posters of European American children and one poster of a African American child. That's less than 20 percent and would be considered tokenism.

In addition, many other cultural groups present in the community are invisible in this classroom.

Use the classroom to help you introduce children to the diversity in their community, state, or region that may or may not be reflected in the racial/ethnic identities of their classmates and teachers. Display images of children and adults from the major racial and ethnic groups. Choose images that accurately portray their daily lives. Check to make sure there is a numerical balance in representation of racial and ethnic groups in your classroom. Remember to reflect the here and now, that is, life in the United States today. Leave long ago and far away (other countries and historical materials) for later elementary school years.

Here is a list of materials to add to your classroom environment that will help you promote positive attitudes toward diversity:

Photographs of people from racial and cultural groups in your community, state, and region

Photographs of diverse people actively involved in everyday life

Different forms of music

Set of multiethnic block play people

Collection of multiethnic children's books

Set of multiethnic children's dolls

Multiethnic, nonsexist puzzles

Art materials that include a variety of skin colors

Prevent and Reduce Bias and Stereotypic Thinking

Prejudice is based on stereotypic thinking. Stereotypes have a powerful influence on children's perceptions of reality. Many commercial teaching materials are outright stereotypic. Children's books can be problematic. They may look good at first glance, but contain one or two stereotypic images or references. Holiday decorations are also notorious for containing stereotypes. Older materials, especially those more than ten years old, often contain stereotypes. Go through all of your teacher materials and pull out any that contain stereotypes or seem questionable to you. But don't throw them out just yet. You may be able to use them in an activity to help children differentiate between fair and unfair pictures. Here is a list of materials to set aside:

Materials with cartoon images that inaccurately portray human beings and human diversity

Materials with poor-quality images such as simple line art in which all characters look the same

Materials that contain tokenism (for example, a photograph with four white children and one child of color)

Materials that are stereotypic (portray ethnicity through traditional dress and cultural artifacts)

Materials that use Native Americans as objects (alphabet sets in which "I" is for Indian)

Materials that focus on *long ago* and *far away*

Promote Social Skills and Social Action

Classroom materials can also encourage children to engage in pro-social skills and social action. Display a peace pledge or kindness pledge in the large group area. Set up a peace table in a quiet corner of the room. Post the steps for nonviolent conflict resolution above the table to guide children in problem solving their disagreements with one another. Create a bulletin board dedicated to recognizing people in your classroom, school, and local community who are helping one another and working for social change. Here are some suggestions for materials that encourage social skills and social action:

Photographs and posters of individuals and groups working for social justice

Photographs and posters of people working together

Charts that list steps for problem solving or nonviolent conflict resolution

A peace table where children can go to resolve their problems

Children's books about community, cooperation, problem solving, human rights, and social action

Music about community, peace, freedom, cooperation, and problem solving

Guidelines for Selecting Culturally Relevant and Anti-Bias Materials

Begin implementing culturally relevant and anti-bias education in your classroom by removing stereotypic materials. You may be unsure of what is stereotypic and what is not. Ellen Wolpert (1999), author of *Start Seeing Diversity,* has created lists of common stereotypes associated with people of color. Use this list to help you evaluate classroom materials such as posters, books, manipulatives, bulletin board materials, and videos.

African Americans

Men	*Women*	*Occupations*
Shuffling, eye-rolling, fearful, super-stitious comic	Big-bosomed mammy, loyal to whites	Chauffeur
Gentle, self-sacrificing older man	Big, bossy mother or maid, com-mander of the household	Cook
Athletic super jock	Sexy temptress	Maid
Smooth-talking con man	Stupid, but sweet little girl	Laundry worker
Super stud, but comical little boy		Elevator operator
Rough, dangerous criminal		Waiter
Loudly dressed, happy-go-lucky buf-foon		Unemployed ghetto-dweller
Exotic primitive		Preacher
		Athlete
		Entertainer

Latinos/Latinas

Men	*Women*	*Occupations*
Wearing sombreros	Hard-working, poor, submissive, self-sacrificing, religious mother of many	Campesino (rural farm worker)
Serape-clad	Sweet, small, shy gentle girl	Migrant farm worker
Wearing sandals	Sexy, loud, fiery young woman	Unemployed barrio dweller
Taking siesta near cactus, under a tree, or near an overburdened burro	Undereducated, submissive, nice girl	
Ignorant, cheerful, lazy person		
Sneaky, knife-wielding, mustached bandit		
Teenage gang member		

Asian Americans

Men	Women	Occupations
Smiling, polite, small, servile, bowing	Sweet, well-behaved girl	Laundry worker
Bucktoothed and squinty-eyed	Shy	Restaurant worker
Mystical, inscrutable, and wise	Smiling	Curio shop worker
Expert in martial arts	Dainty	Railroad worker
Cruel, sneaky, sly, evil	Sexy, sweet ("China Doll")	Gardener
Super student	Sexy, evil ("Dragon Lady")	Florist
Places no value on human life	Overbearing, old-fashioned	
Model minority who worked hard and made it	Grandmother	

Native Americans

Men	Women	Occupations
Bloodthirsty, stoic, loyal follower	Heavyset, workhorse	Hunter
Drunken, mean thief	"Indian princess" depicted with European features, often in love with a white man for whom she is willing to sacrifice her life	Cattle thief
Drunken comic		Warrior
Stealthy hunter-tracker	Obedient, submissive "squaw"	Unemployed loafer
Noble child of nature		Craftsperson
Wise old chief		
Evil medicine man		
Brave boy, endowed by nature with special "Indian" qualities		

Suggested Materials

Children learn more through free-choice play than group times and structured activities. Interest centers organize children's free play and provide them with many choices. Through these areas children engage in open-ended activities that have few set rules and procedures. In addition, these areas are flexible and always changing to fit the children's interests and abilities or the curriculum theme.

Begin introducing children to diversity by adding materials that reflect the home cultures of the children in your classroom. Then add materials that represent the diversity present in your local community. Later, add a variety of materials and objects to represent diversity in the United States today. You can also teach through the interest centers by adding materials to each area that support the unit theme.

Art Area

The art area gives children opportunities to explore various art materials and to express themselves. In early childhood education the emphasis is on the process of exploring different media, learning to use art materials, expressing feelings and sense of self, and making representations of the world and one's experience in it. In a culturally relevant and anti-bias classroom the art materials must include colors, patterns, and textures from the children's home cultures and cultures in our communities.

Basic materials to have on hand include skin-colored markers, crayons, tempera, craft paper, and felt. People Colors art materials from Lakeshore are the best of what is currently available. They have the widest range of colors and the most realistic colors. Children who have very light skin and children who have dark skin are able to find and mix a shade that matches the color of their skin.

Consider setting out hand mirrors so that children can look at themselves and notice their skin color and facial features before drawing pictures of themselves or other people. Try adding origami paper for folding, rice paper for painting, and different types of clay for modeling. Collage materials could also be available (items such as magazines with pictures of people from different cultures, a file of pre-cut pictures, or fabric scraps of cloth from different cultures). Include visual displays illustrating the art work, color schemes, and visual patterns of other cultures.

Block Area

Blocks adapt well to a culturally relevant and anti-bias environment because they are the most versatile piece of equipment in an early childhood classroom. Through block play, children explore math, science, and spatial relations concepts. They also engage in fantasy play and make representations of the real world. In addition, the flexibility of blocks is characterized by the fact that children can play alone, side by side, or cooperatively with one another. If you add multicultural accessories and props to a full set of hardwood unit blocks, you will guide and expand children's play.

Block play people by Lakeshore are made of a hard rubber that is durable and easy to clean. The people are dressed in street clothes and have very realistic features, including facial expressions. People of every age, body size, and physical ability are represented. Some of the female figures wear skirts or dresses, while others wear pants. All of the major ethnic groups that make up American society are represented.

Props can also include a variety of transportation toys such as trains, buses, double-decker buses, planes, jets, cars, horses and carts, ferries, barges, canoes, snowmobiles, and sleds. Lincoln Logs, building blocks, and raw materials such as cardboard, boxes, canvas, string, and masking tape encourage children to build their own buildings and houses. Try adding palm leaves, coconut branches, corn husks, pine branches, bark, pine needles, craft sticks, stones, and straw for creating roofs, houses, and fences. Display pictures of buildings from different parts of the world such as a pagoda, tree house, adobe, hogan, thatched hut, log home, sod home, tent, earth-sheltered home, apartment building, trailer, and hotel. Rubber, plastic, wooden, cloth, and carved-bone animals representing the jungle, tropical forest, desert, ocean, and forest will also enhance the children's play.

Music Area

The music area offers children a chance to experiment with and enjoy a variety of music. In this area, children listen to music, create their own music, compare and contrast sounds, move to sound, and learn about and play different instruments. Build up a broad selection of both vocal and instrumental music. Ask parents to make a cassette tape of the music their family and children enjoy at home. Use music from different cultures as background music during free play and naptime. Teach children songs with simple words and melodies from other cultures and teach them songs that encourage differences, acceptance, and cooperation. Add instruments such as kalimbas, maracas, Tibetan bells, gongs, gourds, metal and bongo drums, woven jute rattles, wooden flutes, brass bells, conch shells, castanets, wooden xylophones, and guitars to the set of traditional rhythm instruments. Many cultures use drums and drumming as their primary instrument. Though expensive, a good drum provides a wonderful sound that can serve as the basic background instrument for many music activities.

Dramatic Play Area

In this interest area, children act out their everyday experiences, play out their perceptions of the world, try on adult roles, and explore relationships among people. Like the block area, the dramatic play area encourages cooperative play among children. Here, children come to a greater understanding of themselves and gain a sense of the lifestyles that are available to them. The dramatic play area, like other areas, must allow children to explore a variety of lifestyles, including family systems, economic class, disability, and culture. In this context, children try on the roles of people of different ages, skills, and occupations.

Add a full-length mirror, large plastic crates, hollow blocks, planks, and large pieces of fabric to the basic housekeeping equipment. This allows children to create a variety of homes, floor plans, or places to visit away from home. With older children, consider designing a two- or three-room dramatic play area that includes a living room and a bedroom along with the traditional kitchen. Rather than teaching a particular culture, the dramatic play props should emphasize the cultures of the children in your class, and the many ways of going about our daily lives such as kinds of food to eat, types of eating utensils, and ways of dressing. Begin with items children have in their homes and expand from there. Consider adding the following accessories and props to the dramatic play area:

DOLLS

Dolls continue to be a source of frustration for many teachers and parents. While there are many multiethnic doll sets to choose from, none of them realistically capture children's facial features or expressions. Lakeshore's multiethnic school dolls are some of the best childlike dolls available. They are plastic with movable arms and legs and rooted hair. A boy and girl from each of the major ethnic groups is available. They look like young children and come dressed in nonstereotypic play clothes. Lakeshore also sells a doll with a prosthesis and adaptive equipment, such as wheelchairs, protective helmets, dog guides and harnesses, leg braces and crutches, walkers, hearing aids, and eyeglasses.

Baby dolls (which look like babies rather than children) are available through most of the major catalog suppliers, often called "feels real" or "just born" baby dolls. Environments' twenty-inch newborn dolls are particularly realistic in both size and facial expression. Look for dolls that are a softer vinyl and anatomically correct. Cloth dolls are also a wonderful addition to a classroom, either as accessories in the dramatic play area or as persona dolls. People of Every Stripe makes a variety of cloth dolls; one of the benefits of cloth is that it offers a wider range of skin colors. Their dolls have hand-painted faces and realistic hair. Send them a photo and they'll make a doll to match your specifications. Their dolls really meet the needs of biracial children and children from underrepresented ethnic groups.

PLAY FOOD AND COOKING UTENSILS

Many of the catalog companies carry similar sets of ethnic play food. Constructive Playthings sells the most complete and the varied food sets, including the international bread set and Hispanic, Asian, Middle Eastern, dim sum, taco, and Italian food sets. They also have European American meal sets and produce. Lakeshore has Chinese and Japanese food sets and sells the most complete pretend cooking sets. Their Asian and Hispanic cooking sets include actual cooking utensils that can be used for either dramatic play or classroom cooking experiences.

You don't have to stock the dramatic play area with commercial props. You can collect a variety of accessories and props from the children's families and local ethnic stores in your community. For example:

Food containers: tea boxes and tins, canned foods, cardboard food containers, plastic bottles; stuff rice, flour, and potato bags with batting and sew them closed; make cardboard or wooden slices of bread and stuff them into various bread bags

Food storage containers: baskets, gourds, mesh bags, pottery

Cooking utensils: tortilla presses, molenellos, tea balls, rolling pins, strainers, ladles, woks, steamers, food grinders, mortars and pestles, cutting boards, frying pans, kettles

Eating utensils: silverware, wooden spoons, spatulas, graters, egg beaters, whisks, rice bowls, wooden bowls and plates, tin plates, plastic plates, teacups, chopsticks, tea pots, coffee pots

Dresses, skirts, jackets, large pieces of fabric for clothing in squares, rectangles, and triangles. Pick out different patterns such as batik, tie-dyed, madras, *kente,* and mud cloth; include saris, kimonos, serapes, dashikis, *kentes,* grass skirts, woven vests, shawls, ponchos, tunics, kaffiyeh scarves; include seasonal clothing such as heavy coats, scarves, mittens, boots, and hats for winter

> *Shoes:* sandals, mukluks, clogs, moccasins, huaraches, getas, wooden shoes, boots, slippers, dress shoes
>
> *Hats:* berets, turbans, sombreros, straw hats, black caps, *kuan,* skull-caps, baseball caps, felt hats, knit hats
>
> *Beds:* woven mats, futons, cots, mattress, blankets, hammocks

MISCELLANEOUS

Placemats, vases, trivets, masks, bags, scarves and kerchiefs, sashes, coins, fans, hair combs and brushes, umbrellas, fishing nets, area rugs, baby carriers, and jewelry.

Manipulative Area (Table Toys)

In the manipulative area, children work alone and with friends to put together puzzles, play board games, and complete classification and sequencing activities. Through these purchased and homemade activities and games, children explore concepts of alike and different, whole-part relationships, one-to-one correspondence, and skills such as sequencing, visual discrimination, and recognizing symbols. This area can be enhanced with multiethnic, nonsexist puzzles available through many common toy catalogs. Sets of graduated items from other cultures such as wooden dolls or animals make fun sequencing games. Make your own activities, such as sorting foreign coins, shells, dried beans, ethnic fabric squares, and other raw materials. Make lotto, classification, and matching games such as "Which One Is Different?," "Match-Ups," and "Fair and Unfair" as presented in chapter 9. Because of stereotypic packaging, make it a practice to take toys out of their original container and display them in plastic tubs or trays.

Science Area

This area offers children an opportunity to examine the elements and properties of the natural world. It's a wonderful area for observing differences and learning the importance of respect and care for all living things. Multicultural activities might include a collection of rocks, semiprecious stones, and shells from different parts of the world; terrariums and miniature indoor gardens that model different types of soil, ground covering, and vegetation. The display might include a small cactus garden in sand, a planting of ferns in soil heavy with peat and sphagnum moss on the top, a bonsai display with smooth pebbles, a fish tank with plants that grow under the water, a Norfolk Island pine tree with bark chips, a dwarf citrus tree in sandy loam, a palm tree, a bamboo tree, or a tropical flowering ornamental such as hibiscus or azalea. Include pictures and photographs of gardens from around the world. Grow herbs that are used in cooking traditional foods familiar to the children in your class in a sunny window. Cilantro, lemongrass, oregano, basil, mint, sage, sweet grass, and parsley are good choices. Add smells and scents from other cultures to the smelling jar kit. Create collections of different kinds of grains, beans, and soils. Examples of grains include wheatberries, rye berries, oats, millet, corn, couscous, barley, white rice, brown rice, red rice, and wild rice. A complete assortment of dried beans would include black-eyed peas, baby limas, black beans, adzuki beans, pinto, kidney, great northern, soybeans, and lentils. Look for bulk grains and beans at your local food co-op or health food store. (Some teachers may choose not to use food as a teaching tool. This decision is based on personal values and each teacher must make her own choice.)

Sensory Table

Children are introduced to different textures and fluid media at the sensory table. They learn about comparing and measuring amounts and the characteristics of various materials, so alter the materials in the sensory table to correspond with the curriculum. Try to include textures and smells that represent the experiences not only of the children in the class but of other cultural groups as well. Many of the grains and dried beans can be purchased in large quantities to fill the sensory table. Other dry materials for the table include whole nuts in the shell, bark, dry leaves, coffee beans, soils, different kinds of flour, sawdust, raw cotton, raw wool, raw silk, and flax. When exploring liquids with the children, try adding a scent to the water. Small bottles of essential oils can be purchased at health food stores, food co-ops, or stores that sell bath and body products. They come in a variety of floral, wood, citrus, and herbal scents.

The sensory table can also be used for dramatic play. The addition of small people figures, transportation toys, twigs, rocks, and miniature plastic plants to a base of sand, soil, or water allows children to create environments that are unfamiliar as well as re-create environments that are common in their everyday lives. For example, children in northern Minnesota and parts of Kentucky may be very familiar with mines. They could play "mine" with wet sand, rocks, and a collection of small trucks, front-end loaders, shovels, and small people figures. Likewise, a high-rise construction site could be created with a layer of dirt, a crane, trucks, small building blocks, and play figures. A desert could be created with sand, rocks, and small desert animal figures. Other options include a dam, a beach with sand and shells, a river or lake, mountains, or a farm.

Book/Quiet Area

The quiet area provides children with a cozy, inviting place to look at books. Here children learn to care for and appreciate books; they also develop skills in turning pages, telling stories, sequencing events, recalling events, imaginative thinking, and listening. Begin by creating a soft and cozy setting. Large floor pillows and cushions in ethnic prints invite children to snuggle up with a friend and look at books. Large overstuffed chairs, mattresses, or love seats encourage adults to gather a child on their laps for an individual story time.

Too often, when teachers think of multicultural children's books, they think of folk tales. In fact, there are many different types of multicultural children's books. In the following section, I will highlight the different types of books to include in a classroom and the curriculum. These book suggestions are grouped by the curriculum goals for early childhood education that are based on child development principles, which we discussed in chapter 7. Let's review the four goals:

Developmental Issue	Corresponding Educational Goal
Culture	To foster each child's positive, knowledgeable, and confident self-identity within a cultural context.
Prejudice	To foster each child's comfortable, empathetic interaction with diversity among people.
Prejudice and Racism	To foster each child's critical thinking about bias.
Racism	To foster each child's ability to stand up for himself and others in the face of bias.

BOOKS THAT CONNECT CHILDREN TO THEIR HOME CULTURE

Children need to see themselves and their lives reflected through literature. These books help children identify with and feel proud of their home culture. These books promote goal one: foster each child's positive, knowledgeable, and confident self-identity within a cultural context.

Sari Games, by Naina Gandhi (Andre Deutsch Ltd., 1990)

Cornrows, by Camille Yarbrough (Geoghegan, 1992)

Two Pairs of Shoes, by Esther Sanderson (Pemmican, 1998)

On Mother's Lap, by Ann Herbert Scott (Clarion Books, 1992)

Giving Thanks: A Native American Good Morning Message, by Chief Jake Swamp (Lee and Low, 1997)

Soul Looks Back in Wonder, by Tom Feelings (Puffin: reprint edition, 1999)

Our People, by Angela Shelf Medearis (McGraw Hill, 2003)

Brown Angels, by Walter Dean Myers (HarperCollins Juvenile Books, 1993)

Families: Poems Celebrating the African American Experience, selected by Dorothy S. Strickland and Michael R. Strickland (Boyds Mill Press, 1994)

Daydreamers, by Tom Feelings (E.P. Dutton: reprint edition, 1993)

Mama, Do You Love Me? by Barbara M. Joosse (Chronicle Books, 1998)

Thirteen Moons on Turtle's Back, by Joseph Bruchac and Jonathan London (Paper Star: reprint edition, 1997)

Lee Ann: The Story of a Vietnamese-American Girl, by Tricia Brown (Putnam, 1999)

Daniel's Dog, by Jo Ellen Bogart (Scholastic Paperbacks, 1992)

Pueblo Boy Growing Up in Two Worlds, by Marcia Keegan (Puffin: reprint edition, 1997)

New Shoes for Sylvia, by Johanna Hurwitz (Mulberry Books, 1999)

CULTURALLY RELEVANT CONCEPT BOOKS

These books reflect one specific culture and also teach a concept such as counting, the ABCs, seasons, colors, or shapes. These books also support goal one: foster each child's positive, knowledgeable, and confident self-identity within a cultural context.

The Path of Quiet Elk, by Virginia A. Stroud (Dial, 1996)

Antler, Bear, Canoe: A Northwoods Alphabet Year, by Betsy Bowen (Houghton Mifflin, 2000)

A Prairie Alphabet, by Jo Bannatyne-Cugnet and Yvette Moore (Tundra Books, 1994)

Coconut Mon, by Linda Milstein (William Morrow, 1995)

Can't Sit Still, by Karen E. Lotz (Puffin: reprint edition, 1998)

Where Did You Get Your Moccasins? by Bernelda Wheeler (Peguis Publishers Ltd., 1995)

BOOKS THAT TEACH CULTURAL PRACTICES AND HOLIDAYS

These books teach children about cultural holidays, celebrations, or practices within a culture. These books encourage goal one: foster each child's positive, knowledgeable, and confident self-identity within a cultural context.

Fiesta! by Beatriz McConnie Zapater (Modern Curriculum Press, 1993)

Carnival, by Denise Burden-Patmon with Kathryn D. Jones (Modern Curriculum Press, 1993)

Too Many Tamales, by Gary Soto (Scott Foresman, 1996)

Lion Dancer: Ernie Wan's Chinese New Year, by Kate Waters and Madeline Slovenz-Low (Scholastic, 1991)

Têt: The New Year, by Kim-Lan Tran (Modern Curriculum Press, 1993)

The Sacred Harvest: Ojibway Wild Rice Gathering, by Gordon Regguinti (Lerner, 1992)

A Trip to a Pow-Wow, by Richard Red Hawk (Sierra Oaks Publishing Company, 1992)

BILINGUAL/DIALECTS

These books may be fully bilingual, incorporate words and phrases from another language into the text, or may be written in a specific English dialect. These books promote goal one: foster each child's positive, knowledgeable, and confident self-identity within a cultural context.

Abuela, by Arthur Dorros (Scott Foresman: reprint edition, 1997)

Working Cotton, by Sherley Anne Williams (Voyager Books: reprint edition, 1997)

Pablo's Tree, by Pat Mora (Simon and Schuster, 1994)

Dumpling Soup, by Jama Kim Rattigan (Little, Brown and Co.: reprint edition, 1998)

Walk about: Life in an Ahtna Athabaskan Village, by John E. Smelcer and Tricia Wilson (Ahtna Heritage Foundation, 1998)

The Park Bench, by Fumiko Takeshita (Kane/Miller Book Publishing: reprint edition, 1998)

Tonibah and the Rainbow, by Jack L. Crowder (Upper Strata Ink, 1986)

Flossie and the Fox, by Patricia C. McKissack (Scott Foresman, 1986)

MAIN CHARACTER IS A CHILD OF COLOR

These books focus on the daily life and themes of contemporary American children. Topics might include cleaning up toys, getting a new baby brother, sharing toys, spending time with dad, bringing something for "Show and Tell." Theses books are unique in that the main character is a child of color rather than a white child or a cartoon animal. These type of books foster goal one for children who share the main character's identity and they also advance goal two: foster each child's comfortable, empathetic interaction with diversity among people.

Bright Eyes, Brown Skin, by Cheryl Willis Hudson and Bernette G. Ford (Just Us Books, 1990)

Tomás and the Library Lady, by Pat Mora (Dragonfly, 2000)

I Want to Be, by Thylias Moss (Puffin: reprint edition, 1998)

How Many Stars in the Sky? by Lenny Hort (William Morrow, 1991)

Tar Beach, by Faith Ringgold (Crown Publishers, 1991)

Just Us Women, by Jeannette Caines (Bt Bound, 1999)

Tell Me a Story, Mama, by Angela Johnson (Bt Bound, 1999)

Cherries and Cherry Pits, by Vera B. Williams (Mulberry Books, 1991)

Bet You Can't, by Penny Dale (Lippincott, Williams, and Wilkins Publishers, 1988)

What Mary Jo Shared, by Janice May Udry (Harcourt, Brace and Company, 1997)

A Chair for My Mother, by Vera B. Williams (Scott Foresman, 1984)

Jamaica Tag-Along, by Juanita Havill (Houghton Mifflin, 1989)

DIVERSITY

These books explore similarities and differences, and celebrate differences. These books promote goal two: foster each child's comfortable, empathetic interaction with diversity among people.

Friends in the Park, by Rochelle Bunnett (Checkerboard Press, 1993)

This Is the Way We Go to School, by Edith Baer (Scott Foresman, 1992)

How My Parents Learned to Eat, by Ina R. Friedman (Houghton Mifflin, 1987)

Everybody Cooks Rice, by Norah Dooley (Scott Foresman, 1992)

Black Is Brown Is Tan, by Arnold Adoff (HarperCollins Juvenile Books: reprint edition, 1992)

Welcoming Babies, by Margy Burns Knight (Tilbury House Publishers, 1998)

Potluck, by Anne Shelby (Orchard Books, 1991)

Day Care ABC, by Tamara Phillips (Albert Whitman and Co., 1989)

At This Very Minute, by Kathleen Rice Bowers (Little, Brown, 1983)

All the Colors We Are, by Katie Kissinger (Redleaf Press, 1997)

CROSS-CULTURAL AND CROSS-RACIAL FRIENDSHIPS

These books model positive, respectful cross-racial and cross-cultural friendships. They give children the message, "You can be friends with anyone." These books encourage goal two: foster each child's comfortable, empathetic interaction with diversity among people.

Smoky Night, by Eve Bunting (Harcourt: reprint edition, 1999)

Mrs. Katz and Tush, by Patricia Polacco (Picture Yearling, 1994)

Pink and Say, by Patricia Polacco (Philomel, 1994)

Chicken Sunday, by Patricia Polacco (Paper Star: reprint edition, 1998)

The Bracelet, by Yoshiko Uchida (Paper Star, 1996)

Yo! Yes? by Chris Raschka (Orchard Books, 1998)

Friends at School, by Rochelle Bunnett (Star Bright Books: 2nd edition, 1996)

BIAS

These books tell stories of children who experience bias or people who have biases against others. There are the fewest books in this category. This is unfortunate, because books such as these are very useful in starting discussions about bias and helping children recognize bias. These books support goal three of a culturally relevant and anti-bias curriculum: foster each child's critical thinking about bias.

Why Does That Man Have Such a Big Nose? by Mary Beth Quinsey (Parenting Press, 1986)

Who Belongs Here? An American Story, by Margy Burns Knight (Bt Bound, 1999)

Baseball Saved Us, by Ken Mochizuki (Lee and Low, 1995)

Angel Child, Dragon Child, by Michele Maria Surat (Scholastic, 1989)

Billy the Great, by Rosa Guy (Bt Bound, 1992)

STANDING UP FOR ONESELF AND OTHERS

These books focus on community, standing up for oneself, and social action. Books about heroes and sheroes also fall into this category. These books support goal four of a culturally relevant and anti-bias curriculum: foster each child's ability to stand up for himself and others in the face of bias.

For Every Child, a Better World, by Kermit the Frog, in cooperation with the United Nations (Goldencraft, 1993)

Pearl Moscowitz's Last Stand, by Arthur A. Levine (William Morrow, 1993)

Madame Curie: Brave Scientist, by Keith Brandt (Troll Communications, 1990)

The Day Gogo Went To Vote, by Elinor Batezat Suslu (Little, Brown and Company, 1999)

Rose Blanche, by Roberto Innocenti (Harcourt, 1996)

Elizabeth Blackwell: The First Woman Doctor, by Francene Sabin (Troll Communications, 1990)

Rosa Parks: Fight for Freedom, by Keith Brandt (Troll Communications, 1998)

Harriet Tubman: The Road to Freedom, by Rae Bains (Troll Communications, 1990)

Let the Celebrations Begin! by Margaret Wild and Julie Vivas (Orchard, 1996)

Let Freedom Ring: A Ballad of Martin Luther King Jr., by Myra Cohn Livingston (Holiday House, 1992)

Aunt Harriet's Underground Railroad in the Sky, by Faith Ringgold (Crown, 1995)

Follow the Drinking Gourd, by Jeanette Winter (Knopf, 1992)

Happy Birthday, Martin Luther King, by Jean Marzollo (Scholastic Trade, 1993)

Sadako, by Eleanor Coerr (Putnam, 1993)

Peace Crane, by Sheila Hamanaka (William Morrow, 1995)

Rebel, by Allan Baillie (Ticknor and Fields, 1994)

Locating appropriate culturally relevant and anti-bias children's books has become easier. Geographic location is no longer a factor due to the Internet. In addition, reference librarians at the local public library can order any book you request through its interlibrary loan system. Another option is to get to know a local bookseller. As you work with your local librarian and bookseller, you will educate them about what it is that you need, and they'll begin contacting you when they come across new titles in their publisher's catalogs. Recent curriculum guides such as *Start Seeing Diversity, Kids Like Us, That's Not Fair, and Big As Life* all contain excellent lists of children's books that can guide you in your selection of culturally relevant and anti-bias children's literature.

Selecting Children's Books

When choosing children's books, pay particular attention to the illustrations and avoid stereotypic images. Don't use cartoon images or animal characters to teach about human diversity. Or at least minimize the use of cartoon characters to teach about reality. Look for books with color photographs. Sometimes these are called photo documentaries. Photographs are the best way to depict and visually represent human diversity. *Lion Dancer: Ernie Wan's Chinese New Year* is one good example. Choose books with bright, colorful, full-page illustrations. This will allow you to use the book at large group time. Finally, look for books that have won awards, such as the Coretta Scott King Award.

There are many checklists available to guide you in the selection of culturally relevant and anti-bias children's literature. I developed the following checklist to help you select children's books. It is based on *Ten Quick Ways to Analyze Children's Books for Sexism and Racism,* by the Council on Interracial Books for Children (1980) and Ellen Wolpert's (1999) "Handout 9: Bias Related to Race and Ethnicity" in her book *Start Seeing Diversity.*

Illustrations

Are the illustrations stereotypic?

Are the illustrations so simplistic that all the characters look alike except for a "color wash" to differentiate skin tone?

Do the illustrations exaggerate facial characteristics and hairstyles?

Are people of color depicted accurately?

Do the illustrations depict diversity within a racial or cultural group?

Do the illustrations place people of color in the background or sidelines?

Is the color black, or darker colors, associated with evil and dirtiness?

Is white associated with goodness and cleanliness?

Characters of Color

Are people of color used as animals or objects (like Native Americans in alphabet and counting books)?

Do people of color wear suitable clothing for the setting and occasion?

Are the people of color in leadership or action-oriented roles?

Do the people of color have to exhibit extraordinary qualities to gain acceptance?

Do the people of color have to give up their culture and act "white" to get ahead?

Relationship between White People and People of Color

Are people of color underrepresented compared to whites?

Are the people of color in passive or subservient roles to whites?

Does the white character take care of, protect, or watch out for the person of color?

Is the person of color more concerned about a white character than herself, or others?

Is prejudice presented as an isolated incident rather than a common occurrence in a racist society?

Do the white characters blame people of color for their own difficulties?

Story Line

Does the book contain stereotypic language or loaded words?

Is standard English portrayed as better than other languages or other forms of English?

Does the story line focus on holidays and celebrations rather than daily life?

Are people's lives depicted in the past rather than the present?

Is the setting, behavior, speech, and clothing accurate for the historical period or cultural context?

Are the family relationships stereotypic?

Does this story or its characters limit a child's self-concept or aspirations?

Is the story written from a viewpoint within a culture or from the viewpoint of a white person looking in?

Author and Illustrator

Is the author qualified to deal with the subject matter?

Is the illustrator qualified to deal with the subject matter?

Bulletin Boards and Visual Displays

Visual displays add the final touch to creating a culturally relevant and anti-bias classroom. Remember that we want children to notice and interact with the materials on the shelves and the displays on the tables. We don't want them wandering around or flitting from area to area because they can't tell what their options are. The overuse of visual displays creates "visual noise" that distracts children from the materials. Rather than filling every inch of wall space with bulletin boards, pictures, and posters, try using these materials as if you were decorating a home environment. Use and create visual displays to match, reinforce, and expand the materials and learning that takes place in each of the interest centers. For example, display works of art in the art area; posters of buildings and environments in the block area; and pictures of people, families, and daily life scenes in the dramatic play area. Classroom entrance areas, parent sign-in tables, hallways, cubby areas, and bathrooms can become warmer, more welcoming spaces with the use of a few well-chosen and well-placed visual displays.

Creating an aesthetically pleasing environment that is also multicultural means avoiding the use of cartoon characters such as dolls in costumes, animal characters dressed in ethnic costumes, and stereotypic pictures of people in their traditional dress. Appropriate display materials include the following:

Photographs of children and their families
Photographs of people from magazines
Posters of people engaged in daily life
Artwork
Fabric banners
Rugs
Wall hangings
Musical instruments
Sculpture
Windsocks, wind chimes
Kites

Acquiring Visual Materials

Today, it is much easier and less time consuming to acquire a large selection of culturally relevant and multicultural display materials for the classroom. Most educational supply catalogs now carry modern, accurate teaching posters and picture sets. Large cities offer resources at educational supply centers, third world craft shops, ethnic gift shops, museum gift shops, and alternative or women's bookstores. Now, with the Internet, these resources are available to teachers regardless of where they live.

The following are some other suggestions for sources of multicultural materials for classroom use:

Travels. Another way to acquire multicultural materials is to purchase materials when traveling. Ask friends who may travel internationally to pick up materials for the classroom. I have a good friend with an early childhood background who travels to Japan and Europe regularly. Our center gave her $200 from the equipment budget to purchase children's books, toys, posters, and other interesting items for our classrooms. She brought back wonderful things and was able to purchase them at a much lower cost than if we had purchased them here.

Photographs and magazine pictures. Making homemade materials and visual displays is perhaps the most viable way to create a culturally relevant and anti-bias classroom environment. Photographs from magazines provide pictures of people living out their daily lives in the present. In addition to the picture file that teachers commonly maintain, consider starting a multicultural picture file. When enough photographs have been gathered, they can be mounted and laminated. Display the photographs separately or create a collage on poster board. Collages may focus on a specific theme such as boys and girls, babies, faces, grandparents, families, homes, or workers. Create a collage of pictures of people from a specific ethnic group. This type of collage is particularly useful because it shows the diversity and individuality within an ethnic group.

Not all magazines are useful sources of multicultural pictures. Thumbing through many popular women's magazine for appropriate photographs proves that people of color are excluded in mainstream media. Be careful, too, of publications that cover international and out-of-the-way parts of the globe because many of these tend to highlight people in faraway places dressed in traditional dress at special celebrations, which can be counterproductive to your attempts to show multicultural aspects of the here and now. Magazines that tend to include useful photographs include regional magazines, airline magazines, department store magazine advertisements, and Sunday newspaper magazines.

Postcards and greeting cards. Postcards and greeting cards are also sources of pictures for visual displays and teaching materials. Some greeting card lines are likely to carry traditional stereotypic cards such as cartoon turkeys wearing an Indian headdress wishing you a happy Thanksgiving. However, these cards can be useful in teaching what is untrue and unfair. Independent card shops may carry a greater selection of cards and postcards with wonderful color photographs of people from all over the world.

Polaroid, video, and digital cameras. It can take a long time to develop a comprehensive picture file. Create visual displays as well as children's books by taking photos with a camera. Take the camera on home visits or loan it to families so they can take pictures of their family at home that can then be used in the classroom. Take the camera along on field trips and take pictures of special visitors to the classroom. Also take pictures of the local neighborhood and community. A teacher at a rural early childhood program may want to take pictures of a local migrant child care program. A teacher at a suburban program could take pictures at a local inner-city program. Of course, permission would need to be granted. But perhaps a relationship between the programs could develop as a result.

Using Materials as Teaching Tools

Multicultural teaching materials can be used to stimulate children's awareness of themselves and others. I have four materials that are my favorite: teaching pictures, children's music, children's books, and persona dolls.

Teaching pictures
The picture file is a useful teaching resource. Teaching pictures can enhance the environment, promote a sense of belonging, reflect children's experience, reflect reality, and promote learning goals and objectives.

To make a picture file, follow these steps:

1. Cut out large (8 by 10 inches) photographs from magazines, catalogs, posters, newspaper ads, greeting cards, or other displays. Look for pictures and create a set of images that positively represent human diversity in the United States today.

Do not use cartoons or pictures that portray stereotypes. Consider all of the major areas of human diversity: race, culture, gender, age, economic class, sexual orientation, ability/disability, and religion.

2. Glue each picture to a piece of construction paper, oak tag, or poster board (8 by 12 inches). Pick a frame color that enhances the picture.

3. On the back of the teaching picture note the theme(s) or topic(s), and three to five open-ended questions you could ask children when using the picture as a group discussion starter. Here are some sample questions:

What do you see in this picture?

What do you think is happening?

What do you think was happening before the picture was taken?

What do you think will happen next?

How is this like you? How is it different?

What do you like about the picture?

What would you change about this picture?

4. Laminate the picture or cover both sides with clear, self-adhesive paper.

Children's music

Another one of my favorite materials is music. A lot of good early childhood music is available for young children. Music is important for many reasons: music touches our hearts and souls in a way that other media does not, and music is both culturally specific and universal.

There are at least two types of music to include in the classroom. The first type of music is from the children's home cultures, which includes instrumental music, folk songs, and children's songs. Culturally relevant music can be played as background music throughout the day. It can be used in conjunction with movement and music activities. It can also be used to introduce children to the home cultures of their classmates. Here are some examples:

Fiesta Musical, with Emilio Delgado. 1994. Music For Little People.

Friends, by Nelson Gill. 1992. Etcetera.

Cada Niño/Every Child, by Tish Hinojosa. 1996. Rounder.

Hippity Hop, 1999. Music For Little People.

Positively Reggae, 1994. Sony Music.

I Got Shoes, by Sweet Honey in the Rock. 1994. Music For Little People.

The second type of music addresses human diversity. I try to find songs with strong positive messages. These songs help me stay focused on what it is I am trying to accomplish with children. They also give me hope, even when I'm feeling discouraged. Even though young children may not understand all the words, I believe the music is planting seeds in their hearts and minds. Here are some examples:

Nobody Else Like Me, by Cathy Fink and Marcy Marxer. 1994. A & M.

Teaching Peace, by Red Grammer. 1986. Smilin' Atcha.

I'm Gonna Let It Shine, by Bill Harley. 1990. Rounder.

One Voice for Children, by Jack Hartmann. 1990. Educational Activities.

Peace Is the World Smiling. 1989. Music for Little People.

Two Hands Hold the Earth, by Sarah Pirtle. 1984. Gentle Wind.

Peace by Peace, by Sally Rogers. 1991. Western.

What Can One Little Person Do? by Sally Rogers. 1992. Round River.

Big Ideas! by Patricia Shih. 1990. Glass Records.

All for Freedom, by Sweet Honey in the Rock. 1989. Music for Little People.

Walk a Mile, by Vitamin L. 1989. Lovable Creature.

Songs with strong positive messages can also be played as background music or introduced and taught at circle time. I also like to take phrases from songs and incorporate them into the daily life of the classroom. For instance, the song "Use Your Words," by Red Grammer includes the phrase, "Use your words." That's a phrase that can be spoken to children throughout the day to remind them to solve their problems verbally rather than physically. Another one of my favorite songs is "Walking Tall, Walking Proud" by Jack Hartman. When walking a class down the hall to lunch, I like to remind them to "walk tall and proud."

Children's books

You can use books in a number of ways to help promote culturally relevant and anti-bias education:

- Introduce or conclude activities. For example, you can read the book, *All the Colors We Are,* prior to doing an art activity with skin-color art materials. You can also conclude an activity by reading a multicultural children's book. Ask the children to cut out magazine pictures of families and make a collage of all kinds of families. Conclude the activity by reading the book, *Black Is Brown Is Tan,* or the book, *All Kinds of Families.*

- Promote problem solving. If superhero play in your classroom is getting out of hand, try reading *Amazing Grace* to introduce other heroes into the children's play. If name-calling is a problem in your classroom, or if you want to prevent name-calling, try acting out a skit with puppets and read the book, *Angel Child, Dragon Child.* If children are avoiding responsibility by saying, "It's not my fault!" or blaming others try reading the book *Chicken Sunday.* Follow up with a discussion about how it feels to be blamed for something you didn't do and what we can do instead of blaming others.

Read a variety of books on the same topic. Examine three to four counting books or alphabet books from different cultures. Talk about how they are alike and how they are different. Combine stories that are similar yet different. For instance, consider reading *Mama, Do You Love Me?* and *The Runaway Bunny,* by Margaret Wise Brown. These are both stories about a child testing his or her mother's love. Or try reading two or three versions of the same story. This works particularly well with older children and folk tales. You can compare similar tales across cultures. Unfortunately, young children may simply get lost in the stereotypic illustrations of the folk tales.

Consider these resources if you are interested in more ideas about using literature to foster culturally relevant and anti-bias education.

Building Bridges with Multicultural Picture Books: For Children 3–5, by Janice Beaty (Prentice Hall, 1996).

Children and Books I: African American Story Books and Activities for All Children, by Patricia Buerke Moll (Hampton Mae Inst., 1991).

Persona dolls

Louise Derman-Sparks introduced this powerful teaching method in the anti-bias curriculum, though it originated with Kay Taus, a kindergarten teacher who participated with Louise on the Anti-Bias Task Force. Recently, Trisha Whitney further refined this method in her book *Kids Like Us.* Persona dolls are simply dolls with a personality. Begin with a childlike doll (not a baby doll). Give it a name, family, racial and cultural identity, and a few personality traits. Bring the doll to large group time and introduce the doll to the class: "Children, I want to introduce you to a new friend. This is Maribel. Maribel is four, just like you. Can you all say, 'Hi' to her? She lives in an apartment with her mom, dad, and twin sisters. Maribel is Mexican American and she speaks English and Spanish. She goes to a school that is a lot like ours. She loves ice cream, pizza, and riding her bike."

Then in future weeks, bring the doll back to group time on a regular basis, each time telling stories about her life. Sometimes the stories will introduce children to the doll's culture, sometimes the stories will help children learn to recognize stereotypes and biases, and other times the stories will give children practice in solving problems and responding to incidents of bias.

Persona dolls have been found to be very effective with children. When you have one child in your class who is the only representative of his culture, you may be afraid of discussing differences for fear the child will become the object lesson and be made to feel "different." The persona doll takes the pressure off isolated and underrepresented children and makes it easier to learn about their cultures. Persona dolls can help you overcome segregation and lack of diversity. What racial and cultural groups are missing from your classroom this year? A persona doll can introduce children to cultural groups absent from your school, but present in the local community or region. Persona dolls also help children develop problem-solving skills. Have the persona doll or a pair of dolls act out an incident of discrimination such as name-calling or teasing. Ask the children to help the dolls solve their problem.

This is a very brief introduction to the use of persona dolls. I highly recommend *Kids Like Us: Using Persona Dolls in the Classroom,* by Trisha Whitney. She provides specific guidelines for creating a collection of persona dolls, many examples of stories, and lots of resources for purchasing or making persona dolls.

By changing the classroom environment as well as the people who teach in it, we can quickly add or improve culturally relevant and anti-bias education in our classrooms. Helpful changes in the classroom environment can include everything from changing the room arrangement to teaching through interest areas, devising a criteria for reviewing books and materials for stereotypes, making your own visual displays, and selecting culturally relevant and anti-bias materials.

The next chapter will give you many ideas for planned activities that you can group together to form the curriculum. These culturally relevant and anti-bias activities will help you meet the needs of individual children through your curriculum, and help you decide what is developmentally appropriate.

Questions to Ponder

How are your program's goals reflected in the classroom?

How are your own attitudes and values reflected in your classroom?

What groups of people and ways of life are missing from your classroom?

List five things you can do to eliminate stereotypes from your classroom.

List five things you can do to increase diversity in your classroom.

References

RESOURCES FOR NON-STEREOTYPIC CLASSROOM MATERIALS

Constructive Playthings. U.S. Toy Company, Constructive Playthings, 13201 Arrington Road, Grandview, MO 64030, 800-448-7830, www.consplay.com

Environments, Inc., P. O. Box 1348, Beaufort, SC 29901-1348, 800-342-4453, www.eichild.com

Lakeshore Learning Materials, 2695 E. Dominguez Street, Carson, CA 90810, 800-421-5354, www.lakeshorelearning.com

BOOKS AND ARTICLES

Council on Interracial Books for Children. 1980. *Ten quick ways to analyze children's books for sexism and racism.* New York: Council on Interracial Books for Children.

Derman-Sparks, Louise. 1989. *Anti-bias curriculum: Tools for empowering young children.* Washington, D.C.: NAEYC.

Kendall, Frances E. 1993. *Diversity in the classroom: A multicultural approach to the education of young children.* New York: Teachers College Press.

Moll, Patricia Bueker. 1991. *Children and books: African American story books and activities for all children.* Vol. 1. Tampa: Hampton Mae Institute.

Pelo, Ann, and Fran Davidson. 2000. *That's not fair! A teacher's guide to activism with young children.* St. Paul: Redleaf Press.

Ramsey, Patricia G. 1987. *Teaching and learning in a diverse world: Multicultural education for young children.* New York: Teachers College Press.

Whitney, Trisha. 1999. *Kids like us: Using persona dolls in the classroom.* St. Paul: Redleaf Press.

Williams, Leslie R., and Yvonne De Gaetano. 1985. *Alerta: A multicultural, bilingual approach to teaching young children.* Menlo Park, Calif.: Addison-Wesley.

Wolpert, Ellen. 1999. *Start seeing diversity.* St. Paul: Redleaf Press.

York, Stacey. 1998. *Big as life: The everyday inclusive curriculum.* Vols. 1 and 2. St. Paul: Redleaf Press.

Any genuine teaching will result, if successful, in someone's knowing how to bring about a better condition of things than existed earlier.

John Dewey

Culturally Relevant and Anti-Bias Activities

Early childhood educators teach through planned activities as well as a culturally relevant and anti-bias prepared environment. These planned activities are then grouped together to form the curriculum. Curriculum planning requires some decision making. Early childhood teachers must ask themselves: What messages do I want to convey to young children? What information would be developmentally appropriate? How might I organize a multicultural curriculum?

This chapter will help you plan curriculum units and meet the needs of individual children through curriculum. It will also help you decide what is developmentally appropriate and what information should be saved for presentation when children are older. Most important, this chapter provides you with over eighty culturally relevant and anti-bias activities for use in your classroom.

Unit Themes

Unit themes are probably the most popular way to organize learning in early childhood programs. Themes provide a focus, a topic around which to plan and choose activities. Ideas for themes may come from the teacher and manifest concepts she believes children should learn. Themes may come from the children, too, representing things they are asking questions about and are interested in learning more about. Themes also come from the physical and social world. For example, you probably plan themes about winter during the winter season, and children learn about Valentine's Day in February.

Many common early childhood themes can be expanded to include multicultural values (and the activities in this book). The following themes support and provide opportunities to explore multicultural concepts:

I'm Me and I'm Special

Books

Boys and Girls

Places People Live

Friends

Toys and Games

Families

Transportation

Our Community

Clothes We Wear

Food We Eat

Alike and Different

Day and Night

Light and Dark

Feelings

Holidays and Celebrations

Five Senses

Heroes and Sheroes

Music

Weather

Folk Tales

Animals

Dance and Movement

Pets

Bodies

Colors

In *Big As Life: The Everyday Inclusive Curriculum* (two volumes), I show how culturally relevant and anti-bias concepts can be incorporated into curriculum units. For example, a culturally relevant/anti-bias approach to learning about food could include the following topics:

What foods do you eat? Which are your favorite foods?

Are there any foods that you can't eat? Why?

How do you eat your food?

What are all the ways to eat food?

What meals do you eat? When and where do you eat meals?

With whom do you eat meals?

Who cooks food?

Where and how do people cook?

What tools and equipment do people use to cook food?

Who works to help us have food?

Who grows food? How is food harvested?

Who prepares and processes food?

How and where is food processed?

Who buys and sells food?

Where and how is food bought and sold?

Where does food come from?

Which food comes from animals? From plants?

How do our senses help us learn about food?

How does food taste, smell, feel, and sound?

What are the shapes, sizes, and colors of food?

Why do we eat food?

Which foods are healthy? Which foods are unhealthy?

How can we eat a balanced diet?

What are all the kinds of food?

What are all the kinds of fruit? Vegetables? Meat? Dairy products?

What are all the kinds of grains, cereal, and bread products?

How are foods similar to one another? How are foods different from one another?

What are real/pretend foods?

What are pretend foods?

How does food stay the same/change?

What are stereotypes about food?

How can we work together to challenge the stereotypes about food?

What are people's food wants and needs?

What is hunger?

How can we work together to help people who don't have enough food to eat?

When does your family eat special foods?

What special foods does your family eat?

How can we celebrate food?

Avoid themes such as "children around the world" or "let's visit Hawaii." They encourage activities that focus on countries, artifacts, traditional clothing, and ceremonies. They teach children to be tourists (outsiders visiting an unknown culture that is totally irrelevant to their daily lives). This method of curriculum planning teaches children trivia, ignores that people of other cultures really exist today and live normal everyday lives, and does nothing to build a foundation for living in a multicultural world. Children learn about the culture for a week, two weeks, or a month and then they move on to unit themes, such as the circus or dinosaurs. And the culture they just studied may not be talked about for the rest of the year.

Planning Multicultural Curriculum

Whether planning curriculum alone or with a teaching team, you'll want to consider all of the elements of an early childhood classroom. The curriculum planning form on the next page will help you consider such details as theme and concepts, important dates, parent newsletter articles, field trips, bulletin boards, cooking projects, and the room arrangement. It will give you a broad framework of the unit plan, be it a two-week time period or a month. Each team member can then take a copy of the general plan and use it to write up specific activities for free play and group time.

Curriculum Planning Form

Theme _____   Week _____

	Monday	Tuesday	Wednesday	Thursday	Friday
Large Group					
Free Choice					
Small Group					
Large Group					
Art Area	Dramatic Play Area			Manipulatives	
Block Area	Sensory Table			Science	

Using the Curriculum Planning Form

Theme. Decide on the theme and the length of time the class will spend on that unit. Select a theme from the list in this chapter or use one of your own.

Basic concepts. Write down the basic concepts and ideas to which the children will be exposed through the activities offered in this unit. Remember that the early childhood years are not the time to emphasize learning facts and information. Use the theme to expose children to new experiences and invite them to explore new materials.

Special dates. Go through the calendar and write down any special dates that take place during the time the class will be focusing on this particular unit. Also include children's birthdays if you celebrate them in your program.

Field trips/visitors. Try to take one field trip each month. If you live in an area with harsh winters, substitute a field trip with a special visitor. Use the form to list places you might take the children, or visitors you might invite into the classroom to emphasize the curriculum theme.

Cooking activities/snack. Some programs offer cooking as a weekly activity. These experiences are fun for children if they can actively participate in the preparation and cooking of food. Plan cooking experiences that support the unit theme. Plan a few special snacks or meals to go along with the theme if the center has a food service program. Remember, parents are a good source for recipes.

Visual displays. Often teachers change the bulletin boards to go along with the curriculum theme. Bulletin boards can be important teaching tools. Think of displays that support the concepts you are trying to teach the children. Remember to include visual displays that show a variety of people in everyday situations. Use photographs and homemade displays as often as possible. Try to avoid cartoon figures that may be stereotypical and serve no purpose other than decoration.

Parent newsletter. Most programs have some form of written communication with parents, be it a monthly classroom newsletter or an all-program newsletter. Write an article on the current theme and how you incorporate multicultural concepts and activities into the daily activities. Use this section to list ideas for newsletter articles and other information such as requests for materials, reports on a field trip or visitor, and sharing recipes.

Classroom environment. The next section of the planning form lists the interest areas or learning centers often found in early childhood classrooms. Rotate and add materials that support the theme for each of the interest areas. In addition, use the curriculum planning form to delegate staff responsibilities for setting up or rearranging interest areas to go along with the theme. For example, one person may be responsible for returning and checking out new library books. Another person takes the art area and changes the colors of the paint and construction paper and makes new playdough.

Individualized Planning

Multicultural education means that early childhood education professionals include, accept, and respect each child as an individual. It means that we recognize what each child values and holds dear, and then build those things into the daily life of the early childhood program. New teachers often teach to their class as a group and are overwhelmed by the thought of considering and planning for individual children. Experienced teachers who have become comfortable and confident in their curriculum planning can take their skills one step further by designing curriculum based on individual children's developmental abilities and interests. The curriculum that results from this practice is both child centered and emergent evolving: it comes from the child. It is naturally respectful and mindful of multicultural values because it takes each child's culture into account from the beginning.

The individualized planning form on the following page helps you focus on each individual child in your class. It is written for a teaching team to complete together as a group. This activity can also be done by individual teachers who work alone with their own class.

Individualized Planning Form

Theme _____   **Week** _____

Planning Multicultural Activities

As adults, we may think of countries, governments, languages, and customs when we hear the term *multicultural education*. We remember our own experience of learning geography, making relief maps, and writing our first big report on the country of our choice. These are appropriate activities for elementary, junior high, and high school, but because of their cognitive development, young children are not ready to learn "facts" about different cultures, and they are easily confused by events that happened long ago or that occur in faraway places. As a result, teachers should avoid focusing on the following:

Names of countries

Locations of countries

National flags

Historical events

The concept of city, state, and nation

Revolutions and wars

Past presidents and rulers

In addition, young children may not believe that people from other cultures are real, or they may believe that they lived long ago and are no longer living in the world today. Activities that portray characteristics of other cultures as unusual, weird, abnormal, or extreme encourage children to believe in stereotypes. Young children may not recognize real people from other cultures when they see them on the street. They may say, "No, that's not an Indian. Indians wear feathers and ride horses." "No, she's not Japanese. She doesn't have a kimono or those funny shoes on."

Teachers of young children should limit the amount of multicultural activities planned around these topics, because using the elements of a culture with which children have no actual experience can strengthen stereotypes rather than breaking them down.

Foreign foods

Traditional costumes

Holidays and celebrations

Cultural artifacts

As early childhood educators, we know that children learn best when they are actively exploring materials, experiencing the world with their whole bodies and all of their senses, and interacting with a variety of people. According to Louise Derman-Sparks (1989), author of *The Anti-Bias Curriculum,* we need to use a new perspective to examine existing activities and use good early childhood practices to deal with new issues.

Rather than simplifying elementary school activities and social studies lessons, try adapting proven early childhood activities. Avoid using worksheets, coloring pages, and craft projects. Go through your own activity files and curriculum books. As you review the activities you currently use every day in the classroom, think about how they might be modified to teach multicultural concepts. The activities presented in this chapter provide many examples of how to use basic early childhood activities to emphasize multicultural concepts.

Multicultural Concepts Young Children Can Understand

Appropriate multicultural activities for young children focus on things children are interested in and the concepts they are struggling to understand. Build your multicultural curriculum around activities that focus on these concepts:

Everyone is worthy.

Everyone is lovable and capable.

Everyone is equal.

Everyone deserves respect.

Everyone is important.

Everyone has feelings.

People are similar.

People are different.

Some physical characteristics stay the same. Some physical characteristics change.

It is important to try new experiences.

We can learn about the daily life of people we know.

Culture comes from parents and family.

There are different kinds of families.

Families live in different ways.

Many different people live in our community.

People work together and help one another.

Some things are real and some are pretend.

Some things are fair and some things are unfair.

People have different points of view.

Introducing Multicultural Activities

As teachers, we spend long hours making learning games, teaching aides, and rotating materials. Sometimes, we become frustrated that children do not notice or use the materials. How we introduce new materials and activities is an important part of teaching. Take time to introduce materials and activities to children. A clear introduction builds interest and helps children be successful. Keep in mind these two ideas when introducing multicultural activities and materials.

1. Help children appreciate multicultural materials by introducing them as such. Talk about who the object belongs to, who made it, where it came from, and how it is used. Children may not remember the information but will "catch" the feeling that this is something important and special. Sensing the teacher's interest and respect increases children's interest in activities and materials.

2. When introducing materials or activities, avoid making sweeping generalizations. For example, don't say, "All Japanese people eat with chopsticks," or, "All black people love to dance." These kinds of statements are stereotypical. Whenever possible, introduce a multicultural activity or material in relation to a person or a family that the children know, such as "Sato's family is Japanese and sometimes they eat with chopsticks."

Activity Ideas

The following activities illustrate how you can take common early childhood materials and activities and adapt them to multicultural concepts. These activities are designed to help children explore, examine, and talk about their feelings and perceptions. These activities are developmentally appropriate for preschool and kindergarten children. Not all of the activities may be appropriate for an individual child or for your particular group of children. Some may be too simple, others too difficult. What works with a group of three-year-olds may not work with a group of five-year-olds. Use discretion in selecting which activities to include in your curriculum.

The activities are grouped by the goals of a culturally relevant/anti-bias curriculum. The goals are

1. To develop positive, knowledgeable, and confident self-identity within a cultural context
2. To demonstrate comfortable, empathetic interaction with diversity among people
3. To think critically about bias
4. To stand up for oneself and others in the face of bias

Goal 1 Activities

CULTURALLY RELEVANT ACTIVITIES strengthen children's connections to their family and home culture. Activities may include demonstrations by parents or grandparents, learning to count or recite the alphabet in a child's home language, or learning about a child's home country. Parents and grandparents are wonderful sources for culturally relevant activities. Look for more culturally relevant activity ideas in these resources:

Kaleidoscope: A Multicultural Approach for the Primary School Classroom, by Yvonne De Gaetano, Leslie R. Williams, and Dinah Volk (Merrill Prentice Hall, 1998).

Children and Books: African American Story Books and Activities for All Children (vol. 1), by Patricia Buerke Moll (Hampton Mae Institute, 1991).

Baby Pictures

THEMES   Bodies, Families, Our Class

OBJECTIVES   Recognize and celebrate one's own physical features

Feel special and unique

MATERIALS   Baby photographs of each child, a current photograph of each child

DESCRIPTION   Collect pictures of each child as a baby. At circle time, tell the children you have pictures of them as babies. Say, "I'm going to hold up the baby pictures, one at a time. Look at it carefully and see if you can guess who it is." When the children make a guess, ask them to explain their reasoning. Then set out the baby photos and the current photos of the children. Invite children to match the baby and current photo. Display the baby photos and current photos side by side on a bulletin board in the classroom. If you are concerned about damaging or losing the baby photos, make a color photocopy of them.

VARIATIONS   1. Include baby and current pictures of the teaching staff.

2. Make a memory matching game by gluing a photocopy of each picture onto a blank index card. Laminate the cards. Lay them out face down and invited children to find a match.

Cultural Communities

THEMES   Community, My People

OBJECTIVES   Recognize one's own cultural dress

Recognize one's own cultural foods

Recognize one's home language

Identify with one's culture

MATERIALS   Photographs, brochures, flyers, menus, posters, newspapers, and other items from each of the cultural communities represented in your class

DESCRIPTION   Identify the cultures of the children in your class. If possible, take a walk through a culturally specific neighborhood or business district in your community that reflects one of the children in your class. Arrange for your class to visit a retail store, restaurant, bakery, social service agency, or other business. Take photographs of the neighborhood. When you return back to the classroom, make a community book with the children. Include what you saw, smelled, tasted, heard, and touched in that culture's community.

VARIATION   Ask a parent from that culture to assist you in making the community book bilingual.

Who Am I? Board Game

THEMES   Our Class, My People, Friends, Heroes and Sheroes

OBJECTIVES   Identify one's own culture

Identify one's own cultural traditions and customs

Accept one's cultural identity

MATERIALS   File folder, felt-tip pens, construction paper, game board spinner or dice, game pieces

DESCRIPTION   Use a file folder to make a simple board game. Make a path 2 inches wide that weaves back and forth across the page. Write the words *start* on the left side and *end* on the right side. You may want to also write the words "Who Am I?" Board Game on the folder. You can also decorate the game board with pictures and images representing the children's home cultures. Make a set of game cards by writing questions related to cultural identity on each card. For example, include the following questions:

What's the name of your culture?

What's your home language or what is a language that people from your culture speak?

Where did your relatives come from?

Name one food people from your culture eat?

Name one instrument people from your culture play?

Name one piece of clothing that people from your culture wear?

Name one holiday or celebration from your culture?

Name one hero or shero from your culture?

Name your favorite thing about being from your culture?

You may need to make duplicates of the cards in order to have enough to play the game. To play, give each child a marker. It could be a different-color button. A child takes a turn by rolling the dice and turning over the top card. The teacher reads the question. If the child is able to answer the question, he or she moves forward the number on the dice.

VARIATION   Make a board game for other themes such as my family, our class, or my friends.

Cultural Dances

THEMES   My People, Bodies, Music, Community

OBJECTIVES   Recognize and celebrate cultural dress

Identify one's own cultural traditions and customs

Appreciate one's own cultural heritage

DESCRIPTION   Send a note home to parents asking if they, their older children, extended family members, or anyone they know would be willing to come to your classroom to demonstrate a traditional dance from their child's home culture. You could also ask someone who participates in an ethnic dance group. Remember to focus on the cultures represented in your classroom, as the purpose of this activity is to connect children to their home cultures. Ask the parents or dancers to join your group time in their street clothes and talk with the children about when and where they dance, how they feel when they dance, what it means to them, and how they learned the dance.

Cultural Feast

THEMES   Food, My People, Friends, Alike and Different

OBJECTIVES   Recognize and celebrate one's own diet and style of eating

Identify with one's culture

Share one's own cultural experiences with others

MATERIALS   Tables, chairs, tableclothes, serving utensils, eating utensils, place mats, napkins

DESCRIPTION   Send a note home with the children announcing a special multicultural feast. Ask that each child bring a dish from their family's home culture to share with the rest of the class. Schedule the feast for lunch or dinner. This activity works well around Thanksgiving or Christmas, or at the end of the year when children and families have experienced their culture through many other activities.

VARIATIONS   1. Invite parents to join the children at the feast.

2. Ask parents for the recipe of their ethnic dish.

3. Make a cookbook and distribute it to all the families.

4. Adapt the recipes so that they meet the USDA requirements and can be included in the center's daily food service program.

Cultural Ways Feeling Box

THEMES   Senses, Our Class, My People, Alike and Different

OBJECTIVES   Identify one's own culture's artifacts

Appreciate one's own culture

MATERIALS   Collections of small objects and fabric swatches representing the home cultures of the children in your class, a feeling box or bag

DESCRIPTION   Collect the cultural objects and place them in the feeling box. At circle time, invite each child to take a turn to reach into the feeling box and guess one of the objects without looking at it. After guessing, the child takes it out to see if she is correct. Ask the child, "What culture uses this object? Who in our class is from that culture?" Repeat this process until everyone has a turn.

VARIATION   Keep the feeling box in the manipulative area so that children can use it during free play. Place pretend food from each of the children's home cultures in the feeling box.

Culture Calendar

THEMES   Families, My Culture, Our Class

OBJECTIVES   Recognize one's own family's celebrations

Accept one's own cultural identity

Experience an opportunity to contribute to classroom life

MATERIALS   Twelve calendar grids (8 by 11 inches or larger), fine point felt-tip pens

DESCRIPTION   Prepare to make a calendar of the families' holidays and celebrations by sending a note to parent. Ask them for a list of the holidays and celebrations their family observes each year. Display the calendars on the wall side by side so that they create a time line. Mark all of the families' holidays and celebrations on the calendar. Keep the calendar up all year long. This will help children recall the past, identify the present, and anticipate the future.

VARIATION   Include local neighborhood or community holidays or celebrations that the school participates in.

Fables, Morals, and Proverbs

THEMES	Communication, My People, Families
OBJECTIVES	Promote identification with one's own culture
	Foster connections between families and schools
	Promote values of children's home culture
MATERIALS	Fables, morals, or proverbs from the cultures of the children in your class; chart paper; felt-tip marker
DESCRIPTION	Use fables, morals, and proverbs to bring the culturally based values of your children into the classroom. Collect a variety of children's fables, moral stories, or proverbs from the cultures of the children in your class. Ask parents to help you identify those that are appropriate for the age of the children.

Introduce children to the fables. Tell them, "Fables are stories that teach us how we are supposed to behave. Each fable has a lesson to help us learn good behavior." Identify the culture that the fable comes from and the children in the class who share that cultural identity. Read the fable.

Afterward, facilitate a discussion with the children. Post a sheet of chart paper. Ask them what the fable means. If the moral of the story is to respect elders, ask the children, "What do you think it means to respect your elders?" Write their answers on the chart and post it in the classroom. Ask them, "How can we show respect to our elders?"

VARIATION	Make a book of your class's favorite fables and proverbs.

Face Puzzles

THEMES	Bodies, Our Class, Boys and Girls
OBJECTIVES	Recognize and celebrate one's own physical features
	Recognize one's beauty
	Experience self-worth
MATERIALS	Color close-up photograph of each child's face, oak tag or poster board, glue, scissors
DESCRIPTION	Help children recognize themselves and notice their own unique facial features. Take a close-up photo of each child's face. Use a color photocopier to enlarge each photo. Glue the photocopies to pieces of oak tag or poster board. Cut each picture into pieces, making a puzzle. Place each child's puzzle in a resealable plastic bag. At small group time, give each child his or her picture puzzle. Ask the children, "I wonder what is in the bag I just gave you? Does anyone know what it is? Open the bag and empty it." Once children realize it is a puzzle, challenge them to put the pieces together to see what's on the puzzle. Take turns looking at each child's face puzzle. Ask the children to put the pieces back into the bag. Store the puzzles in a basket in the manipulatives area so that children can play with the puzzle during free choice time.
VARIATIONS	1. Make a puzzle of each child's family.
	2. Make a puzzle of a child's drawing or painting of himself.

Family Foods

THEMES	Families, My People
OBJECTIVES	Recognize and celebrate one's own diet and style of eating
	Identify with one's own culture
	Share one's own culture with others
MATERIALS	Ingredients and cooking utensils will depend on the recipe
DESCRIPTION	Ask parents to share one of their family's favorite recipes from their home culture. Invite the parent into the classroom to prepare the recipe with the children. You could even schedule a "Favorite Family Food" cooking experience each week.

Get the recipe from the parent ahead of time. Purchase the ingredients. Buy enough so that children can explore the raw ingredients.

Introduce the parent and cooking activity at group time. Ask the parent to show the children some of the ingredients that are special or might be unfamiliar to the class. They may also want to talk about the cultural significance of the recipe such as when the dish is eaten or how the dish came to be part of their family.

Set up the cooking activity at the table during free choice play. This way, children can come and go according to their interests. Remind the children to wash their hands prior to joining the activity. Serve the dish with lunch or afternoon snack.

Later that day, dictate a letter from the children. Thank the parent for sharing his or her culture with the class. Include comments from the children about how much they liked the dish and enjoyed the activity.

VARIATION	Take pictures of the parent and children cooking. Display the photographs on a bulletin board near the sign-in sheet or make a book about the different foods.

Famous People

THEMES	My People, Community, Heroes and Sheroes
OBJECTIVES	Learn about role models within one's culture
	Set high expectations for oneself
	Identify with one's own culture
MATERIALS	Posters of "famous people" from each of the cultures represented in your classroom
DESCRIPTION	At group time introduce children to members of their home culture who have accomplished great things and made important contributions to American society. Each day focus on the contributions of people from a different culture.

Show children a picture of the person and ask them, "Do you know who this is? Why do you think we have a poster of this person? What do you think this person did that was helpful to all of us?" After looking at all of the pictures, ask the children if they can remember some of the good and helpful things the people we learned about did? Ask them, "How could you be like these people?"

VARIATION	Make your own set of local important people from the cultures in your classroom by cutting out pictures from local magazines and newspapers.

It's Me!

THEMES	Bodies, Our Class
OBJECTIVES	Recognize and celebrate one's own physical features
	Recognize one's own beauty
	Experience dignity and pride
MATERIALS	Small unbreakable mirrors; skin-color paints, markers, or crayons; construction or drawing paper
DESCRIPTION	Invite children to look at themselves in the mirror. Help them notice and name their physical features. For instance, "Your hair is brown, curly, and short. Your eyes are brown and round." Encourage children to draw or paint a self-portrait. Encourage them to continually refer back to their mirrors if they forget what their face looks like. Ask each child to share his or her picture at group time.
VARIATION	Using larger unbreakable mirrors, invite children to draw their face on the mirror.

Language Books

THEMES	Our Class, Friends, Communication
OBJECTIVES	Recognize and celebrate one's own home language
	Use one's own home language
	Experience dignity and pride
	Experience an opportunity to contribute to classroom life
MATERIALS	Magazines, crayons and markers, glue, felt-tip pen, hole punch, yarn
DESCRIPTION	Identify the home languages of the children in your class. With the children, make a book for each of the home languages represented in your classroom. Invite the children to think of one or two of their favorite things. Challenge them to find a magazine picture or draw a picture of it. Glue the magazine pictures onto construction paper. Write the word for the object in English directly below the picture. Ask a parent, staff member, or older student to write the word in a child's home language. Punch holes in the pages and tie the book together with yarn. Use the book at circle time to begin to learn some basic words in each child's home language.
VARIATIONS	1. Make language posters to display in the classroom.
	2. Create an audio tape to go along with the book.

Language Sounds

THEMES   Communication, My People, Friends, Our Class

OBJECTIVES   Recognize and celebrate one's own home language

Use one's own home language

Experience dignity and pride

MATERIALS   Cassette tape recorder, microphone, blank cassette tapes

DESCRIPTION   Identify the home languages spoken by the families of the children in your class. Make a cassette tape of people (children or adults) speaking in the child's home language. Try to have brief (two to five minutes) segments of three or four different languages (including English) on the tape. Invite children to listen to the tape and see if they can identify the languages spoken.

VARIATION   Have each speaker recite the same poem, chant, finger play, or short story that is familiar to the children.

Listen to Our Elders

THEMES   Families, My People, Community, Heroes and Sheroes

OBJECTIVES   Learn about role models within one's own culture

Appreciate one's own cultural heritage

Feel special and unique

MATERIALS   Invitations, adult-size chair

DESCRIPTION   Send a note home to parents asking if any of the elders in their family might be interested in coming to school to talk with the children, tell them a story about their culture, or share some cultural artifacts with them.

Prepare children for the elder's visit. Ask the children, "So you know what an elder is?" "An elder is an adult who has lived a long time. Elders are wise because they have done many things in their lives and they know a lot. Elders deserve our respect." Ask the children if they know how to show respect to an elder. Have them practice greeting an elder. Encourage them to model how their parent(s) have taught them to greet and address elders. When the elders visit your classroom, bring the children together for large group. Give the elder a place of honor in front of the group. Introduce the elder to the children and ask each of them to introduce themselves. At the end of their time with the elder, the children could sing a song or recite a poem. As a follow-up, have the children draw pictures and write a class "thank-you" letter to the elder.

VARIATION   Invite elders from the community to visit and share with your class.

My Family Comes from . . .

THEMES   Families, My People, Changes, Communication

OBJECTIVES   Identify one's own culture

Recognize the concept of homelands

Identify with one's own culture

MATERIALS   Colored construction paper (12 by 18 inches), hole punch, yarn, felt-tip pen, photographs of children's families

DESCRIPTION   Make a book for each child to record his family history and culture. Include photographs of grandparents and extended family members. The book could also include information such as which family members came to the United States, what country they came from, languages spoken at home, simple words or greetings in their family's home language, favorite foods, and customs practiced at home. Each page could include their drawings and responses to the following questions:

Who are your people?

What's the name of your ethnic group?

Which ancestors came to America?

When did they come here?

Where did they come from?

What languages does your family speak?

What are your favorite foods?

Which foods do you eat most often?

What are some cultural customs practiced in your family?

How do you feel about your culture?

What do you like best about your culture?

VARIATION   Collect information about families by asking parents to fill out a family questionnaire.

My Family

THEMES	Families, My People
OBJECTIVES	Recognize and celebrate one's own family
	Experience self-worth
MATERIALS	Large sheets of construction paper (11 by 18 inches), skin-colored construction paper cut into people shapes, glue, crayons, or felt-tip markers.
DESCRIPTION	Introduce the topic of family. Define family as people we live with and love. Ask children to name the members of their family. Invite the children to pick out a people shape for each person in their family, glue the shapes to the construction paper, and decorate the people. Offer to write the names of the family members on each child's paper. Display the children's family pictures or send them home.
VARIATIONS	1. For older children, expand the definition of family. Include things such as family members who care for one another, do things together, and share responsibilities.
	2. Older children could draw or paint a picture of their family rather than using the people shapes.

My Homeland

THEMES	My People, Families, Community, Planet Earth
OBJECTIVES	Recognize the concept of homelands
	Appreciate one's own cultural heritage
MATERIALS	Globe or world map, photographs of the countries that children in your class are from, construction paper, scissors, glue
DESCRIPTION	Ask parents what countries they or their ancestors are from. Make a chart listing the children and their family's home country/countries. Set out a globe or a map. Help the children locate the countries their families are from. Help them find magazine pictures to cut out and glue onto construction paper to make a homeland poster or collage. Display the collages near the globe so that children can associate places on the globe with the pictures.
VARIATION	Some parents may go back and forth between their homeland and the United States. Ask them to share pictures and artifacts from a recent trip with the children. Make color photocopies of parents' photographs and create a collage representing their homelands.

Name Game

THEMES   Families, Friends, Our Class, Communication

OBJECTIVES   Recognize and celebrate one's own name

Identify the meaning of one's name

MATERIALS   Strips of poster board (6 by 24 inches), glue, felt-tip marker, glitter, sparkly or shiny collage materials; books on the meaning of names (can be checked out from the library)

DESCRIPTION   Prior to this activity send a note home to parents asking them if there is a story attached to their child's name. In other words, what does it mean? Who is the child named after?

Use the marker to write each child's name on a poster-board strip. At circle time, hold the strips up, one at a time. See if the child recognizes his or her name.

Together with the child, write the meaning of his or her name on the back of the poster board strip. Look up the child's name in baby name books to identify the meaning of the name.

Give each child a strip of poster board and invite them to write their name in glue and cover the glue with glitter. Let the name tag dry. Once it is dry, children could decorate it with a variety of sparkly and shiny collage materials.

VARIATION   Invite a parent to talk with the children about how people in their culture are given their names.

Self-Portrait

THEMES   Bodies, Our Class

OBJECTIVES   Recognize and celebrate one's own physical features

Recognize one's own beauty

Experience dignity and pride

MATERIALS   Photograph of each child, a color enlargement of each photo, a plexiglass easel or clear acetate, skin-color paints, a variety of other colors of paint, paint brushes, smocks

DESCRIPTION   Take a picture of each child's face. Enlarge the photograph on a color copy machine. Lay it on the table and put a piece of clear acetate over it, or tape it to the back of a clear plexiglass easel. Invite the child to paint a picture of themselves. When they are done, get out the unbreakable hand mirrors. Encourage the child to compare and contrast their face in the mirror with the photograph and their self-portrait.

VARIATION   Take a full-body picture and invite children to paint their whole selves.

Sing My Songs

THEMES   Families, My People, Music, Our Class

OBJECTIVES   Identify with one's own culture

Share one's own culture with others

Experience an opportunity to contribute to classroom life

MATERIALS   Cassette tape player, blank audio cassettes, chart paper, felt-tip pens

DESCRIPTION   Invite parents to share children's songs, chants, and musical games from their home culture. Ask them, "What songs, chants, and musical games did you sing as a young child? Would you share them with our class?" Ask the parents to teach the song, chant, or musical game to the children. If it isn't possible for the parent to volunteer in the classroom, give the parent a tape recorder and ask him to record the song on audio tape. Parents may also have cassette tapes of children's songs from their home culture that they would be willing to share with the class. Make a "Big Book of Songs from My Culture" by writing the lyrics on chart paper and hanging it on a chart rack in the classroom.

VARIATION   Invite staff to share children's songs, chants, and games from their home culture.

Body Paintings

THEMES   I'm Me and I'm Special, Boys and Girls, Alike and Different, Colors, Bodies

OBJECTIVE   Help children become aware of their body, skin color, and facial features

MATERIALS   Unbreakable full-length mirror, tempera paint mixed with soap, paintbrushes, paint containers

DESCRIPTION   This is an activity for children to do one at a time. Have the child stand in front of the mirror. Ask the child to draw his body on the mirror using a paintbrush and paint. Encourage the child to trace the outline of the body first and then fill it in. Talk with the child about his body shape and physical features.

VARIATIONS   1. Put a piece of clear plastic film over the mirror. This allows the child to save the picture. Put it up to the sunlight or on a window and see the light come through.

2. Ask the child to stand up against the mirror and then trace her body. The child then colors it in.

3. Make a body sculpture. Have the children lay on butcher paper and trace their bodies. Give them paint, crayons, or felt-tip pens to color it in. When the drawing is complete, put a plain sheet of butcher paper underneath. Cut out the body drawing, cutting both sheets of paper at the same time. Staple the two "bodies" together around the edges and stuff with newspaper.

I'm Special Book

THEMES	I'm Me and I'm Special, Friends, Books, Alike and Different
OBJECTIVES	Help children feel good about themselves and notice how each of the children in the class is special
MATERIALS	Construction paper (12 by 18 inches), yarn, hole punch, camera, film, felt-tip marker, glue
DESCRIPTION	Make a book for each child by folding three sheets of construction paper in half. Punch holes half an inch from the fold. Thread the yarn through the hole and tie in a bow to secure the book. Take a photograph of each child and glue it to the cover. Fill the book with information about and photographs of the child. Include physical characteristics (height, weight, skin color, eye color), favorite toys, family size and members, languages spoken at home, pets, nickname, birth date, and age. Set the "I'm Special" books in the classroom's book corner for all the children to look at and read.
VARIATIONS	1. Make the book so that it can be filled in at home by the parent and child.
	2. Make a book of the entire class with a page or two for each child.

Sock Puppets

THEMES	I'm Me and I'm Special, Boys and Girls, Friends, Alike and Different, Colors, Feelings, Folk Tales, Books, Bodies
OBJECTIVES	Give children an opportunity to make a three-dimensional object to represent themselves
	Gain skills in verbal self-expression
MATERIALS	Collection of tan, beige, cream, brown, peach, and other skin-colored socks; felt scraps; assorted fabric trim, yarn, buttons, glue, mirrors
DESCRIPTION	Say to the children, "I brought some materials so that you can make a sock puppet that looks just like you." Let the children select the color of sock they want to use for making a puppet. Encourage them to choose one that is similar to their skin color. Set out the mirror and materials on a table. The children may want to look in the mirror when deciding how to make their puppet's facial features and hair. Talk about the similarities and differences between the puppets. For example, you could say, "Each puppet is different because it looks like the person who is making it."
VARIATION	Set up or make a puppet stage and encourage the children to act out a story or classroom situation.

Goal 2 Activities

DIVERSITY ACTIVITIES PROMOTE the goals and objectives of goal two. That is, they foster each child's positive, empathetic interaction with diversity among people. In an anti-bias curriculum, diversity activities would address all areas of human diversity. This includes age, gender, economic class, culture, race, disability, body size, and sexual orientation.

Diversity activities are usually the easiest activities for teachers to plan and implement with children. Most teachers are used to helping children explore the concepts of alike and different. Look for more diversity activity ideas in the following books:

The Affective Curriculum: Teaching the Anti-Bias Approach to Young Children, by Nadia Saderman Hall and Valerie Rhomberg (Nelson Canada, 1995).

Creative Resources for the Anti-Bias Classroom, by Nadia Saderman Hall (Delmar, 1999).

Mixing Playdough

THEMES I'm Me and I'm Special, Alike and Different, Colors, Five Senses, Light and Dark, Bodies, Changes

OBJECTIVES Explore similarities and differences

Appreciate the physical characteristics of others

MATERIALS Mixing bowls, measuring cups, measuring spoons, large spoon for stirring, flour, salt, alum, oil, powder tempera paint or paste food coloring

DESCRIPTION With the children, prepare five batches of playdough, one in each of the following colors: black, brown, red, yellow, white. Use this recipe or one you're familiar with.

> *Playdough*
>
> 2 cups flour
>
> 1 cup salt
>
> 2 tablespoons alum
>
> 1 1/2 cups warm water
>
> 1 tablespoon oil
>
> paste food coloring or powder tempera paint

Mix one to three tablespoons of powder tempera with the liquid ingredients. Add mixture to the dry ingredients and stir. Knead until smooth. Store in an airtight container.

Tell the children there are five different colors of playdough and they can make different colors by mixing two or three colors together. For example, combining red playdough with white playdough will make pink playdough. Ask the children to look at the color of their skin. Encourage them to mix different colors of playdough so that their ball of playdough matches their skin color. As the children experiment with combining the playdough, talk with them about the concepts of new colors, shades of color, and lighter and darker.

VARIATIONS 1. Make a recipe chart that shows how to mix colors.

2. Put each child's ball of skin-colored playdough in a plastic bag and allow them to take it home.

3. During group time, see if the children can order the balls of playdough from light to dark.

4. Leave the five colors of playdough out on the art shelf for two weeks so that children can continue to experiment with mixing colors to match their skin color.

Fingerpaint Mix-Up

THEMES I'm Me and I'm Special, Changes, Alike and Different, Five Senses, Light and Dark, Bodies

OBJECTIVES Explore similarities and differences

Develop positive attitudes toward human differences

MATERIALS Liquid starch; black, brown, red, yellow, and white powder tempera paint; fingerpaint paper; paint smocks; small plastic bowls; teaspoons

DESCRIPTION Put a small amount of each color of powdered tempera paint into separate bowls and set them out on a table with a teaspoon in each. Show the children the five colors of paint. Ask the children to look at their skin colors. Prompt discussion of the difference between the paint colors and skin colors by asking them questions such as, "Are those paint colors the same colors as the skin of any of the children around the table?" "How are they different?" "What do you think will happen if you mix the colors together?" or "How could you use these colors of paint to mix paint that's the same color as your skin?" Give each child a piece of fingerpaint paper and pour about three tablespoons of liquid starch onto the paper (or allow them to mix paint directly on the table). Tell the children they can spoon a little bit of the powdered tempera onto their papers or onto the table and mix the colors and starch together with their fingers. Encourage the children to mix the colors to make fingerpaint that matches their skin color. Compare the color of the fingerpaint with each child's skin color and help them figure out how to mix paint that matches their skin color by asking them questions or making comments such as, "Is the paint darker or lighter than your skin color?" "What color do you think you need more of to make the paint match your skin?" or "Hmm, that paint *is* pinker than you are, isn't it?"

VARIATIONS 1. After the painting has dried, encourage the children to draw a face on their artwork.

2. Allow the children to fingerpaint directly on the table. When they are finished, lay a piece of paper on top of the area. Press down and lift the paper off quickly, making a print of the finger painting. This gives children a chance to freely experiment without using up a lot of paper.

Use Lakeshore's people-color paints.

Skin-Color Match-Ups

THEMES I'm Me and I'm Special, Alike and Different, Colors, Clothes We Wear, Light and Dark, Bodies

OBJECTIVES Explore similarities and differences

Understand that all people are similar to and different from one another

MATERIALS Collection of nylon knee-hi stockings in many shades of tan, black, white, pink, yellow, and red.

DESCRIPTION Set out the collection of stockings at the discovery table or introduce them to the children at group time. Tell the children you have stockings in many different shades of brown and some stockings in other colors. Encourage the children to try them on their hands and arms or their feet and legs. Ask these questions to help the children increase their awareness of skin color: "Can you find a stocking that is the same color as your skin?" "What color is that stocking you have on your arm?" "Try the _____ stocking. Is it lighter or darker than your own skin?"

VARIATIONS 1. Set out the stockings in the dramatic play area.

2. Have children match the same-colored stockings to make a pair.

3. Have the children order the stockings from light to dark.

4. Talk about how no one's skin color is purely white, pink, yellow, or red.

Light and Dark

THEMES Alike and Different, Colors, Light and Dark, Bodies

OBJECTIVES Explore similarities and differences

Appreciate physical characteristics of others

Understand that all people are similar to and different from one another

MATERIALS Colors Around Us study prints (available through Afro-American Publishing company) or your own set of pictures of people with different skin colors, easel, easel paper, paintbrushes, four shades of the same color paint (preferably brown).

DESCRIPTION During group time, show children the pictures of people with different skin color. Tell the children to look at their skin. Ask questions such as: "Is your skin light or dark?" "Does it ever get darker than it is now?" "Does it ever get lighter?" Also ask the children if they know how to make a color darker or how to make a color lighter. Show them the four containers of paint. Talk about how each container holds a different shade of the color brown. Ask, "Which one is the lightest?" and "Which one is the darkest?" Tell the children that they can experiment with the light and dark shades of paint at the easel during free choice play.

VARIATIONS 1. Use paint swatches instead of a picture set.

2. Older children can experiment with mixing shades of paint for use at the easel. Have them choose a color and slowly add white paint to create lighter shades. This gives children the experience of beginning with dark and changing it to light. (Note: A child may express discomfort by saying, "I want a lighter color." Consider this response: "Are you wanting your skin to be lighter? What do you like about light-colored skin?" Once you discover what the child is responding to, you can provide accurate information.)

What Color Are You?

THEMES	Colors, Bodies, I'm Me and I'm Special, Our Community
OBJECTIVES	Explore similarities and differences
	Appreciate physical attributes of others
	Develop positive attitudes toward human differences
MATERIALS	Pictures of people from a variety of racial groups (or the "Colors Around Us" study prints)
DESCRIPTION	Hold up one picture at a time. Ask questions such as: "Who can tell me about this picture?" "Who is this person?" "Is this person a boy or a girl?" "How do you know?" "What color is this person's skin?" "What color is their hair?" "Where do you think this person lives?" Write down the children's answers. Make a bulletin board display by posting the pictures along with the children's descriptions.
VARIATION	Mix up the pictures and lay them face down. Select a child to come up and choose a picture from the pile. Ask the child to show it to the class and describe the person in the picture.

Draw Me/Draw You

THEMES	I'm Me and I'm Special, Friends, Alike and Different, Five Senses
OBJECTIVES	Appreciate the beauty and value of others
	Appreciate the physical characteristics of others
	Experience positive, respectful interactions with people who are different
MATERIALS	Drawing paper, felt-tip pens, crayons
DESCRIPTION	Have the children find a partner and ask them to sit across from one another at the table. Encourage the children to draw a picture of their partner's face. Ask them to look at their partner. Then ask: "What color is his skin? What color are her eyes? Does he have freckles? What color is her hair? How long is his hair? Is her hair straight or curly?" The drawing probably won't look like the partner. That's all right—looking at the features of another person is the important part. Ask the children to exchange the drawings when they are done.
VARIATIONS	1. Have the children describe themselves to each other before they begin drawing.
	2. Have the children share their drawings with the class at group time.
	3. Play a guessing game during group time. Have the children look at the drawing and guess who it is.

Thumbprints

THEMES   I'm Me and I'm Special, Alike and Different, Five Senses, Bodies, Our Community

OBJECTIVES   Understand that all people are similar to and different from one another

Recognize that human differences make people unique and special

MATERIALS   White paper (3- by 5-inch cards), black ink pad, pen, magnifying glass

DESCRIPTION   Encourage the children to make prints of their thumbs by pressing them on the ink pad and then on the paper. Label each print with the child's name. At group time, show the children the prints. Talk about how everyone has patterns of lines on the skin of their fingers, how each person has a different pattern, and how each person's fingerprints are different from everyone else's. No two are alike. Set out the prints and a magnifying glass on the table so the children can examine the similarities and differences in the fingerprints.

VARIATION   Make two sets of prints for each child. Mix them up and see if the children can match them.

Hair

THEMES   I'm Me and I'm Special, Boys and Girls, Alike and Different, Clothes We Wear, Bodies

OBJECTIVES   Appreciate the beauty and value of others

Appreciate the physical characteristics of others

Learn about similarities and differences

MATERIALS   Pictures of a variety of people with different hairstyles, a hand mirror, empty hair-care containers, wigs, scarves, turbans, rubber bands, hair clips, combs, old hair dryers, old curling irons, old crimping irons

DESCRIPTION   Show pictures of different hairstyles to the children. Ask them to touch their hair. Talk about how hair has texture and curl; how some people have fine hair and some people have coarse hair. Some people have straight hair and other people have curly hair. Pass around the mirror so that children can look at their hair. Talk about how people differ in the color and length of their hair. Set out hair-care materials in the dramatic play area for children to use during free choice play.

VARIATION   As an introduction to the activity, read the book *Cornrows*, by C. Yarbrough (New York: Putnam, 1979).

Photo Masks

THEMES   I'm Me and I'm Special, Boys and Girls, Friends, Changes, Alike and Different, Feelings

OBJECTIVES   Experience human diversity

Appreciate human diversity

MATERIALS   Close-up photographs of people's faces (choose people in your center that exemplify a variety of differences), rubber cement, poster board, hole punch, scissors, string

DESCRIPTION   Have the photos enlarged to 8 by 10 inches. Cut out the photo around the hair and face. Mount the photo on poster board using rubber cement. Punch a hole on both sides above the ear. Tie a 12-inch piece of string through each hole. Introduce the masks at group time. Set them out on a "discovery table" with a mirror, or in the dramatic play area. Observe the children and notice their conversations as they try on different masks.

VARIATIONS   Record the children's voices or write down what they say as they take on other people's identities. (Adapted from *Constructive Play*, Forman and Hill, 1984.)

Face Puzzles

THEMES   I'm Me and I'm Special, Bodies, Alike and Different, Friends

OBJECTIVES   Appreciate the physical characteristics of others

Develop positive attitudes toward human differences

MATERIALS   Camera, film, rubber cement, poster board or foam core, mat knife, pencil, ruler

DESCRIPTION   Take a close-up photo of each child's face. Have the photos enlarged to 8 by 10 inches. Glue the photo to the foam core and let dry. Using a ruler, mark off the photo in fourths, vertically and horizontally. With a pencil, lightly draw lines for cutting out the pieces. This results in sixteen 2-inch squares. Cut out the pieces with the mat knife and put the child's name or initials on the back of each piece. During group time, give the pieces to each child in a plastic bag. Encourage them to try to put together their face puzzle. As they work on their own puzzle, talk about where the eyes, nose, and mouth are located on a person's face. When children have completed their puzzle, ask them to hold up the piece that shows their mouth. Talk about how each person's mouth is different. Continue with the other facial features.

VARIATIONS   1. Combine three or four puzzles. Have children unscramble them and make the correct faces.

2. Set out the puzzle pieces in a tub and let children freely explore putting the pieces together to create different faces.

Line Up

THEMES   Bodies, I'm Me and I'm Special, Friends, Alike and Different

OBJECTIVES   Learn about similarities and differences

Recognize that the class is made up of many different people

MATERIALS   Large sheet of butcher paper, masking tape, felt-tip marker, crayons

DESCRIPTION   Tape the butcher paper to a wall or fence. Have the entire class line up next to one another with their backs to the paper. Draw around their bodies with a felt-tip pen. The children can stand away from the wall as soon as you finish tracing their body. They'll enjoy looking at their outline as well as watching you trace the rest of the class. When finished, encourage the children to look at the mural. Can they recognize each person's outline? How do they know? Distribute crayons or markers, and encourage the children to draw their face, color in their skin and hair, and decorate their clothes. Display the mural in the hallway or classroom.

VARIATION   As a group, decide how each person's body should be colored in.

Felt Friends

THEMES   I'm Me and I'm Special, Bodies, Boys and Girls, Alike and Different, Families, Colors, Feelings, Clothes We Wear

OBJECTIVES   Develop positive attitudes toward human differences

Recognize that the class is made up of many different types of people

Increase comfort with human diversity

MATERIALS   Felt squares in a variety of skin colors, gingerbread-person cookie cutter, scissors, fine black felt-tip marker, assorted felt scraps, flannelboard

DESCRIPTION   Show children the different colors of felt and tell them that you are going to make a felt doll for each of them to use on the flannelboard. Say, "Pick the color of felt that is most like the color of your skin."

Use the cookie cutter to trace the doll on the felt and cut it out. Write the child's name on the back of the doll. Make clothes for the dolls out of the felt scraps. Introduce the dolls to the class during a group time. See if the children can match the doll with the child. Set the dolls and the flannelboard out during free play.

VARIATIONS   1. Make a small flannelboard for each child.

2. Cut out, mount, and laminate magazine illustrations to make scenery and props to use with the felt friends.

3. Make a felt doll to represent each family member.

People Paper Dolls

THEMES   I'm Me and I'm Special, Boys and Girls, Friends, Bodies, Alike and Different, Feelings

OBJECTIVES Experience positive, respectful interactions with people who are different

Recognize that our class and community are made up of many different types of people

MATERIALS   Camera, film, cardboard, half-round molding (1-inch diameter), mat knife, saw, rubber cement

DESCRIPTION Take a full-length picture of each child. Have it enlarged so that it measures 10 inches high. Mount the photo on cardboard and cut it out with a mat knife. Cut a short piece (2 inches) of molding and saw a groove in the rounded side for a stand. Slide the paper doll into the groove. Set out the dolls in the block area or with the doll house. Encourage children to create situations and dramas with their dolls.

VARIATIONS 1. Use the dolls to act out conflicts between children.

2. Make dolls of people from different cultures.

3. Make a doll for each member of a family.

Family Photos

THEMES   Families, Changes, Alike and Different, Clothes We Wear, Bodies

OBJECTIVE   Recognize ways people grow and change

MATERIALS   Photographs of children's parents, photographs of each child, resealable plastic bags

DESCRIPTION Collect photos from the parents, assuring them that they will be returned in a week or two. This activity may bring up questions about different types of families (single parent, gay/lesbian, and blended families). Put them in individual resealable plastic bags for safekeeping. Tell the children they are going to play a guessing game and that you are going to set out the photos of parents for all the children to see. But everyone must be quiet and not tell the others which photo is of their parent. Give each child the photo of herself to hold. One by one, ask the children to come up in front of the group with their pictures. Encourage the child to show the photo to the class. Then ask the class to look at the photos of parents. Ask, "Who can guess which photo is of _____'s parents?"

Encourage the children to notice hair color, skin color, and other physical similarities. When a correct match has been made, place the child's photo next to the one of the parents. After everyone has had a turn, encourage the children to look at all the pictures. Ask the children, "What do you think you will look like when you grow up?" Talk about how children get their skin color and physical looks from their biological parents. Also talk about how many of our physical characteristics such as skin color and eye color stay the same as we grow older.

VARIATIONS 1. You may need to vary this activity if you have adopted or multiracial children in your group. Ask parents how they explain the origin of skin color and physical features to their children.

2. Set out the photos for the children to look at and match on their own.

3. Make a bulletin board display of the photographs at the children's eye level.

4. Make a class book of children's families.

5. Repeat the activity with baby pictures and current photographs of each child.

Washing

THEMES	Changes, Colors, Bodies, Five Senses, Light and Dark
OBJECTIVE	Help children discover that skin color is a physical characteristic that does not wash off
MATERIALS	Brown fingerpaint or mud, sink or water table with soapy water, towels
DESCRIPTION	Encourage the children to fingerpaint. Talk about the brown paint on the children's hands. Notice how it looks on different colors of skin. Ask: "What will happen to your skin when you wash your hands?" "Will you wash off your skin color?" "Does it make a difference if your skin is light or dark?" Talk about how skin color doesn't wash off and how it always stays the same.
VARIATIONS	1. Read the book *The Marvelous Mud Washing Machine,* by Patty Wolcott (New York: Scholastic Books, 1974).
	2. Experiment with washing dolls, rocks, and other objects.
	3. Make a list of things that keep their color when washed and things that lose their color when washed.

Same As Me

THEMES	Alike and Different, Our Community, Bodies, Friends
OBJECTIVES	Learn about similarities and differences
	Develop positive attitudes toward similarities and differences
MATERIALS	One large piece of paper, felt-tip marker
DESCRIPTION	Display the paper on a wall. Ask the children to look around at all of the people in the classroom. Say: "Look at their faces and look at their bodies. Let's see if we can name all of the ways we are like one another." Ask the group: "What is one way that our bodies are the same?" Ask an individual child: "Kimong, what is one way that your body is the same as Asumpta's body?" Write the children's answers on the paper. When the list is complete, show the children pictures of people from other cultures. Ask the children: "How is this person like you?"
VARIATION	Repeat the activity, focusing on differences.

Which One Is Different?

THEMES	Alike and Different, Boys and Girls, Bodies, Colors, Places People Live, Toys and Games, Clothes We Wear, Food We Eat
OBJECTIVES	Appreciate the physical characteristics of others
	Notice human similarities and differences
MATERIALS	Strips of oak tag or poster board (4 by 20 inches), magazine pictures, rubber cement, clear self-adhesive paper
DESCRIPTION	For each strip, draw or glue on four pictures that are similar, discarding the one that is different. Here are some examples:

1. Four pictures of African American children
2. Four pictures of Hispanic American children
3. Four pictures of different Asian American children
4. Four pictures of European American children

Start with pictures that show obvious differences. Later, add pictures with less distinct differences. Encourage the children to see if they can find both similarities and differences among the pictures. Ask the child to find the ways in which the people in the picture are alike.

VARIATIONS	1. Older children can make their own "alike" and "different" picture strips.

2. Trace appropriate drawings or pictures of people. Duplicate them on a copying machine and color them.
3. Use picture strips of objects such as Native American baskets or pottery.

Sound Choice

THEMES	I'm Me and I'm Special, Boys and Girls, Friends, Five Senses, Alike and Different
OBJECTIVES	Recognize that human differences make people unique and special
	Appreciate people who are different
MATERIALS	Cassette tape recorder, blank cassette tape
DESCRIPTION	Tape the children's voices one at a time. With a small group of children play the tape and see if they can guess whose voice they hear on the cassette tape. Ask them how they know who it was.
VARIATIONS	1. Blindfold children and see if they can identify their friends by the sound of their voices.

2. Tape parents and staff, in addition to children.
3. Make a tape of people speaking in different languages and accents. Include someone speaking languages of the cultures represented in your program or community.

Match-Ups

THEMES   Families, Our Community, Alike and Different, Places People Live, Toys and Games, Transportation, Clothes We Wear, Food We Eat, Holidays and Celebrations

OBJECTIVES   Recognize some of the cultural groups within the United States

Recognize that people do things in different ways

MATERIALS   Photographs of people from various cultures, actual objects from each culture or a photograph of common objects, rubber cement, oak tag or poster board, fine felt-tip marker

DESCRIPTION   Make five sets of matching cards by cutting out ten oak tag rectangles that are 4 by 6 inches. Draw or glue a photograph of a person onto one of the cards and an object from that person's culture on the other card. Use current examples and avoid pictures of people in their native costumes. Show children the pictures of the objects. Talk about how people use these things. Show children the pictures of the people. Talk about where these people come from and how they live. Place the cards face up in two sets: objects and people. Tell the children that one of the objects matches one of the people. Encourage the children to match a person with an object. Choose people and objects that the children are already familiar with. Note, however, that you should not use this activity to introduce a culture.

Daily Life and Celebrations

THEMES   Alike and Different, Folk Tales, Dance and Movement, Clothes We Wear, Holidays and Celebrations

OBJECTIVES   Learn about similarities and differences

Learn about the cultures of the other children in the class

MATERIALS   Manila file folder, 4- by 6-inch or 5- by 8-inch index cards, 5- by 8-inch manila clasp envelope, felt-tip markers, clear self-adhesive paper, magazine pictures, rubber cement

DESCRIPTION   Make a file folder game for children to sort pictures of people into two categories: everyday life and celebrations. Open up the file folder. Label the left side "Everyday Life" and affix magazine pictures that represent everyday life. Label the right side "Celebrations" and affix magazine pictures that show people celebrating special occasions. Collect twenty pictures of people of different cultures in daily life activities (wearing street clothes, living in the here and now) and celebrating special events (wearing ethnic costumes). Glue each picture to an index card. Write the culture and the event on the back of the card. Cover both the file folder and the index cards with clear self-adhesive paper. Attach the small manila envelope to the outside of the file folder with a metal fastener. Store the cards in the envelope. Introduce the game to the children during a group time and set it out for the children to use during free play.

VARIATION   Play the game as a group with each child taking a turn and the others watching.

Guess Who?

THEMES   Bodies, Five Senses, Friends, Alike and Different

OBJECTIVES   Appreciate physical characteristics of others

Develop positive attitudes toward human differences

MATERIALS   Scarf or mask for a blindfold

DESCRIPTION   Introduce this activity by talking with the children about the ways in which people are different from one another. For example, our hair is different. The shape and size of people's eyes, nose, and mouth are different. When we use our eyes, we see that people look different from one another. We can also know that people are different by feeling their face and body with our hands. Tell the children they can play a guessing game. One person is blindfolded and tries to identify children by touching and feeling. Ask: "How did you know?" when a child guesses the identity of a classmate.

VARIATION   Have children feel their own faces and bodies before the game begins.

We're All Human

THEMES   Boys and Girls, Friends, Families, Alike and Different, Places People Live

OBJECTIVES   Learn about the cultures of other children

Understand that all people are similar to and different from one another

Feel empathy for others

MATERIALS   Pictures of children from around the world in everyday settings, books about children from other cultures

DESCRIPTION   Display the pictures on a bulletin board near the book corner or group area. Show the children the pictures and talk about them. Read two stories about children from other cultures. Say: "People live in many different places. People have different-colored skin and different colors of eyes. But in many important ways, we are all alike." Ask the children if they can think of some ways that they are like the children in the story. Children's answers may include: "We have mommies and daddies, go to sleep, play, go to school, eat, wear clothes, have families, go to work, cry, get sad." End the group discussion by talking about how people are alike even though they look different and live in different places.

Group Tree

THEMES   I'm Me and I'm Special, Friends, Our Community, Alike and Different

OBJECTIVES   Recognize that our community is made up of many different types of people

Name some of the racial and cultural groups that make up the United States

MATERIALS   Five dead tree branches, five large coffee cans, sand or plaster of paris, magazines, scissors, glue, construction paper, hole punch, yarn, photographs of each child and staff members

DESCRIPTION   Make five "trees" by securing each branch in a can filled with sand or plaster of paris. Let the plaster of paris dry and harden. Bring the trees to group time. Introduce them by explaining the concept of a group: groups are more than two people, a family is a group, and our class is a group. Each of the trees is like a group: there is a tree for African Americans, Hispanics, Asians, Native Americans, and European Americans. One by one, show the class a photo of each child and staff member. As a group, decide which tree to hang the photo on. If the class is not multicultural and some of the trees are bare, talk about how no children from these ethnic groups are in your class, but these people do live in your city and go to another school. Tell the children there will be magazines, scissors, glue, and construction paper out in the art area during free choice time. The children can cut out pictures of people and hang them on the appropriate tree. Leave the trees out for a few weeks so that children can continue to add pictures.

VARIATION   Make group posters instead of "trees."

Try It, You'll Like It

THEMES   I'm Me and I'm Special, Changes, Alike and Different

OBJECTIVE   Develop an openness to new experiences

MATERIALS   Selection of foods that may be unfamiliar to children (kiwi, mango, papaya, pomegranate, jicama, date), knife, napkins

DESCRIPTION   Introduce the activity by telling the children you brought some foods that may be new to them. Ask them if they can think of ways to get to know these foods. Answers might include, "We could touch them, smell them, taste them, hold them, look inside them." Focus the conversation, keeping an open mind and trying new things. Ask the children what would happen if you said "Yucky" and walked away? Explain how we miss out on a lot when we are afraid or don't like new things. Encourage the children to explore the foods with their senses. Cut open the fruit and let the children taste the different foods. Talk about other things that may be new or different in their lives.

Just Like Me

THEMES   Alike and Different, I'm Me and I'm Special, Friends, Bodies

OBJECTIVES   Recognize human similarities and differences

Develop a positive attitude toward human similarities and differences

MATERIALS   A mirror and a variety of pictures of people that represent different cultures, gender, hair color, eye color

DESCRIPTION   Display the pictures on a wall or table. Ask the children one at a time to pick out all of the pictures of people who look like them. If a child seems unsure, encourage him to look in the mirror. Describe the child's physical characteristics. Then ask, "Do you see any pictures of people with skin color and hair like yours?" Pick out all of the pictures and show them to the child. Talk about the common features between the people in the pictures and the child.

VARIATIONS   1. Have the children pick out pictures of people who are not like them.

2. Ask the children to find a partner. Encourage the children to look at their partner and find pictures of people who look like their partner.

Who Is Missing?

THEMES   Our Community, Alike and Different, Friends, Five Senses

OBJECTIVE   Help children recall members of a group

MATERIALS   A picture of a boy and girl from each of the following groups: African American, Hispanic, Asian, Native American, and European American; or a set of multicultural dolls

DESCRIPTION   Set all of the pictures face up for the children to see. Pick up the pictures, shuffle them, take out one, and lay down the rest for the children to see. Ask the children to look at the pictures and guess which one is missing. The child who guesses correctly may shuffle the pictures, pull out one, and lay out the pictures again.

VARIATIONS   1. Do the same activity with dolls.

2. Play a memory/matching game by setting out the pictures face down. Have each child take a turn by turning over two cards for all to see. If there is no match (a boy and girl from the same culture), then the cards are put back in their places face down. A child who makes a match may keep the pictures.

Classroom Scrapbook

THEMES   Friends, Books, Holidays and Celebrations, Our Community

OBJECTIVES   Provide a visual and written record of the year's classroom events

Help children learn about remembering past events through pictures and words

MATERIALS   Large three-ring binder or bound scrapbook, camera, and film

DESCRIPTION   Use the scrapbook as you would a diary, capturing the celebrations, special events, field trips, visitors, and multicultural activities that go on through the year. The scrapbook must include and represent everyone in the class. Keep a camera handy at all times to take pictures. Children can contribute by dictating their own experiences of classroom activities and drawing pictures.

VARIATIONS   1. Allow children and families to check out the book and take it home.

2. Leave it out on the bookshelf, and encourage children to "read" the stories and retell the events to others.

Family Tree

THEMES   I'm Me and I'm Special, Families, Alike and Different

OBJECTIVE   Help children understand that every family is different

MATERIALS   A photograph of each child's family, a large piece of butcher paper, a felt-tip marker

DESCRIPTION   Display the family photos on a bulletin board in the classroom. Together with the children, count the number of people in each child's family. Make a chart showing how many people are in each family. Who has the most people in their family? Who has the smallest number of people in their family? Look at the photographs again. Ask the children to name the family members (mother, father, sister, aunt, grandmother). Write down all of the names a child uses to describe family members. Talk about the many different ways of being a family. Some families are small and some are large. Families differ in who lives together and the names they call their members. Include culture when appropriate. For example, Anna's family is German and she calls her aunts "Tante."

Houses

THEMES	Places People Live, Families, Alike and Different, Our Community
OBJECTIVES	Help children understand that families live in different kinds of dwellings
MATERIALS	Pictures of different types of dwellings: homes, apartment buildings, high-rises, houseboats, huts, trailers, tents, cabins, cottages
DESCRIPTION	Show children the pictures of different types of houses in which families live. Ask each child to talk about what kind of house their family lives in. Display the pictures in the block area and encourage the children to build different types of houses during free choice time.
VARIATIONS	1. Set out boxes and a variety of art materials so that the children can make houses.
	2. Take a picture of each child's house or ask the parents to bring in a picture of their child's house.
	3. As a class, make a house collage by cutting and pasting pictures of dwellings onto a large sheet of butcher paper.

Smelling Jars

THEMES	Five Senses, Alike and Different
OBJECTIVES	Help children develop their awareness through smell
	Introduce children to the smells of other cultures
MATERIALS	Small containers such as margarine tubs, baby food jars, or film containers; a variety of spices, incense, or essential oils (such as ginger, coriander, anise, five-spice powder, garlic, sesame oil, cilantro, cumin, hot pepper sauce, cardamom, sandalwood, patchouli)
DESCRIPTION	Place one ingredient in each container. Tell the children you have some things for them to smell. Say, "Some of these smells will be familiar. You may have smelled them before at your house. Some of the smells will be new to you." Ask the children to close their eyes and smell the contents of each container. Encourage the children to guess the smell. Talk about how people all over the world use different spices for cooking and have different smells in their homes. Ask the children which ones they like the best.
VARIATIONS	1. Make two sets of smelling containers and see if the children can match them.
	2. Do a cooking project with some of the spices used in this activity.
	3. Make picture labels to go with the smelling jars.

My Family Comes from . . .

THEMES   Families, Changes, Places People Live, Books

OBJECTIVE   Help children understand that every family comes from another place and every family has a cultural heritage

MATERIALS   Colored construction paper (12 by 18 inches), hole punch, yarn, felt-tip pen, photographs of children's families

DESCRIPTION   Make a book for each child to record her family history and culture. Include photographs of grandparents and extended family members. The book could also include information such as which family members came to the United States, what countries they came from, languages spoken at home, simple words in their family's home language, favorite ethnic foods, and ethnic customs practiced at home.

VARIATION   Collect information about families by asking parents to fill out a family questionnaire. (See chapter 6.)

Multicultural Feast

THEMES   Food People Eat, Holidays and Celebrations, Friends, Alike and Different, Families

OBJECTIVE   Expose children to other types of food and give them an opportunity to share their culture with others

MATERIALS   Tables, chairs, eating utensils, plates, and napkins

DESCRIPTION   Send a note home with the children announcing a special multicultural feast. Ask that each child bring a dish from their family's native culture to share with the rest of the class. This activity works well at Thanksgiving, Christmas, or at the end of the year when children and families have experienced their culture through many other activities.

VARIATIONS   1. Invite parents to join the children at the feast.

    2. Ask parents for the recipe of their ethnic dish. Make a cookbook and distribute it to all the families.

    3. Adapt the recipes so that they can be included in the center's daily food service program.

Slide Show

THEMES Places People Live, Transportation, Clothes We Wear, Friends, Families

OBJECTIVE Help children develop an awareness of and empathy for people from other parts of the world

MATERIALS Slide projector; screen; and slides of children, families, family dwellings, and towns from different parts of the world

DESCRIPTION Early childhood programs often show films or videos one day a week or when the weather prevents children from going outside. Use this time to expose the children to children and families that live far away. Put together your own multicultural slide show using slides from trips and vacations. Select and duplicate slides of people, children, and families involved in everyday activities such as bathing, eating, cooking, playing, sleeping, and working. Avoid slides that focus on places of interest or famous buildings. If you have not traveled, ask to make copies of slides from friends who have traveled out of the country. If you know someone who is going on a trip, you might buy them a roll of slide film and ask them to take pictures for you.

VARIATIONS 1. Make a slide show of people who live in the city or people who live in the country.

2. Make up stories about the lives of the children and families.

3. Go to local ethnic communities that the children may not have an opportunity to learn about (local migrant camp, local reservation, nearest metropolitan area).

4. Visit a multicultural child care center as a source of photographs.

Breads

THEMES Food We Eat, Alike and Different, Five Senses, Holidays and Celebrations

OBJECTIVE Help children experience different types of bread

MATERIALS Samples of various types of bread (cornbread, tortillas, Mexican sweet bread, matzo, rusk, lefse, pita bread, steamed buns, chapatis, scones, black bread, fry bread, piki bread)

DESCRIPTION Plan a bread-tasting party for snack time. Talk with the children about how some people from other cultures eat different kinds of bread. Introduce the different breads. Ask the children if they have ever eaten any of them before. Give each child a sample to try. Talk about the name of the bread and where it comes from. Follow up the activity with stories about bread or baking bread for another snack.

VARIATIONS 1. Find out what kinds of bread the families from your class eat and use them for exploring different types of breads.

2. Visit an ethnic bakery.

3. Set out jars with different grains and flours and talk about the fact that people eat bread that they make from the grains that they grow. People living in different places grow different grains and make different kinds of bread.

What Do You See?

THEMES   Places People Live, Transportation, Books, Friends, Alike and Different, Families, Feelings

OBJECTIVE   Help children use expressive language and explore their perceptions of people from other cultures

MATERIALS   A large picture book, pictures of contemporary people from other cultures engaged in everyday activities, large sheets of paper, felt-tip pen

DESCRIPTION   Read the story to the children, emphasizing how the pictures show us what is happening in the story. Hold up one of the pictures for the children to see. Ask the children "What do you think is happening in this picture?" Encourage the children to tell a story about the people in the picture. Write their stories down on the paper. Display the picture and written stories in the book area.

VARIATIONS   1. Stack the pictures face down and invite a child to pick a picture. Encourage the child to make up a story from looking at the picture.

     2. Choose one picture and ask each child in the group to say what they think is happening in the picture.

Face Masks

THEMES   I'm Me and I'm Special, Friends, Families, Changes, Alike and Different, Colors, Folk Tales, Light and Dark, Bodies

OBJECTIVES   Help children explore and express their feelings about differences of skin color through creative dramatics

MATERIALS   Poster board, tempera paint, clear self-adhesive paper, scissors, wax crayons, paper towels

DESCRIPTION   Cut four to six masks out of poster board. Paint each mask a different shade of tan to correspond with the skin colors represented in the classroom. When the masks are dry, cover both sides with clear self-adhesive paper. Introduce the masks during group time. Tell the children that they may take the masks, draw faces on them, and use them during free play. Show them how to wipe off the crayon "face" with a paper towel when they are done or want to change the expression. Encourage the children to form small groups to use the masks in their dramatic play.

VARIATIONS   1. Use the masks to tell a story or retell a discriminatory incident in the classroom. Change roles by switching masks.

     2. Set out full-length mirrors so that children can see themselves.

Goal 3 Activities

BIAS ACTIVITIES ARE likely to be the most unfamiliar to you. Rarely have early childhood teachers talked with their children about bias, much less planned and implemented activities to prevent or reduce biased attitudes. Goal three activities differ from diversity activities in that they rely much less on teaching materials. You can set out multicultural dolls, posters, books, and art materials to help children increase their comfort level with diversity. You can't just set out non-stereotypic and stereotypic materials and expect children to figure out what is fair and what is unfair. So bias activities rely much more on the adult.

In order for these types of activities to be effective, we need a teacher who is willing to open his or her mouth and talk about bias with children. So in many ways, you are the most important element in these types of activities.

Here are sources for additional bias activities:

Kids Like Us: Using Persona Dolls in the Classroom, by Trisha Whitney (Redleaf Press, 1999).

Start Seeing Diversity, by Ellen Wolpert (Redleaf Press, 1999).

Real and Pretend

THEMES   Feelings, Holidays and Celebrations

OBJECTIVE   Help children tell the difference between real people and discriminatory pretend images of people

MATERIALS   Manila file folder, 4- by 6-inch or 5- by 8-inch index cards, 5- by-8 inch manila clasp envelope, felt-tip markers, clear self-adhesive paper, magazine pictures, greeting cards, rubber cement, metal fastener

DESCRIPTION Make a manila file folder game. Label one side of the folder "Real" and the other side "Pretend." Underneath each word, glue pictures to illustrate the concept. Make a number of cards (sixteen or more) with actual pictures of people from various cultures. On an equal number of the cards, glue cartoons and other pretend images of people (such as animals wearing a feather head dress or a sombrero). Introduce the game by asking questions such as, "How do you know if something is real?" "How do you know if a person is real?" "How do you know if something is pretend?" Talk about pretend pictures of people, and how it can be hard to tell if the person in the picture is real. Some pictures make animals look like people. Encourage the children to look at the picture cards and see if they can sort them. (Adapted from *Anti-Bias Curriculum,* by Louise Derman-Sparks, 1989.)

VARIATION   Tell the children that when animals are dressed up to look like people they are really making fun of people. Say, "These pretend pictures hurt people's feelings and make people mad because they are not true."

Victim Aid

THEMES   Friends, Feelings

OBJECTIVES   Help children recognize unfair behavior when it occurs

Help children recognize that name-calling hurts

MATERIALS   Adhesive bandage strips

DESCRIPTION Intervene every time a child is discriminated against either by name-calling or because of physical characteristics. Bring the children together. Ask the victim, "How does it feel to be called _____?" Talk about how name-calling makes us sad, and it hurts our feelings. Ask the victim what he would like to say to the child making discriminatory remarks, and ask the child how you can help. Give the child an adhesive bandage strip for their "owie" and tell the child they can put it anywhere on their body they want.

How Would You Feel If . . .?

THEMES　　Friends, Feelings, Our Class

OBJECTIVES　Help children recognize that some people treat others unfairly because of differences

Help children recognize that name-calling, teasing, and rejecting hurts

Help children put themselves in another person's situation

MATERIALS　Oak tag, scissors, metal fastener, fine-tip marker, multicultural photographs or pictures of people in various everyday settings

DESCRIPTION　Cut an 8-inch circle out of oak tag. Divide the circle into six sections. In each section, draw one face to represent each of the following emotions: happy, sad, afraid, angry, ashamed, and proud. Label the drawings. Make a spinner by cutting an arrow out of the oak tag and attaching it to the center of the circle with the metal fastener. Show the child one of the teaching pictures and tell them a simple story about what is happening in the picture. Example: Two boys, Jake and Tacoumba, are painting at the easel. Jake looks around to see what Tacoumba is painting. He says, "You're not my friend. You yucky. You muddy." Ask the children, "How do you think Tacoumba felt when Jake said he was muddy because he is black? How would you feel if someone called you muddy?" Pass the spinner around so that each child can make the spinner point to the picture and show the other children how they would feel in this situation.

VARIATION　Discuss actual situations from your classroom using the spinner.

Fair and Unfair

THEMES　　Friends, Feelings, Heroes and Sheroes, My People

OBJECTIVES　Help children begin to recognize stereotypes

Help children compare fair and unfair

MATERIALS　"Feeling box" or paper sack; collection of actual ethnic objects; pictures that accurately portray people from other cultures; stereotypical objects such as greeting cards, cartoons, holiday decorations, and small toy figures

DESCRIPTION　Mount the pictures on oak tag. Place the pictures and objects in the "feeling box" or a paper sack. Tell the children they can play a guessing game about the many things inside of the "feeling box." Say some of the things are pretend pictures of people. These unfair pictures make people look stupid and silly. They make people sad and seeing them hurts their feelings. These pictures are unfair because what they show is not true. Other pictures and objects in the box are fair because they show people as they really are. Seeing fair pictures makes people happy and proud. Encourage children to close their eyes as they put their hand inside the box. Continue to talk about the concepts of unfair and fair as children pull an item from the box. (Adapted from Louise Derman-Sparks, *Anti-Bias Curriculum*, 1989.)

VARIATIONS　1. Put all of the pictures and objects into two piles: fair and unfair.

2. Introduce the word *stereotype*.

What Would You Do If . . .?

THEMES   Friends, Feelings, Heroes and Sheroes, Our Class

OBJECTIVES   Help children recognize that some people treat others unfairly because of differences

Help children recognize that rejecting others hurts

MATERIALS   Teaching pictures that show a variety of people in everyday situations

DESCRIPTION   Show the children one of the pictures. Describe the situation. For example: It's snack time and Tara doesn't want to sit next to Loann because her eyes are funny. Ask the children, "What would you do if you were Loann? How do you think she feels? Is it fair to not like someone because of their eyes?"

VARIATION   Use the photo paper dolls to tell a story for children to think about.

Mistaken Thinking

THEMES   Friends, Boys and Girls, Our Class, Community, Work, Senses

OBJECTIVES   Help children recognize that some people have misconceptions about others

Help children learn simple, truthful information about human diversity

MATERIALS   Chart paper and markers

DESCRIPTION   Introduce the activity by telling the children, "Sometimes we make mistakes with our bodies. For example, I spilled when I was pouring milk in cups at snack this morning. Sometimes we can also make mistakes with our heads. I think I know something, and then I find out I was mistaken. When I was little, I thought girls and women couldn't drive trucks. Then my mom and dad showed me how lots of women drove trucks. I had made a mistake with my thinking. And I changed my thinking. Sometimes, we have mistaken ideas, or biases, or stereotypes about people." Ask the children if they can think of any mistaken or silly ideas they have had about people. Then, show the children a large sheet of chart paper with three to four sets of these fill-in-the-blank sentences written on it.

I used to think_____.

Then I found out_____.

Now I think_____.

Ask children to volunteer to share a mistaken idea they have had about people (what people can do, where people live, what people eat, what makes people alike and different). Use their examples to fill in the blanks for all of the children to see.

Conclude the activity by reinforcing that we all make mistakes. As we are growing and learning, we make mistakes with our thinking. Getting new and real information helps us learn and grow. With new information, we can change our thinking.

VARIATION   For older children, given them a handout with the three sentences and have them write down their answers. Collect all of the handouts and create a book.

Pick a Friend

THEMES Friends, Boys and Girls, Feelings

OBJECTIVE Help children recognize the importance of not making judgments based on appearance

MATERIALS Pictures of boys and girls from a variety of cultures

DESCRIPTION Show the children the pictures. As the children are looking at the pictures ask, "Of all these children, who would you like to be your friend?" After the child chooses, follow up with another question such as, "What makes this child look like a friend to you?" "Do you see any other children who could be your friend?" "Do you see someone that you would not like to have as a friend?" Notice if the children are selecting potential friends of the same gender and race. Affirm children who willingly choose pictures of children from other cultures as friends.

VARIATION Have the child sort the pictures into two groups: friend and not friends. (This activity can be used as a diagnostic tool to help you learn more about children's understanding of differences.)

True or False

THEMES Feelings, My People, Our Community

OBJECTIVE Help children begin to recognize stereotypes

MATERIALS Collections of accurate and stereotypical pictures of people. Examples include the following:

Asian—coolie hat, person bowing, martial arts, geisha girl

Black—tribal warrior, mammy, athlete

Hispanic—sombrero, bandito, siesta, migrant worker

Native American—warrior, chief, squaw, papoose

DESCRIPTION Show the children one picture at a time. Ask, "What is this a picture of? Is this picture true or false?" If a child answers incorrectly, repeat the answer along with a correcting statement. For example, "False. Not all Native Americans are chiefs. And they only wear headdresses with feathers at special ceremonies."

VARIATIONS 1. Sort the pictures into two piles: true and false.

2. Encourage the children to look for false pictures in magazines and books.

What's the Bias?

THEMES   Friends, Boys and Girls, Feelings, Heroes and Sheroes, Our Class

OBJECTIVES Help children recognize stereotypes

Help children recognize that some people treat others unfairly because of differences

Help children think for themselves

MATERIALS   A children's storybook that contains a situation of bias, chart paper, and markers

DESCRIPTION Introduce the story by telling the children that this is a book in which a child is treated unfairly because others have biases and believe in stereotypes. Challenge them by saying, "As I read the story, see if you can find the stereotypes and biases." You may decide to list the stereotypes as you read the story. Older children will be able to listen to the entire story and reflect back on the stereotypes and biases. Talk about the effect the stereotypes had on the main character and her relationship with others.

VARIATION   Tell the story again and remind the children of the stereotypes and biases put on the main character by others. In your class discussion, focus on how it feels to be misunderstood, limited, and rejected because of stereotypes.

Break the Stereotype

THEMES   Friends, Alike and Different, Boys and Girls, Feelings

OBJECTIVE   Help children explore their preferences in picking friends

MATERIALS   Children's book in which the main character challenges stereotypes such as *Amazing Grace*, by Mary Hoffman; drawing paper; and crayons.

DESCRIPTION Introduce the story. Tell the children that this is a story about a little girl named Grace. She believes that she can be anyone and anything that she wants to be. Some other people believe in stereotypes and they try to use the stereotypes to keep Grace from being who she is. Read the story. Discuss the stereotypes and how Grace rejected the stereotypes others tried to put on her. Talk about how everyone learned new ways of thinking. They grew and had a positive experience because Grace did not believe in stereotypes.

After the story, invite the children to come to the table. Give each child a piece of drawing paper. Write across the top, "([underline]child's name) is amazing because . . ." Go around the table, ask each child why he or she is amazing. Write down their answers to complete the sentence. Give the children crayons or markers and invite them to draw a picture of their amazing selves.

VARIATION   Encourage the children to brainstorm ways in which they have experienced stereotypes. Write each one on an index card. Mix up the cards and invite a child to pick one. Read the card out loud. Have the child pick one to three classmates and act out the stereotyping incident written on the card. When they are done, invite another child up to pick a card and act out another incident.

You Don't?

THEMES   Friends, Boys and Girls, Feelings, Our Class

OBJECTIVES Help children recognize that some people have misconceptions about others

Help children learn simple, truthful information about human diversity

MATERIALS   Pictures of boys and girls from a variety of cultures

DESCRIPTION Children have a tendency to assume that everyone else lives the way they do. For example, they often believe that everyone eats the same food, uses the same eating utensils, speaks their language, and celebrates their holidays. Children may respond negatively when faced with a child, parent, or teacher whose lifestyle is different. Begin with the diversity present in your center, school, neighborhood, or community. Identify four or more biases children may have about the human diversity they are experiencing.

For example, some may believe that the "handicapped" kids down the hall are babies. The kids who don't speak English are stupid. The girls who wear traditional clothing that covers their heads and veils their face are scary. The kids who can't eat pepperoni pizza are weird.

Create a chart with three columns. Label the first column "differences," the second column "stereotypes," and the third column "truth." At group time, show children the chart. Point out that as they grow and get older, they spend more time away from home and in the community. Ask them to think about all the places they go and all the different kinds of people they see. There are all kinds of people at school, at the park, at the library, at the medical clinic, at the grocery store. It's great that we can share our lives with so many different kinds of people. Invite the children to brainstorm all the different kinds of people they have contact with. You may need to help them name the forms of diversity (racial, ethnic, gender, age, class, ability, religion, sexual orientation). Once the left column is complete, talk with the children about biases and stereotypes. "Sometimes people have mistaken ideas about people that they don't really know. Sometimes these mistaken ideas keep us from being respectful and friendly to one another. So over the next couple of weeks, we will fill in our chart—so we can make sure we don't have stereotypes about others and so we can really know about the people in our lives." Go through one or two of the differences and identify some of the stereotypes. Then, as a group, figure out how you will get some actual information about people. As you and the children collect actual information, fill in the right column. This is an activity that will be ongoing for a period of weeks. You could come back to it once or twice a week until the chart is complete.

VARIATION   Assign each child or a small group of children to find out accurate information for column three. Invite classroom visitors who represent various aspect of human diversity to address the stereotypes and provide accurate information.

Cartoon Stereotypes

THEMES   Friends, Boys and Girls, Feelings, Communication, Our Class

OBJECTIVES   Help children begin to recognize stereotypes

Help children compare respectful and disrespectful images

MATERIALS   Collection of stereotypic cartoon images of people or cartoon animals dressed up as a person, magazines and newspapers with photographs of actual people, construction paper, glue

DESCRIPTION   Gather a variety of materials with stereotypic images such as puzzles, flannelboard figures, bulletin board figures, bulletin board border, a ruler, greeting cards, and other holiday decorations. At group time, show the children the materials one by one. Lay them out together. Ask the children, "What do these materials all have in common?" How are they alike?" The children may focus on other attributes, such as they all go in a classroom or they all have people. Tell them that all of these materials have stereotypes. Point out each of the stereotypes. As you do, ask the children if the stereotype is true. For example, show them an old puzzle of a child dressed as an Indian dancing with a headdress. Ask the children, "Do all Indians or Native Americans wear feathers?" Invite and encourage the children to answer with a loud and enthusiastic "No!" Invite the children to go through the magazines and look for pictures of people that are not stereotypic. Encourage children to cut out the images and glue them onto construction paper. Remind the children that we only have posters with photographs of real people on the walls of our classroom because we don't want to stereotype people. We want to respect and appreciate all people.

VARIATION   Invite children to go through educational supply catalogs and look for toys and classroom materials that have stereotypes.

Rewrite the Stereotype

THEMES   Friends, Boys and Girls, Feelings, Communication

OBJECTIVES   Help children recognize stereotypes

Help children learn about the importance of doing something about discrimination

Help children think for themselves

MATERIALS   Children's books with stereotypes (Fairy tales often include many stereotypes.)

DESCRIPTION   Introduce the book to children and tell them that it includes stereotypes. After reading the story, have children brainstorm a group list of the stereotypes. Then, as a group, change each of the elements so that it is no longer stereotypic. Together rewrite the story so that you have a non-stereotypic version. Give each child a role and have the children act out their new and improved version as you narrate the story.

VARIATION   Invite children to continue thinking about the story and rewrite their own version. Have an adult sit in the writing area during free play and take dictation as individual children retell their own "non-stereotypic" version of the story. Set aside some time at the end of the morning or in the afternoon for children to reenact their stories.

Toy Box Bias

THEMES   Friends, Boys and Girls, Feelings, Our Class

OBJECTIVES   Help children recognize stereotypes

Help children recognize who is left out and who is included

MATERIALS   A variety of toys and games in their original packaging

DESCRIPTION   Bring the toys and games to group time. Introduce the activity by telling the children that they have learned a lot about stereotypes and biases. You were wondering what they thought of the boxes that toys come in. Ask them, "Have you ever really looked at the boxes that toys come in? Today we are going to look at the pictures on the boxes. Some people think that the color of the box or the type of people on the box tells us who the toy is meant for. Some people believe the pictures. If they only see boys on the box, they think the toy is for boys. If they only see African American children on the box, they think the toy is only for African Americans."

Take out a box and show all the sides to the children. You could even pass it around for each child to look at. Ask them whose picture is on the box. Does it include both girls and boys? Does it include all the racial groups? Who is not included on this box? Who is playing with the toy and who is watching? Does the box give us the idea that only some kinds of children can play with this toy? Does it give us the idea that this toy is meant for all kinds of children? What kinds of mistaken ideas about the toy could children get by looking at this box?

VARIATION   Have the children gather plastic containers, baskets, or plain cardboard boxes for displaying or storing toys. They could cover the cardboard boxes with clear self-adhesive paper and make their own labels for the toy boxes as a way to remove stereotypes from the classroom.

Bias Hurts

THEMES	Friends, Our Class, Boys and Girls, Feelings
OBJECTIVES	Help children recognize that some people treat others unfairly because of differences
	Help children learn about the concept of fair and unfair behaviors
	Help children put themselves in another person's situation
	Help children associate feelings with biased behaviors
MATERIALS	Persona dolls, people puppets, or people flannelboard figures
DESCRIPTION	This activity will help children recognize and empathize with how it feels to experience bias. Trisha Whitney describes bias to children as "being unfair to someone because of who they are (1999, 87)." At group time, gather the children together and tell them, "Today we are going to talk about how it feels to be treated unfairly. Another word for unfair is bias. Bias means being unfair to someone because of who they are. I've got a story to tell you. In this story one child is biased toward another child."

Tell the children the story. Make up a simple story based on bias incidents in your own classroom or school.

In her book *Kids Like Us*, Trisha Whitney provides a variety of simple stories to use as discussion starters:

"Julio could hardly wait for lunch because he had some special yummy tamales left over from the party the day before. But when he got out his lunch, Elizabeth looked at his tamales and asked, 'What's that blucky thing?' " (p. 90)

"When Lucia got mad at Mei Lin, she pulled her eyes into little slits and said, 'I don't have to do what you say. You have ugly eyes.' " (p. 92)

After the story, ask questions to help the children focus on how bias hurts people's feelings. How does Julio feel? Reinforce the children's use of feeling-related vocabulary such as *sad, mad, hurt, rejected, embarrassed,* or *ashamed.* Has this ever happened to you? How did it feel? What does this story mean to you?

VARIATION	Invite the children to use puppets to act out bias incidents for the class to discuss.

Don't Believe It

THEMES Friends, Boys and Girls, Feelings, Our Class

OBJECTIVES Help children recognize one's misconceptions about human diversity

Help children think for themselves

MATERIALS Pictures of boys and girls from a variety of cultures

DESCRIPTION Children are susceptible to believing biases or stereotypes about themselves. Use a persona doll, puppets, or flannelboard characters to tell a brief story about a child who has come to believe a stereotype about herself. Here are some examples:

Javier speaks Spanish very well. But when he went to school, none of the children and none of the teachers spoke Spanish. He thought the reason no one spoke Spanish was because English is better. Now the teacher and children are trying to get Javier to teach them Spanish, but he refuses to speak Spanish at school.

Umoja hates her name. She wishes she could change it to Susan. Or maybe Hillary. When she first came to her school and the teacher told the class her name, some of the kids laughed. Now Umoja is afraid someone will laugh again. (Whitney 1999, 92)

Maya hates her black curly hair. She wishes she had blond hair like Faith Hill, her favorite singer. She only likes to play with the dolls that have blond hair. Maya says she is ugly because she doesn't have blond hair.

After the story, ask the children a series of questions to help them recognize the bias, develop empathy for the child, and challenge the bias. "Who was using mistaken thinking? What was the mistaken thinking? What was the bias in this story? How did the child in our story feel about herself? How can we help her feel better about herself?"

VARIATION Invite the children to identify things they've come to believe about themselves that are not true.

Bias Choices

THEMES   Friends, Families, Boys and Girls, Feelings

OBJECTIVES   Help children resist name-calling, teasing, and rejecting others

Help children practice distinguishing right from wrong

MATERIALS   People puppets, finger puppets, or flannelboard figures

DESCRIPTION   This activity helps children reject biases and stereotypes. Use a puppet, finger puppet, or flannelboard figure. Introduce the character, tell a brief story, and ask the children if the main character should commit an act of bias.

Michael walks over to the snack area where Woubi and her mom are making Ethiopian food for snack. Should Michael say, "Oooh, that's some yucky food"?

Ari sings a song in Hebrew for the class. Imini has never heard anyone speak Hebrew before. Should Imini say, "Oooh, you talk funny"?

Kahlid is biracial. His mom is white and has light-colored skin. His dad is African American and has dark-brown-colored skin. Kahlid's skin is a medium brown color. When the class is talking about families and skin color, Kahlid says his mom is white and his dad is black. Should Mikaela say, "You're mom's not white. Look at you, you got brown skin"?

VARIATION   Repeat the activity with biased behavior instead of biased comments. Have the children practice how they would respond to these and other incidents of bias.

What's on the Inside

THEMES   Friends, Boys and Girls, Feelings, Senses, Food

OBJECTIVE   Help children recognize the importance of not making judgments based on appearance

MATERIALS   A variety of ready-to-eat canned food with the labels removed

DESCRIPTION   Set out a variety of canned foods for the children to taste. Peel off the labels beforehand so that all the cans look the same. Ask the children if they can tell what is inside the can by looking at it? Tell them that they can't tell what kind of food is inside by looking at the can and they don't know if they will like what's inside or not. Place the cans in front of the children and ask, "What do you think is inside these cans?" Help the children to open their cans and invite them to try the food inside the can.

Ask the children, "How are cans and people alike? Can you get to know a person by how they look on the outside? Some people think they can tell if they will like someone, or not, based on how they look. That's not fair. We can't judge people by looking at them. We have to get to know them. What's on the inside is what counts."

VARIATION   Invite children to continue thinking about how it's what's on the inside that counts. Ask them to think of examples of how people judge others based on looks. Ask them to think of questions that they could ask someone in order to get to know them on the inside.

Bias Behaviors

THEMES   Friends, Boys and Girls, Feelings, Communication, Our Class

OBJECTIVES   Help children recognize unfair behavior when it occurs

Help children resist rejecting others

Help children recognize that some people treat others unfairly because of differences

MATERIALS   Children's books with stereotypes (Fairy tales often include many stereotypes.)

DESCRIPTION   This activity will help children recognize some of the forms that biased behavior can take. Create a set of role-play cards. Write a biased behavior on one side of the card and the description on the other. Include these behaviors and add others that you have experienced or can anticipate experiencing in your classroom.

Hurtful questions. A child asks a question with mean words and in mean voice: "Why do your eyes look like that?"

Avoidance. A child stays away from another child. He won't sit next to, hold hands with, talk to, or play with the child.

Name-calling. A child calls another child mean names as a put-down: "You're a stinky." "You're a dirty Mexican."

Exclusion. A child refuses to allow another child to play or join an activity because of a physical feature or cultural characteristic. You can't play because you talk funny. You can't play because you dress weird. You can't play because you have dirty skin.

Invite children up in pairs. Have them pick a card. Read it to them and help them understand the situation they are to act out for the class. After the pair has acted out the bias, ask the class, "What happened? What was the bias behavior? Why isn't that behavior okay? What could we do instead?"

VARIATION   For younger children, use puppets or dolls to act out the situation for them and follow up with a group discussion.

Back of the Bus

THEMES Friends, Boys and Girls, Feelings, Heroes and Sheroes, My People, Community

OBJECTIVES Help children put themselves in another person's situation

Help children think of ways to respond to discrimination

Help children recognize unfair behavior when it occurs

MATERIALS Large open space, 8–10 child-size chairs, steering wheel

DESCRIPTION Simulate a bus by arranging two rows of chairs so they are all facing in the same direction. Include enough seats for everyone to participate. Set out an additional chair and a steering wheel. Pretend to be the bus driver and ask the children where they would like to go. Once you get to the pretend destination, stop the bus and tell the children that you want to talk to them about something that happened on a bus a long time ago. Ask them to look around and see where they are sitting on the bus. Ask them, "How did you choose where you were going to sit on the bus?" Tell them that there used to be a rule in many communities that African Americans had to sit in the back of the bus. Ask the children if they think that rule is fair. How would they feel if there was a rule that said all boys have to sit in the back of the bus? Or all children with blond hair have to sit in the back of the bus? Help children recognize that it wasn't a good rule because it was unfair.

VARIATION Simulate other historical situations of bias such as going to school together, eating lunch together at a restaurant, drinking out of the same drinking fountain, or being able to watch a movie together.

Goal 4 Activities

ACTIVISM OR SOCIAL ACTION activities may take many forms. Sometimes when we think of activism, we think of adults protesting, picketing, or sending around petitions in order to promote social change. These can be activism activities. But we have to be very careful not to overburden young children with adult agendas for social change. We must take our cues from the children, from their life experiences, and their concerns. Ideally, social action activities will emerge out of a curriculum project or unit theme. The activities in this section are designed to help the children develop a disposition toward action. Here are some resources for more social action activities.

That's Not Fair: A Teacher's Guide to Activism with Young Children, by Ann Pelo and Fran Davidson (Redleaf Press, 2000).

Linking Up! Using Music, Movement, and Language Arts to Promote Caring, Cooperation, and Communication, by Sarah Pirtle (Educators for Social Responsibility, 1998).

A Kid's Guide to Social Action, by Barbara Lewis (Free Spirit, 1991).

A Kid's Guide to Service Projects, by Barbara Lewis and Pamela Espeland (Free Spirit, 1995).

Superheroes

THEMES	Heroes and Sheroes, Friends, Boys and Girls, Communication, Community
OBJECTIVES	Help children develop a sense of personal responsibility
	Help children relate values and principles to action
MATERIALS	Visual aids such as picture books, films, pictures of popular cartoon superheroes, pictures of people who have made an important contribution such as Daniel Inouye, Chief Joseph, Mohandas Gandhi, Tecumseh, Eleanor Roosevelt, Martin Luther King Jr., Jackie Robinson, Nat Turner, Sojourner Truth, Crazy Horse, Cesar Chavez, Phyllis Wheatley, Harriet Tubman, Lucretia Coffin Mott, Susan B. Anthony, Osceola, Booker T. Washington, Paul Robeson, Pontiac, or Helen Keller.
DESCRIPTION	Show the children pictures of popular cartoon superheroes. Talk with them about how these superheroes appear on TV. Ask the children what they like about the superheroes? Describe heroes as people who make wrong things right. Tell the children that there are real people who are heroes. Say, "Some of the heroes lived a long time ago, but we still remember the good and helpful things they did. Other heroes live today. Sometimes we see them on the news as they work to make the wrong things right. Real heroes care a lot about other people. Real heroes have dreams and hopes of doing important things or making our world a better place. Real heroes work very hard for a long time, and they don't give up." Show the children the teaching pictures and talk about the contributions that each of the real heroes has made. Display the pictures at the children's eye level. Set out books about these people in the book corner.
VARIATIONS	1. Celebrate or commemorate the birthdays of real heroes.
	2. Ask parents who they would like their children to learn about.

Cooperation

THEMES	Our Class, Community, Friends
OBJECTIVES	Help children participate as group members
	Help children recognize that people can work together to help one another
MATERIALS	Large open space in the classroom
DESCRIPTION	Sing this simple song at morning circle time or at clean-up time to foster a sense of group identity and cooperation.

Tune: *Round the Village*

Let's all stand together.
Let's all stand together.
Let's all stand together.
We're all one community.
Let's all hold hands together.
Let's all hold hands together.
Let's all hold hands together.
We're all one community.
Let's all work together.
Let's all work together.
Let's all work together.
We're all one community.

(Adapted from *Sing a Song All Year Long,* Connie Walters and Dianne Totten. 1991. Minneapolis: T.S. Denison & Company. Used with permission.)

VARIATION	Encourage children make up their own verses to this song. For instance, you could sing, "We all belong here," "Let's welcome differences," "Let's treat each other fairly," "No name-calling," "Stand up for one another."

Work It Out

THEMES   Friends, Boys and Girls, Our Class

OBJECTIVES   Help children participate in group problem solving

Help children generate solutions to problems

Help children experience nonviolent conflict resolution

MATERIALS   Poster board, camera, film, markers

DESCRIPTION   Help children learn how to resolve their conflicts with one another. Introduce them to the song, "Shake Your Brains," by Red Grammer. Teach them the following five-step problem-solving method.

1. Find out what happened.
2. Name the problem, our feelings, our wants, and our needs.
3. Think of solutions.
4. Make a choice.
5. Do it!

Take a picture of children at each step in the problem-solving process. Make a problem-solving chart that children can refer to as they attempt to verbally and nonviolently solve their problems.

VARIATION   Set up a "peace table" in a corner of the room. Decorate a table with a cloth, a picture of people getting along, and a poster with the steps for problem solving. When children are in conflict with one another, invite them to come to the peace table and work it out.

Kindness Pledge

THEMES   Friends, Our Class, Our Community, My People

OBJECTIVES   Help children positively contribute to the community

Help children relate values and principles to action

DESCRIPTION   Ask the children, "What does it mean to be kind? What does a kind person do? How can we be kind to one another in our classroom? How can we be kind to one another in our families? How can we be kind to one another in our community?" Invite children to take the kindness pledge each morning at circle time:

I pledge to myself, on this day,

To try to be kind, in every way.

To every person, big and small,

I will help them if they fall.

When I love myself and others, too,

That is the best that I can do!

(*The Kindness Curriculum: Introducing Young Children to Loving Values,* Judith Anne Rice. 1995. St. Paul: Redleaf Press. p. 9. Used with permission.)

VARIATION   Discuss the opposite of kindness. Make a set of affirmation card for each aspect of kindness that children identified.

Stand Up

THEMES	Our Class, Community, Boys and Girls, Bodies, Communication
OBJECTIVES	Help children stand up for themselves
	Help children take action against bias
MATERIALS	Persona doll or puppet
DESCRIPTION	Help children develop assertiveness in the face of name-calling, teasing, rejection, or other forms of discrimination. Use a doll or puppet to role-play the experience of being called names, teased, or rejected. Ask the children, "How do you think the puppet feels? What can the puppet do when others call him names?" Trisha Whitney suggests asking these questions, "What do you think the doll could do to stand up against the bias? What would you do if that incident happened to you (Whitney 1999, 148)?"
	Discuss the children's answers, which may include things such as, "Tell him how you feel. Tell him, 'Don't say stereotypes about me.' "
	Tell the children that you know how to stand up for yourself, which is a strong way to respond and a way that doesn't hurt anyone. You have to stand tall and proud, look at the other person, speak in a strong voice, and speak your truth (what you know, what you feel, and what you need). Use the puppet to model standing up for yourself. Reenact the name-calling incident and have the puppet stand tall, look at the puppet who called him names, and say in a strong voice, "No name-calling! I don't like it when you call me names. Call me by my real name."
VARIATION	Have children brainstorm other ways that they can stand up to name-calling, teasing, and rejection. Give children an opportunity to practice standing up to name-calling.

Courage

THEMES	Heroes and Sheroes, My People, Feelings
OBJECTIVES	Help children develop a sense of responsibility
	Help children relate courage to positive social action
DESCRIPTION	Introduce children to the word *courage*. We think of heroes and sheroes as having courage. You might describe courage as a special quality that each of us can have. Tell the children that courage is doing something even when you are afraid. Courage is standing up for yourself and others. Children demonstrate courage when they stand up to unfair situations. It might be name-calling, teasing, or rejecting. Courage could also be standing up to an unfair situation such as not having a place to live, not being able to go to school, or not having enough food to eat.
	Read stories about children who are courageous. Make it a point to listen to the news, read the paper, and check the Internet for examples of children who demonstrate courage. Bring these examples and share them with the children.
VARIATIONS	1. Make a vocabulary word card for courage and display it in the classroom. Each week introduce a new word related to the values and principles of social action.
	2. Invite children to draw or paint a picture of what courage means to them.

Think and Act for Yourself

THEMES Families, Friends, Boys and Girls

OBJECTIVE Help children think for themselves and act independently

DESCRIPTION Teach children this simple finger play that I learned from Gloria Needleman at a recent NAEYC conference. It's a great way to reinforce thinking and acting for yourself.

Once there was a mother who had four children. (Hold up five fingers.)

One day she had to leave her children at home and go care for a sick friend. She told her children, "I want you to stay home until I return." Then she went to care for her friend. (Hold up four fingers.)

The first child said, "It's a hot, sunny day. I'm going down to the creek to swim and play." (Fold down the first finger, leaving three.)

The second child said, "I don't care what you say. I'm going to my friend's house to play." (Fold down another finger, leaving one.)

The fourth child said, "There goes my friend Mike. I'm going outside and riding my bike." (Fold down the last finger.)

But the fifth child said, "I don't agree. I will not roam. Because I think for myself and act for myself, I will stand alone. (Turn hand and hold up thumb.)

VARIATIONS 1. Reinforce children's independent thinking by giving them a thumbs up when they think for themselves.

2. Introduce children to the song "A thousand times, NO!" by Patricia Shih.

Dove and Eagle Club

THEMES Animals, Our Class, Heroes and Sheroes

OBJECTIVES Help children positively contribute to the classroom and the community

Help children relate values and principles to social action

MATERIALS Bulletin board, 2½ to 3-inch cut-out letters, large picture of a dove, and a large picture of an eagle

DESCRIPTION Make a bulletin board and decorate it with a dove and an eagle. Use the cut-out letters to add the heading "Peace and Freedom Begin with Us." Tell the children that the dove is often a symbol of peace and the eagle is often a symbol of freedom. Every time a child helps another or stands up for another, write up the incident and post it on the bulletin board. Read through them periodically throughout the month.

Reinforce the concept of peace and freedom by teaching children the song "Everybody Ought to Know." The arrangement by Ysaye Maria Barnwell on *All For Freedom*, by Sweet Honey in the Rock, is great for classroom use. Encourage children to insert *peace* in the second verse.

VARIATION Another popular peace education curriculum uses a giraffe as a symbol of courage. Children are invited to become members of the "Giraffe Club" by sticking their neck out for others. You could also make a classroom bulletin board or chart based on this concept.

Martin's Dream

THEMES   Heroes and Sheroes, My People, Community

OBJECTIVES   Help children develop a sense of social responsibility

Help children generate solutions to problems

MATERIALS   Art paper, crayons, markers, and paints

DESCRIPTION   Dr. Martin Luther King Jr. may be one of the first heroes the children learn about. Use this poem to introduce children to Dr. King.

> We remember you, Martin
>
> For all the good things you've done.
>
> You tried to unite all people
>
> And bring us together as one.
>
> We remember your actions and words
>
> For what you believed in was good
>
> love and peace among people
>
> The objectives of true brotherhood.
>
> (Source unknown)

People who want to make changes begin with a dream. Martin Luther King gave a famous speech in which he talked about his dreams for our world. Ask the children to finish the sentence, "I have a dream that . . ." Write down their dreams and encourage them to draw or paint a picture to accompany their dream. Our visions become real when we take action, when we do something to make them real. To follow up, invite the children to "read" their dreams to the class. As a group, brainstorm things we could do to make the dreams become real.

VARIATIONS   1. Invite children to write out their recipe for peace.

2. Introduce children to the song, "What Can One Little Person Do?" by Sally Rogers.

Walk Away

THEMES	Feelings, Friends, Heroes and Sheroes
OBJECTIVES	Help children stand up for themselves
	Help children develop a sense of responsibility to themselves
MATERIALS	Large open space in the classroom
DESCRIPTION	Help children learn how to take care of themselves when experiencing bias. One option is ignore name-calling or teasing by turning around and walking away. Ask the children, "Why do some kids stick out their tongues at people? Why do some kids make faces and say things such as 'Na-na na-na boo-boo'? Do you think they are trying to make us mad? Do you think they are trying to get our attention?" Ask the children what they do when someone makes a face at them. Tell them that there is a way to respond that is strong and proud. It's a special skill that Martin Luther King Jr. and other heroes have used. All you have to do is stand tall and proud, turn your head, and walk away. Ask the children to form a circle, and pick two children to stand in the circle facing each other. One child is the teaser and the other child is the hero. The teaser makes faces at and taunts the hero. The child who is the hero stands tall, turns around, and walks away, leaving the teaser alone in the circle. Everyone cheers for the hero who walked away. The hero picks another child to go into the circle and the teaser becomes the hero in this round. Continue until all the children have had a turn being the hero and the teaser.
VARIATIONS	1. Help children brainstorm all of their options for walking away. They could ignore the person, look for a friend, decide not to listen to them, or look for an adult.
	2. Role-play resisting hurtful or unfair situations by walking away from trouble and telling an adult friend who can help. Use examples from the classroom or the children's lives.

No Name-Calling

THEMES	Friends, Boys and Girls, Feelings, Our Class
OBJECTIVES	Help children resist name-calling
	Help children develop conflict-resolution skills
MATERIALS	Two persona dolls or puppets
DESCRIPTION	Introduce the concept that it is not acceptable to call people names or exclude someone because of their skin color, gender, language, dress, family, or disability. Use puppets or dolls to demonstrate a situation of name-calling and exclusions. Have one puppet say to the other puppet, "Hey, that looks like fun. Can I play?" The other puppet responds, "Get away, you're not one of us." Ask the children, "What did the puppet just say? Is that okay? What could the puppet do instead? What would you do if someone treated you that way?"

Stand by Me

THEMES   Friends, Boys and Girls, Our Class

OBJECTIVES   Help children develop a sense of responsibility to others

Help children stand up for another person

MATERIALS   Persona doll or puppet

DESCRIPTION   Help children explore how they can be a friend to someone who isn't being treated fairly. It is easy to feel alone when you are experiencing bias from others. Use a puppet or persona doll story to help children recognize that they can assist a friend or classmate who is being treated unfairly. After the story, ask the children how they could help the doll with his or her problem. Children's answers might include the following:

"I could stand by him and tell the others, 'Hey, that's not fair.'"

"I could work with him to make things fair."

"I could tell the others, 'You're being biased.'"

"I could tell my friend not to listen to them."

"I'd make sure I didn't laugh when the others are laughing at him."

"I'd stand close to him and hold his hand."

VARIATION   Help children explore how they could get help from a teacher, parent, or other adult.

Thanks and No Thanks

THEMES   Communication, Our Class

OBJECTIVES   Help children coordinate their actions with others to accomplish a shared goal

Help children take action against bias

MATERIALS   Chart paper, homemade cards, school letterhead, and envelopes

DESCRIPTION   As a group, go through classroom materials and identify which ones are respectful and which are stereotypic. As a group, write thank-you letters to educational suppliers that manufacture or distribute quality multicultural, gender-fair, and disability-aware materials. Write a letter to the company and send back any stereotypic materials that you may have purchased for your classroom. Take dictation, writing the children's words on chart paper for all to see. Help the children transfer the group letter onto note cards or letterhead. Together, mail the letters.

VARIATIONS   1. Write letters to children's book authors and publishers. Thank the authors and publishers for the books that you enjoy, or that have been helpful or meaningful.

2. Write letters of objection to authors and publishers whose books you find stereotypic, exclusionary, or offensive. Also consider focusing on children's computer software, which tends to lack both human diversity and realistic images and illustrations.

Don't Leave Us Out

THEMES Communication, Families

OBJECTIVES Help children participate as a group member

Help children participate in group decision making

Help children generate solutions to bias

MATERIALS Wall calendars with children or babies

DESCRIPTION Show children wall calendars with babies or children. See if any culture, race, gender, or disability is missing or underrepresented. Talk about how it feels to be left out. As a group write a letter to the company that manufactures the calendars and request that they make their calendars more inclusive.

VARIATION Go through a collection of magazines, birthday cards, or children's books to identify how well all the ethnic groups in your class, school, or community are represented in mainstream media.

Human Rights

THEMES Community, Friends, Our Class

OBJECTIVE Help children recognize human rights

MATERIALS Children's books on human rights (such as *For Every Child a Better World* or *The United Nation's Declaration of Human Rights for Children*), chart paper, markers

DESCRIPTION Everyone has the right to speak their own language, follow their cultural beliefs and practices, and feel good about their culture and ethnic background. Help children recognize that sometimes there are barriers to these basic human rights. For example, one barrier is that it's easy to feel that our way of doing things is the only way or the best way. Many messages in our society tell us that one way is the best way or the right way, and that disrespects other ways.

Help children think about what people need to be able to respect and get along with one another. Ask them, "What things do people need to respect one another? What things do people need to get along with one another? Why do you think some people don't respect or get along with others? What are some of the ways that people are treated unfairly in our community? What could we do to change these? What choices could people make to encourage respect? How could we help people respect one another?" Make a group flyer based on the class's discussions about human rights and distribute it to all the families. Display it throughout the school.

Bias-Free Zone

THEMES   Our Class, Community, Friends

OBJECTIVES   Help children positively contribute to the classroom

Help children develop a sense of responsibility to one's community

MATERIALS   Large sheet of butcher paper, crayons, markers

DESCRIPTION   It is important that every child in our centers and schools feel safe and as if they belong. Bias in the forms of lack of representations, stereotypes, name-calling, teasing, taunting, bullying, and rejecting denies children this basic human right.

During group time, review the concept of human rights with the children. Ask them, "What would help every child feel welcome in our school? What would help every child feel safe in our school?" Take notes on their discussion using chart paper and markers so that children can see their thoughts and ideas in writing. Challenge the children to find out what other kids in their school think by interviewing as many children as they can. Have them ask other children these two questions:

What would help you to feel safe at our school?

What would help you feel like you belong?

You may want to send the children out in pairs with a cassette recorder to record the children's answers. When the children think they've interviewed enough children, have them listen to their answers, again making notes on large chart paper for all the children to see. Ask the children to come up with a plan to help all children feel safe and as if they belong.

VARIATION   Have the children give their plan a name such as "Racism Free Zone." Design a symbol to represent their plan, and write up and distribute their plan to the children, staff, and parents in your center or school.

Group Think

THEMES   Our Class, Friends

OBJECTIVES   Help children participate in group decision making

Help children generate solutions to problems

Help children experience working cooperatively with others

DESCRIPTION   Teach the children how to make a group decision. Tell the children that sometimes they will all make one choice together. If they wanted to cook, they would need to decide what to make. If they wanted to take a field trip, they would need to decide as a group where to go. If they get tired of the classroom arrangement, they might need to decide on a new way of arranging the furniture. Tell the children that making a decision is like making a choice. You want to use your head and think very carefully when making a decision.

Teach children a process to guide them in making a group decision. Here is one simple step-by-step process:

1. What is the situation?

2. What are the choices?

3. What do we like and what don't we like about each choice?

4. Pick the one best choice.

Sarah Pirtle (1998, p. 201) suggests the following to help children brainstorm together.

Our Agreements When We Brainstorm

1. We're going to give everyone who wants to a chance to speak.

2. Please raise your hand so I can call on one person at a time. I'll put your words into a short phrase and write it down so that we can remember your idea.

3. When we're brainstorming, we're not deciding what we want to do. Deciding on our choice comes second. Right now we're thinking.

4. If you hear an idea you really like or you really don't like, please don't call out and tell us your opinion. Don't say "no" or "hurrah." Right now we're listening to all the ideas. We'll make the list as long as we can.

5. If you don't understand someone's idea, we'll stop and let the person explain how it would work.

VARIATION   Give children an opportunity to role-play group decision making.

Classroom Rights

THEMES   Our Class, Friends

OBJECTIVES   Help children recognize human rights

Help children positively contribute to the classroom

MATERIALS   Chart paper or poster board, markers

DESCRIPTION   Teach children this statement of human rights for the classroom. Post it near the circle time area. Consider using it to help your class write their own statement of human rights.

Our Human Rights

I have a right to be happy and to be

treated with compassion in this room;

This means that no one

will laugh at me or

hurt my feelings.

I have a right to be myself in this room;

This means that no one will

treat me unfairly because of my skin color,

or because I am fat or thin, tall or short, a boy or a girl,

or because of the way I look.

I have a right to be safe in this room;

This means that no one will

hit me, kick me, push me, pinch me, or hurt me.

I have a right to hear and

be heard in this room;

This means that no one will yell, scream, shout, or make loud noises.

I have a right to learn about myself in this room;

This means that I will be free

to express my feelings and opinions without being

interrupted or punished.

I have a right to learn according to my own ability;

This means no one will call me names because of the way I learn.

("Individual Differences: An Experience in Human Relations for Children," by M. Cummings. 1974. Madison, Wisc.: Madison Public Schools. In *Teacher, They Called Me a _____!* by Deborah Byrnes. 1987. Utah State Office of Education and Anti-Defamation League of B'nai B'rith. New York: Anti-Defamation League; pp. 30–31. Used with permission.)

Speak Up

THEMES	Communication, Our Class, Friends
OBJECTIVES	Help children stand up for themselves
	Help children stand up for another person
MATERIALS	Puppet or persona doll
DESCRIPTION	This activity helps children think about when speaking up is helpful and when speaking up would be tattling. Use a puppet or persona doll to describe different situations she's seen. Give each child a turn at deciding if they think the puppet should speak up or keep silent.

Make up a variety of situations and write each one on an index card. Mix them up and have children pick one card at a time.

There is a new kid in class and some children are making fun of his clothes.

One of the kids is jumping in puddles on the playground and the teacher told us not to.

I heard a kid call another kid names because of his skin color.

One kid has been at the computer a long time and no one else has been able to use it.

One kid told another, "Get away from us, you white boy."

There is a new child in the class who has a name some of the kids have never heard before.

One of the kids says, "I don't like you, you've got a weird name."

VARIATION	Have one of the teachers take on the role of the person who is making the mistake rather than simply reading scenarios. (Adapted from Pirtle 1998)

Tributes

THEMES   Heroes and Sheroes, Community, My People

OBJECTIVES   Help children relate values and principles to social action

Help children develop a sense of personal responsibility

MATERIALS   Children's books about heroes and sheroes, chart paper, markers

DESCRIPTION   Help the children learn about people who work to make the world a place where everyone can get along. Children can learn about adults in their families, school, community, nation, and world. Children can begin with one of their family members. Teachers can introduce a few community members. Children can begin to "read" biographies about famous people.

Sarah Pirtle wrote a song to help children honor significant people. One example is the following:

Marian Wright Edelman,

Marian Wright Edelman

You give voice to children.

You started the Children's Defense Fund.

I want to know your name.

As children identify people to honor, create a new verse for them using this format:

Name of the person,

Name of the person

One thing important about what that person did.

I want to know your name.

The chorus of Sarah's song is

I want to know your name.

I want to know your name.

We are links on the chain.

I want to know your name.

I want to know your name.

>   (From *I Want to Know Your Name*. Words and music by Sarah Pirtle. 1997. Discovery Center Music, BMI.)

Follow up by making a paper chain that includes everyone's name on it.

VARIATIONS   1. With older children, you could include three or four things the person did.

2. Make a tribute book of all the people your class recognized and add to it throughout the year.

>   (Pirtle 1998, 122–127)

Special Activities

CHILDREN LEARN FROM real experiences, whether from meeting real people or exploring real materials. "Trips give adults an opportunity to see for themselves something they have heard or read about. Trips serve not only that same function for children, but also its opposite. They give children an opportunity to see for themselves something they will learn more about later in pictures or books or through conversation (Redleaf 1983, 3)." Walks and field trips offer children first-hand, real-life experiences and are a good starting point for learning about people and different ways of living. These experiences are especially appropriate for children in monocultural programs.

Walks and Field Trips

Here are some ideas for multicultural walks and field trips:

Neighborhood walk

House walk

People walk

Homes of children or staff

Ethnic grocery stores

Third world craft stores

Ethnic neighborhoods

Neighborhood community centers

Ethnic museums and cultural centers

Multicultural celebrations or street fairs

Plays and puppet shows

Museum exhibits

Adopt a Classroom

Establish a "sister" relationship with an inner-city early childhood education program, a child care center in another part of the state, or a program in another country. Exchange photographs, artwork, and letters. Get together for picnics or other special events.

Invite Visitors

Also consider bringing in special visitors from the community. Parents and family members are the first choice since the children know them on a daily basis. If your program is not multicultural, try contacting the education and outreach volunteer or staff person within local ethnic/cultural associations. Ask visitors to talk about themselves and their family as they live today, rather than speaking on behalf of their people and focusing totally on the past.

References

Baker, Gwendolyn C. 1983. *Planning and organizing for multicultural instruction.*
   Reading, Penn.: Addison-Wesley.

Derman-Sparks, Louise. 1987. It isn't fair! Anti-bias curriculum for young children.
   Alike and different: Exploring our humanity with young children. Edited by

Bonnie Neugebauer. Redmond, Wash.: Exchange Press.

Derman-Sparks, Louise. 1989. *Anti-bias curriculum: Tools for empowering young children.* Washington, D.C.: NAEYC.

Forman, George E., and Fleet Hill. 1984. *Constructive play: Applying Piaget in the preschool.* Menlo Park, Calif.: Addison-Wesley.

Kendall, Frances E. 1983. *Diversity in the classroom: A multicultural approach to the education of young children.* New York: Teachers College Press.

Pirtle, Sarah. 1998. *Linking up!* Cambridge, Mass.: Educators for Social Responsibility.

Ramsey, Patricia G. 1987. *Teaching and learning in a diverse world: Multicultural education for young children.* New York: Teachers College Press.

Redleaf, Rhoda. 1983. *Open the door, let's explore.* St. Paul: Redleaf Press.

Williams, Leslie R., and Yvonne De Gaetano. 1985. *Alerta: A multicultural, bilingual approach to teaching young children.* Menlo Park, Calif.: Addison-Wesley.

Glossary

Important Terms

It is impossible to talk about culturally relevant and anti-bias education without using specific terms—words that are often misunderstood or misused. The following terms are defined here according to the way they are used throughout this book. Read through the list. Which words are familiar to you? Which words are new? Which words name something you can relate to or have experienced in your own life?

Activism. Taking group action against unfair behaviors or situations based on critical thinking, group decision making, group problem solving, or nonviolent conflict resolution.

Anti-bias approach. A form of multicultural education that helps children explore all types of human diversity (age, race, culture, class, ability, and sexual orientation). It seeks to help children respect differences and recognize and challenge bias.

Assimilation. Modifying one's culture by adapting to another culture; changing or losing your cultural patterns and cultural identity to fit into or be accepted by the society. Also the process by which one cultural group acquires the values, beliefs, language, and behaviors of another culture (usually the dominant culture) and sheds its own culture. Often the result of colonization. Assimilation has been the U.S. government's policy toward cultural diversity.

Bias. Any attitude, belief, or feeling that results in, and helps to justify, unfair treatment of an another.

Bicultural. An individual who has two cultural identities and who can function competently and comfortably within each of the cultures.

Bigotry. A rigid attitude, belief, or behavior that is intolerant of individuals or groups who are different because of race, religion, political views, creed, sexual orientation, ability, gender, and so on.

Bilingual. An individual who has access to two dialects or languages for social communication. Usually one language is dominant. Some define bilingual competences as speaking, reading, and writing two or more languages competently. Over 70 percent of the world's population is bilingual and bilingualism has been associated with more fluid cognitive functioning.

Bilingual education. Programs designed to help English language learners (the fastest growing school-age population in the United States) acquire English and function at their grade level in all subject areas. Includes a variety of approaches; is highly politicized; and has been historically controversial.

Blaming the victim. Justifying social inequality by finding defects in the victims of inequality, or holding individuals responsible for social problems while ignoring the impact and role of victimizing forces in society. It keeps helping strategies focused on changing the victim rather than changing society. It distracts helping energies from focusing or addressing root causes. And it distracts the public from holding leaders accountable.

Child study movement. The period in the mid-1920s, when wealthy American families, such as the Carnegies and the Rockefellers, funded child development departments and research centers at Yale and other universities around the country, which resulted in a decade of significant research that laid the foundation for our understanding of child development and early education today.

Citizenship. Living in a particular country and being a participant in that country's government through birth or naturalization. Participating as a productive member of the country. The role of a citizen is to demonstrate allegiance to the government by obeying the laws and participating in civic life through voting, paying taxes, and so on. In return, citizens have the right to protection by their government.

Classification. A cognitive skill that involves recognizing physical attributes and grouping objects by their shared attributes.

Code switching. Occurs when a bilingual individual alternates between two languages during a conversation with another bilingual person. Can include switching words, phrases, sentences, or entire clauses.

Context/Contextually relevant. The social (cultural, political, economic, and historical) environment in which children grow and live. It includes the cultural, historical, social, and political makeup of the community. Curriculum activities and content should be contextually relevant to children's lives.

Contextual analysis. The process of trying to understand and uncover the social context of the children and families. It may include observing and spending time in the neighborhood, conducting home visits, meeting with community leaders and gatekeepers, reading about the child's home culture, reading about the local neighborhood and community, and confirming information with parents and grassroots leaders.

Cross-cultural effectiveness. An essential skill for all people who work with children and families. Ways of thinking and behavior that enables a professional of one cultural group to work effectively with members of another culture. Conducting one's professional work in a way that is congruent with the behavior and expectations of another culture's members. It does not mean becoming a member of another culture through speech, dress, or behavior.

Cultural identity. Awareness of oneself as a cultural being and a sense of belonging to a cultural group.

Culturally competent. The ability to function effectively in the midst of cultural differences. It includes knowledge of cultural differences, awareness of one's own cultural values, and the ability to successfully and consistently function with members of other cultural groups.

Culturally deprived. An outdated belief perpetuated by European Americans that children of color have home cultures that deprive them of basic life experiences and opportunities for healthy growth and development.

Culturally relevant care and education. Structures and programs that mirror and empower the cultures of the children and families that use them. Caregiving routines, teaching methods, and curriculum are consistent and modeled after the child's home culture and the individual family's style. It requires a positive working relationship with parents.

Culturally responsive. The program represents and supports the home cultures of the families whose children attend.

Culture. The shared values, attitudes, beliefs, and rules for behavior of a group of people. It is who we are on the inside and how we live our lives.

Culture clash. Disagreements between individuals, or individuals and institutions, due to different value systems, beliefs, or practices that are culturally based.

Culture shock. A sense of confusion and disorientation as a result of being immersed in another culture. It includes feeling different, surprised, frustrated, uncomfortable, unsettled, lost, unsure of yourself, and angry. Behaviors may include becoming withdrawn, lethargic, and aggressive, or experiencing increased illness.

Discrimination. Treating a person favorably, or unfavorably, based on racial or cultural stereotypes, rather than treating a person individually based on personal knowledge.

Diversity. The human differences between people including, but not limited to, shape, size, ability, gender, age, skin color, sexual orientation, family background, spiritual beliefs, and political affiliation.

Dominant culture. The culture that exercises social/political authority or influence in a society. The cultural group that controls economic, political, educational, or social service institutions.

Egocentric thought. According to Jean Piaget, this is a characteristic of children's thinking in the preoperational stage of development (ages two through seven). Children see the world from their own point of view and assume that everyone else sees the world as they do. They are incapable of taking another person's perspective.

Enculturation. The transmission of culture within the family from one generation to the next. The process and strategies families use to teach their children the values, beliefs, and behaviors of their home culture.

Ethnicity. The geographic origin or national identity of a person.

Ethnocentrism. The attitudes that one's own culture is superior. A tendency to view other cultures as inferior or deficient. Seeing the world through one's own culture without considering other cultural perspectives. Assuming your form of family, way of doing things, and childrearing practices are the norm or the standard, psychologically healthy, or functional. Judging other styles and patterns as inferior, unhealthy, or dysfunctional.

European American. People in the United States descended from any of the different nations or ethnic groups in Europe.

Eurocentrism/Eurocentric. A worldview that centers on the people, culture, and history of Europe and European Americans. Theories and practices that are European or European American in origin but are held up as the norm, universal, or best practice.

Family. Two or more people with a long-term commitment to one another who share living space and the tasks involved in maintaining the group.

Home language. The primary language spoken in a child's home. The first language that a child learns and the primary language a child uses to think and communicate with and to relate to others.

Identity. Sense of self that includes both an individual and group identity. Largely influenced by the environment and interaction with others. Strengthened by information (self-knowledge) and congruence with one's culture.

Inclusive. Education theory and practices prioritizing openness and acceptance of all children and families.

Internalized oppression. Self-oppression that results from the unconscious acceptance of societal biases by a member of an oppressed group. Taking on and believing stereotypes about one's group that results in feeling shame, hopelessness, or despair. It can cause individuals to distance themselves from, reject, or act aggressively toward members of their own racial/cultural group.

Internalized superiority. Assumption of superior social status and human worth, as well as the right to preferential treatment that results from being a member of the dominant group in a society.

Interracial/Biracial. A child or family from two or more races.

Large group time. A teacher-directed learning experience in which the entire class comes together. It is often conducted on the floor, where children sit cross-legged in a circle. Large group time may consist of music, movement, singing, storytelling, creative dramatics, role-playing, and discussions.

Minority. An outdated, inaccurate, and offensive term used to label a group of people with a separate identity and a lower status from the dominant society. Minorities may be the numerical minority or numerical majority.

Monocultural. Having one cultural identity; an individual, family, institution, or community that consists of individuals from the same culture.

Multicultural education. A setting that includes and serves individuals from many cultures. A multicultural program would include staff, meals, caregiving practices, teaching methods, and a curriculum content that reflects many cultures.

Oppression. The systematic use of social power to keep people of one social group from having equal access to society's good and benefits.

People of color. A term commonly used to describe people who are not European Americans. Attempts to deal with the complexity and limits of language by combining all cultural groups (except European Americans) together under the label "people of color" minimizes the unique history and culture of each cultural group and does not recognize the differences between cultural groups.

Persona doll. A storytelling technique used by teachers to help children learn about identity, culture, and diversity that uses a lifelike doll that has been given a name, personality, and family.

Prejudice. An opinion (usually unfavorable) or attitude about an individual or group without correct or adequate information. Opinions and attitudes based on stereotypes and overgeneralizations that result in discriminatory behavior. Prejudging and disliking an individual or group based on race, ability, gender, creed, sexual orientation, occupation, residence, and so on.

Privilege. An unearned entitlement to a position of high status based on group membership (race) in a society and accompanied by an attitude of superiority and advantage.

Race. A theory of separating human beings into groups based on physical characteristics of skin color. A concept with no scientific or biological basis that is used to assign social status, power, and worth to people. Often confused with culture and ethnicity.

Racism. Prejudice plus power. Attitude, action, and institutional practice backed up by institutional power that subordinates people of color.

Rejecting/Rejection. Strategies parents of color use to support their children in developing positive self-esteem and internal strength to resist racism and internalized oppression.

Small group time. A teacher-directed learning experience in which the class is divided into small groups of five to ten children. The adult plans and facilitates an activity designed to foster one of the curriculum goals.

Socialization. A process, beginning at birth, through which we acquire the knowledge, skills, and behaviors required by the society in which we live. It is the process of preparing individuals to take their place in society in order to maintain society.

Society. The set of systems, institutions, organizations, and individuals that function interdependently based on a set of prescribed values, beliefs, and cultural patterns. American society is the largest (but not necessarily the most important) entity that impacts the development and socialization of children.

Stereotype. Stubborn beliefs, overgeneralizations, myths, and distorted information about groups of people that shape people's thinking and form the basis of prejudice. Stereotypes are projected through the media, become part of the collective consciousness, and are used to justify discrimination.

Telegraphic speech. A form of speech that emerges around twenty-four months in which children begin to speak in two- to three-word utterances such as "go potty" or "me cookie."

Theme. A curriculum topic or unit of study that should be based on children's interests, is relevant to their lives, is concrete, and encourages extended learning in all curriculum areas.

Tokenism. A minimal attempt to diversify that is manipulative and degrading. Includes a little diversity (less than 25 percent) in the curriculum and keeps diversity marginalized. Adding a few multicultural materials such as posters or books to the classroom.

Tourist curriculum. A patronizing approach to multicultural education that teaches children about other cultures through artifacts, food, traditional clothing, and celebrations.

Web/Webbing. A method of brainstorming used to quickly generate ideas, which are written in a circle. Related ideas are connected by lines so that the final result looks like a spider web.

White people. A racial term that refers to people of European ancestry. It is used in highlighting the economic, political, cultural, educational, and legal controls and benefits that European Americans, as a group, have in the United States.

Index

dominant culture approach. *See* human relations approach to multicultural education
Don't Believe It activity, 235
Don't Leave Us Out activity, 248
Dorros, Arthur, 89
Dove and Eagle Club activity, 244
Doyle, Anna Beth, 30
dramatic play
    materials for, 158–160
    People Paper Dolls activity, 213
    Photo Masks activity, 211
    and sensory table, 161–162
Draw Me/Draw You activity, 209
dress-up clothes, 160
dual language approach to bilingual education, 93–94
Dumpling Soup (Rattigan), 88

E

ecological theories, 35, 39, 40
egocentric thought, 29, 262
elders, 199
Elliot, Jane, 41
empathy, 139–140
enculturation, 262
English, Karen, 89
English as a Second Language (ESL) instruction, 92, 93
English language classrooms, 95
enrollment forms, 96, 112, 113–114
entitlement, 46
equality, 52
Erikson, Erik, 15
Espeland, Pamela, 239
ethnicity, 37, 262
ethnocentrism, 45, 262–263
Eurocentrism
    and assimilation, 60–61
    and culturally inappropriate programs, 72
    defined, 262
    and education, xiii, 5, 62
    and European American cultural characteristics, 63
    and families, 109
    and human relations approach to multicultural education, 132
    and single-group study approach to multicultural education, 142
European American children
    effects of racism on, 43–46
    racial awareness, 17
    racial identity, 42
European Americans
    children of color overidentification with, 47
    cultural characteristics, 63
    culturally relevant, anti-bias education as attack on, xii–xiii
    defined, 263
    demographics, 3
    and institutional racism, 38
    See also European American children

"Everybody Ought to Know" (Sweet Honey in the Rock), 244
exclusion. *See* biased behaviors
expectations, 5, 51
exploring, 28

F

Fables, Morals, and Proverbs activity, 196
Face Masks activity, 224
Face Puzzles activity, 196, 211
Fair and Unfair activity, 227
fairness
    and child development, 18
    Fair and Unfair activity, 227
    and nonracist classrooms, 54
    Victim Aid activity, 226
    See also activism (goal 4); bias
false associations, 29
families
    bilingual, 86
    cultural differences, 63, 66, 68
    and culture, 109–111
    defined, 263
    diversity of, 109
    early childhood programs as part of, 111
    young children's awareness of, 12
    See also parent relationships
Family Foods activity, 197
Family Photos activity, 213
Family Tree activity, 220
Famous People activity, 197
fear, 46, 130–131
feeling boxes, 195
feelings, 15–16, 70.
Felt Friends activity, 212
field trips, 184, 255, 256
¡Fiesta! (Guy), 98
Fillmore, Charles, 83
Fillmore, Lily Wong, 59, 94
Fingerpaint Mix-Up activity, 207
finger plays, 244
Finley, Carlos, 55
first language classrooms, 94
First Steps Toward Cultural Difference: Socialization in Infant/Toddler Day Care (Miller), 62, 64
five- and six-year-olds, 18, 21
food
    European American cultural attitudes toward, 63
    Smelling Jars activity, 221
    as teaching tool, 161
For Every Child a Better World, 248
formal learning style, 70
forms
    curriculum planning, 183, 186
    parent questionnaire, 113–114
freedom, 244
free play
    and bilingual education, 98–99
    and classroom environment, 148
Future Vision, Present Work (CRAB), 12, 136

G

games, 193
Garay, Louis, 89
gender, young children's awareness of, 12, 13, 16, 18, 19
Genishi, C., 88
golden rule, 53
Grammer, Red, 174, 242
Grant, Carl, 131, 143
group membership, 19. *See also* racial identity
group-oriented learning style, 70
Group Think activity, 250
Group Tree activity, 218
Guess Who? activity, 217
guilt, 49
Guy, Ginger Fogelson, 98

H

Hair activity, 210
Hall, Nadia Saderman, 204
Hammerstein, Oscar, II, 11
Hart, Marcy, 19
Hartman, Jack, 174
hatred, 46
Head Start Performance Standards, 7
Helms, Janet, 41
Higa, Carol Tanaka, 12
historical situations, 238
Hoffman, Mary, 230
holidays/celebrations, 116–118
    and books, 164
    Culture Calendar activity, 195
    Daily Life and Celebrations activity, 216
    and stereotypes, 152
homelands, 200, 201
home language, 87, 263. *See also* bilingual education
home language stage of bilingual language development, 87
home visits, 115
honor, 69
Houses activity, 221
How Would You Feel If . . .? activity, 227
humanism, 69
human relations approach to multicultural education, 132–133, 142, 143
human rights, 248, 249, 251
Human Rights activity, 248

I

I'm Special Book activity, 204
identification stage of prejudice, 25
identity, 263. *See also* racial identity; self-concept
imitative play, 16
immersion approach to bilingual education, 86, 92
immigrants
    and bilingual education, 85
    demographics, 3, 4
    families, 110
inclusiveness, 263